The Psychology
of Computer Use

Computers and People Series

Edited by

B. R. GAINES

The series is concerned with all aspects of man-computer relationships, including interaction, interfacing modelling and artificial intelligence. Books are interdisciplinary, communicating results derived in one area of study to workers in another. Applied, experimental, theoretical and tutorial studies are included.

The Psychology of Computer Use

Edited by

T. R. G. GREEN
S. J. PAYNE
*MRC/SSRC Social and Applied
Psychology Unit
Sheffield University, UK.*

G. C. van der VEER
*Department of Psychology
Free University of Amsterdam
The Netherlands*

· 1983

ACADEMIC PRESS
A Subsidiary of Harcourt Brace Jovanovich, Publishers
London   New York
Paris   San Diego   San Francisco   São Paulo
Sydney   Tokyo   Toronto

ACADEMIC PRESS INC (LONDON) LTD.
24/28 Oval Road
London NW1

United States Edition published by
ACADEMIC PRESS INC.
111 Fifth Avenue
New York, New York 10003

British Library Cataloguing in Publication Data
The Psychology of computer use.—(Computers and
    people)
    1. Data processing—Congresses
    2. Man–machine systems—Congresses
    I. Green, T.R.G.
    II. Payne, S.J.
    III. Veer, G.C. van der
    IV. Series
    001.64   QA76

    ISBN 0-12-297420-4

    LCCCN 82-73798

Printed in Great Britain by
Whitstable Litho Ltd., Whitstable, Kent

CONTRIBUTORS

ARBLASTER, A. Bell Telephone, Franciswellesplein 1, 2000-Antwerp, Belgium.

BARNARD, P. MRC Applied Psychology Unit, 15 Chaucer Road, Cambridge CB2 2EF, UK.

CLARK, I. Human Factors Laboratory, IBM United Kingdom Laboratories, Winchester, UK.

GREEN, T.R.G. MRC/SSRC Social and Applied Psychology Unit, Department of Psychology, The University, Sheffield, S10 2TN, UK.

HÄGGLUND, S. Software Systems Research Center, Linköping University, S-581 83 Linköping, Sweden.

HAMMOND, N. MRC Applied Psychology Unit, 15 Chaucer Road, Cambridge CB2 2EF, UK.

HOC, J-M. Laboratoire de Psychologie du Travail de l'E.P.H.E., 41, rue Gay Lussac, 75005 Paris, France.

JØRGENSEN, A.H. Institute of Datalogy, Copenhagen University, Sigurdsgaade 41, DK-2200 Copenhagen N. Denmark.

KAHNEY, J.H. Open University, Milton Keynes, UK.

MAASS, S. University of Hamburg, Schluterstrasse 70, D-2000 Hamburg 13, W. Germany.

NAUR, P. Institute of Datalogy, Copenhagen University, Sigurdsgaade 41, DK-2200 Copenhagen N., Denmark.

PAYNE, S.J. MRC/SSRC Social and Applied Psychology Unit, Department of Psychology, The University, Sheffield, S10 2TN, UK.

PINSKY, L. Laboratoire de Physiologie du Travail et d'Ergonomie, Conservatoire National des Arts et Metiers, 41 rue Gay Lussac, 75005 Paris, France.

PREECE, J. Open University, Milton Keynes, UK.

SENACH, B. Institut National de Récherche d'Informatique et d'Automatique, Domaine de Voluceau, Rocquencourt, B.P. 105 - 78150 Le Chesnay, France.

SENGLER, H.E. URW-Unternehmensberatung, Harksheiderstrasse 102, D2000 Hamburg 65, W. Germany.

TIBELL, R. Software Systems Research Center, Linköping University, S-581 83 Linköping, Sweden.

van der VEER, G.C. Subfaculteit Psychologie der Vrije
  Universiteit, De Boelelaan 1115 Prov. I.B. 126,
  1081 HV Amsterdam, Netherlands.

van de WOLDE, G.J.E. Technische Hogeschool Twente, Afd. Toe-
  gepaste Onderwijskunde, Hal A-224, Postbus 217, 7500 AE
  Enschede, Netherlands.

PREFACE

The papers in this book are selected from a conference held at the Free University of Amsterdam in August, 1982, under the sponsorship of Control Data BV. Computer scientists and cognitive psychologists from most parts of Europe met to discuss "Cognitive Engineering", or the problems associated with making use of computers as tools of the intellect.

Both the conference itself and this volume owe a great deal to the efforts of Elly Lammers, who cheerfully gave up a great deal of time to organising one and typing the other and giving painstaking care to both. The editors would also like to thank Cath Pettyfer, of Academic Press, who instantly solved innumerable difficulties and helped to keep us very nearly organised.

Thanks, Elly; thanks, Cath; and of course thanks to all the many other people who helped.

March, 1983

Thomas Green
Stephen Payne
Gerrit van der Veer

By the time all was finished it was clear that special thanks are also due to Sally Oram at Academic Press.

June, 1983   TG/SP/GvdV

CONTENTS

PSYCHOLOGY OF USING COMPUTERS

PSYCHOLOGY OF PROGRAMMING

INTRODUCTION

T.R.G. GREEN, S.J. PAYNE
and G.C. van der VEER

Tools need to be well-shaped. The computer, which according
to some estimates has so far achieved only about 2% of its
eventual penetration of our lives, has become increasingly
more usable by non-specialists, but it still has a way to go:
just like other technological inventions - motor transport,
television, amateur photographic equipment - its history
seems destined to be one of quick technological improvement
with a sharp eye to consumer fashion.

What is different about computers is that technology alone
may not be enough. Technology will be sufficient to achieve
many purposes, perhaps to produce computer systems adequate
for routine uses, such as office word processors or airline
reservation systems, but the computer clearly has another
destiny as an outstanding intellectual tool. Musical hist-
orians might use it to spot borrowings in fifteenth-century
chansons, artists are beginning to use it as a specialist
tool for creating certain graphic effects, scientists might
and indeed do use it to construct and test models of very
complex theories.

Used as an intellectual tool, used for problem-solving
rather than as office furniture, computers raise different
problems from say, cameras. Technological ingenuity has made
light work of modern photography, transforming a complex
system of optics, mechanics, and chemistry into an auto-focus,
auto-exposure, nearly foolproof box of tricks. It cannot
treat computers in the same way. Open any popular computing
magazine, find a computer program, cut it out, and show it -
without the accompanying notes - to a computer person, asking
what it does and how it does it. Or if you have access to a
mainframe installation, observe the difficulties of perfectly
intelligent people trying to get to know the system. Then
ask yourself whether the computer is yet ready to fulfil its
potential, and whether the difficulties you have observed
were difficulties that could be solved just by improving the

PSYCHOLOGY OF COMPUTER USE
ISBN 0-12-297420-4

hardware, or whether they were problems of understanding.
We think you will agree that it ought to be possible to find
simpler ways to do things.

To be sure, some of the problems with computers originate
in their hardware: chip design and disc design, keyboard
design and display design. But even though the computer is
a physical device, many of the problems that plague users are
entirely unphysical. A good analogy would be the practice of
commercial arithmetic before the introduction of arabic numerals. Adding up numbers in the roman system is much harder
than in the arabic system, because the value of a digit is
affected by its neighbours to right and left: whereas in the
arabic system numbers can be lined up in columns of digits
from most-significant to least-significant. Experiment suggests that human information processing is at its best when
abstract properties such as significance can be mapped onto
perceptual properties such as spatial position. Hence it is
hardly surprising that adding up numbers in the roman system
is harder - to say nothing of computing discounts or interest
payments. While roman numerals were in use the basic requirements of commerce demanded much more skill and experience
than today, and if possible the assistance of physical objects
("counters", used for counting), all because of the system
that was used. The difficulties were overcome by changing to
a system that performed the same logical operations, but in
a manner more consonant with the fundamental psychological
design of the human.

Today we are more familiar with the principles that the
meaning of a symbol, such as a digit, should be independent
of its context if possible, and that values and meanings are
perceived more readily if they are coded onto perceptual
dimensions such as position instead of being purely symbolic.
Whether that would make us ready to invent a positional notation for numbers if it had not yet been invented is very
doubtful. But the example illustrates the type of difficulty
that computer users meet, and also how solutions depend on
making the communication and information handling fit better
with human psychology.

What is needed, we believe, is a fusion between cognitive
psychology and computer science. To build really usable
systems we need to know what difficulties users face, and
why: we need to devise ways to circumvent them: and we need
to be able to evaluate the result and discover whether the
new system really has solved anyting. Neither computer
scientists nor psychologists can do it all. Moreover we then
need to mesh the results into the lives of users without
creating misery and poverty at other points in the social
structure - a whole different set of problems which must be

kept in mind, although it goes beyond the scope of this
work.

How can we combine diverse skills and knowledge? Many
European research groups met for the first time at the
Amsterdam conference. Not all the contributions, unfortunately, could be included, but when we review at the end of
this chapter the papers that we could include it will be
clear that a great variety of investigations are in progress.
In order to appreciate them properly it is necessary to have
some understanding of the relevant trends in the underlying
disciplines of computing science and psychology. For instance it would be difficult to understand the significance
of Hoc's study of trainee programmers unless one knew that
the particular method they were taught was an example of the
systematic approach that most professional programmers advocate these days: so that when Hoc finds that the trainees
were unable to keep to the system, it casts doubt on widely-
held and extremely influential beliefs. In the next parts
of this introduction, therefore, we shall sketch some of the
more important features of the intellectual landscape around
us.

SOME TRENDS IN COMPUTING

As everyone knows, we are witnessing a hardware revolution:
machines many times more powerful than those that some of us
did our first research on can now be bought as toys. If the
trends in Britain (where it is reported that twice as many
home computers per head had been sold by Christmas, 1982, as
in the USA) are followed elsewhere, popular computing magazines will flourish and large numbers of enthusiasts will
appear. Those enthusiasts have been given a choice between
Basic and a few alternatives - Pascal, Comal, Forth, C, Logo,
come to mind - and up to now they have voted overwhelmingly
with their feet: Basic Rules OK. If their letters in the
popular magazines are indicative, the reason is simple. They
find the syntax of Pascal too difficult, they find that there
are too many semantic niceties, and above all they do not
want to use a compiled language. They wish to pursue an
"evolutionary" approach to programming. During development
a program is a plastic object, to be moulded gradually into
the desired shape. They may even not know until the program
is nearly finished what that desired shape really is. Experimentation, not forethought, is their watchword.

On the other side of the conceptual water, a different
revolution has happened - a revolution in programming methodology. The computer science fraternity has been working hard
to develop principles of "software engineering". A big

system demands disciplined design, with specified objectives
and careful planning; it demands a professional approach to
information handling, such as passing documents and partial
designs from one stage to the next; and it needs support
tools to help file, interrelate, and retrieve all this information. The construction of programs is rigorously guided,
both at the team level and at the individual programmer level
by the "structured programming methodology" in its various
forms, an approach that could hardly differ more from what
is sometimes disparagingly called "Basic hacking". The
entire design, it is claimed, should be built, working top-
down, deferring actual coding until the design is complete.
Forethought all the way, and no experimentation.

In fact, still stronger arguments are advanced. Forethought alone, it is said, is not sufficient; it may be
mistaken, however careful and meticulous. The only foolproof method is to use formal notations to design a program
and to prove it correct. A number of notation and axiom
systems have been proposed.

The structured programming methodology has not appealed
greatly to amateurs. Perhaps that is not surprising. Even
if they were willing to accept its rigorous discipline, such
a degree of forethought and accurate planning cannot be
achieved without experience to guide the programmer. As for
the axiomatics of program statements and their algebra - it
is impossible to believe that amateurs will ever use them.
Conversely, those of us with computing experience are not
very surprised to learn that "evolution", or hacking if you
prefer, can lead to truly perplexing tangles, programs no
more readable than a crossword puzzle. Such programs all
too often hide obscure bugs.

Naturally there is a lot of rhetoric about these issues.
To find a true balance between these opposed philosophies one
would like to know whether the structured programming methodology can really be taught to novices, or whether it can
only be used by experienced programmers; whether hacking has
real advantages or merely feels good, a pleasurable indulg-
ence; and what advantages might be achieved by structuring
programs in different ways.

Finally, a third revolution is taking place, almost
unnoticed as yet; the software package revolution. Commerc-
ially-produced programs are falling on us like leaves in
autumn. Word-processors, data-bases, spread-sheet calculat-
ors, financial packages, symbolic algebra programs, program
generators, graphics packages, - the air is full of them.
Not so long ago, users glumly accepted that they would have
to write most of their software themselves. Today, that
same toy computer we mentioned before probably boasts a

simple accounting package for the price of a pair of shoes.
A far smaller percentage of users will have to write programs
in the old-fashioned way. Instead they will make extensive
use of command languages and pseudo-codes.

   Packages have their own problems. Quite apart from the
manuals that are often long, diffuse, and ill-written, some
packages are much easier to use than others, despite every
good intention on the designer's part. There is much to
understand about the psychological requirements for a successful software package, but we have learnt a little about
how to choose names for the different functions in a package;
looking ahead, papers will be found here telling us a little
more about the choosing of names, and also about the problems
of displaying the results in a comprehensible manner after
they have been computed.

SOME TRENDS IN PSYCHOLOGY

Diversity within psychology is older than in computing and
perhaps even more deep-rooted. One view has always been that
the best science comes from the controlled experiment, from
comprehensive studies of simple tasks isolated from interference from irrelevant distraction. To study driving, a
first move would be to study the determinants of choice-
reaction time. This has a long and successful history in
many sciences; yet in psychology it has led to more false
starts than we care to list in public, to novel paradigms
and promising developments which generated a huge research
literature and slowly fizzled out. This style of research
has been termed "phenomenon-driven" and has been heavily
criticised at times, but despite all criticisms it has created conceptual frameworks and well-established findings which
have undoubted application to the development of usable computer systems. Above all it has generated research techniques. What is the use of claiming that one computing
system is better than another, if no empirical test can be
made? And how can tests of usability be made, it is argued,
but by the techniques of controlled experiment, in which
sources of confounding are rigorously excluded, randomised,
or balanced?

   The tradition of controlled experiments, as applied to
cognitive activities, has met with two different criticisms.
Some critics concentrate on the problem of individual differences, which are frequently ignored in laboratory studies.
In applied psychology that is indeed sometimes inevitable;
when it was necessary to choose between roman and arabic
numbers, the choice had to be made for all people affected,
and questions of individual differences were less important

than overall effects. So it is now with, say, the Ada language; for the sake of uniformity one single programming language was considered necessary by the US Department of Defense.
In any case, it is almost certainly the case that some notational structures are better than others, in at least some
ways, for virtually everyone (assuming, perhaps, equal practice on different methods). For instance, the arabic number
system, whose advantages we discussed above, may conceivably
be better than the roman, without qualification. And conceivably some programming notations have similar advantages
over others, at least for some tasks.

Still, the criticism remains valid that controlled experimentation too often neglects individual differences. It is
of course true that people are different from each other,
and that a given language design or programming system may
suit some better than others, depending on age, education,
occupation, cultural background, cognitive style, etc. All
these effects can be studied in laboratory settings, and we
can look ahead to van der Veer and van de Wolde's paper for
an example bringing considerations of individual cognitive
style into the analysis. Almost certainly the individual
work-desk could be fitted with a choice of information systems to suit individual tastes and talents.

Nevertheless the goal of psychology is to tell us about
real life, not the psychology laboratory, and recent developments in cognitive science are directing attention to
tasks that are richer, more complex, and more realistic than
those of traditional laboratories. At the same time there
have been attempts to create detailed theoretical formalis-
ations of both the mental representation of knowledge, and
the processes involved in using knowledge. Rather than
record merely how long their subjects took to do a task and
whether they got it right, cognitive scientists today more
often ask how their subjects arrived at their answer, regard-
less of whether it was right or wrong. Much of their work
has been based on studies of "thinking aloud", detailed
studies of small numbers of subjects, during which their
verbal reports are recorded and later analysed in depth.

There has also been increased interest in applying the
techniques of artificial intelligence to theory-building in
psychology. An important tenet in artificial intelligence
is that the problem-solving program needs to contain a model
of its environment, and this view has been imported into cognitive psychology to say that people also need a mental model
of their environment if they are to solve problems successfully. We shall see this in Kahney's paper where he attempts
to elucidate the novice's mental model of the programming
system.

These different approaches to the psychology of cognition are aimed at the same ends, but they are arriving by different routes. Traditional experimental methods are more likely to tell us whether proposed improvements in systems will be successful, by the simple method of try it and see, while the psychology of mental representations is perhaps more likely to bring about fundamental shifts in our viewpoint. We should not suppose that only one approach is right.

SOME QUESTIONS

The psychologists and computer scientists who have contributed to this volume have adopted a variety of approaches, reflecting the vigorous differences in outlook of their disciplines. Their papers were originally delivered to a small conference audience, together with many others that could not be included here, and despite the diversity of outlook it was noticeable that discussion frequently returned to the same questions.

What sort of thinking do computer systems demand?

Algorithmic thinking does not come easily to all. In a paper that could not be included here, Tauber (FEoLL, Paderborn) argued that before programming could be treated as a problem-solving activity, it was necessary to appreciate all its three component parts of problem definition, algorithm design, and coding. At present, he felt, the education of programmers seriously neglected the first of these. Similar concerns were voiced by Dirkzwager (Amsterdam), whose paper also could not be included; he emphasised that people and computers were complementary systems in communication. Too often the view of the joint system was dominated by the computer component rather than by the human component, creating the attitude that the users' work was only "well-defined" when its function in relation to the machine was clear. But if the person were seen as the primary system, then the emphasis would be on creative thinking and constructing, and activities would be evaluated in terms of whether they contributed to the human's goals rather than to the machine's. To achieve such a shift in viewpoint was a major problem in computer education.

Should we set standards and make value judgments, or should we apply our methods wherever we can?

Perhaps this should be rephrased in the form "Should we, as psychologists/computer scientists, take sides in the battle between Basic hackers and structured programmers?" Some felt that we should accept hacking as a natural

approach to programming, and attempt to make hacking easier
rather than to attempt forcible re-education: for instance,
Green (Sheffield University) described plans for a "programmer's Torch" which would illuminate amateur's Basic programs
and help readers to understand them by providing an automatic
analysis. Others felt that if the case for structured programming was sound it should be promulgated, and no encourage-
ment should be given to hackers.

> Is there an alternative to conformist views of
> computing?

A discussion paper distributed by Bjerg (Copenhagen University) emphasised the need to consider cognitive engineering
in the domestic world; not looking at the traditional trends
in computing, derived from administrative computing and gam-
ing, but trying to develop what he jokingly called a "domestic insight accelerator". The "DIA" should be decentrally
developed, he argued, preferably in time for the private
household to outline its conditions for hooking itself into
wider networks. Domestic life is not going to absorb computers easily, and Bjerg stressed the importance of looking
ahead and if possible trying simulations of highly computerised family living.

> While we try to design convenient, friendly tools are
> we unwittingly making deskilled, uncreative jobs for
> others?

This well-founded worry was voiced by many, including
Volpert and Fromman (Technical University, Berlin) in
another paper that could not be included here. Pointing out
how industrial psychology in the past had shown more concern
with profitability than with humanity, they showed that new
technology was narrowing decision latitudes in many jobs,
with severe and detrimental effects. Their theory of the
psychology of action, unlike many other approaches, allows
them to bring out the difficulty experienced in, for instance,
making rapid decisions with inadequate planning time. We
should be conscious of the social impact of what we create,
and concerned to avoid creating misery.

AN OVERVIEW

It is now time to locate the papers in the landscape we have
sketched above. The first section of the book deals with all
aspects of computer working except programming; the second is
devoted to programming, which is the classical problem of the
area.

Our first two papers tackle the conceptual nature of "dialogue" between people and machines; both bring out the problem that our lifetime experience with person-to-person dialogue leaves us ill-disposed to cope with the limitations and unsubtleties of dialogue with computers.

Maass is particularly concerned with the problem that attempts to build friendly tools are in practice likely to reduce job richness, pointing out that conditions in computerised offices are such as to make the users feel that it is they who are tools for running machines. Working from a formal model of natural communication between equal partners she shows how deficient, inflexible, and impoverished existing communications between people and computers are. Her concept of "transparent" systems design would make it easy for users to build an internal model of their communication partner, and she lists some of the necessary requirements for a system to appear transparent.

Pinsky's paper, also concerned with the differences and similarities between natural dialogue and dialogue with machines, comes at it from a different angle. Instead of starting with a formal model he looks at hiatuses that have occurred in actual dialogue between experienced operators and a complex coding system. The effects of these hiatuses or "pathological dialogues" are an increase in workload, as measured by the usual indices. Pinsky examines how the presuppositions and conditions of natural dialogue, have been violated in these hiatuses and attempts to define the elements of the computer's "conversational incompetence". In this way one can arrive at a better understanding of the requirements for a smooth dialogue in which the user will never be at a loss, and indeed at a better understanding of the nature of dialogue.

The next two papers treat the problems of information display. Using computers to help solve problems is pointless if their users face further problems in trying to assimilate the computer's output. Judging by the many stacks of line-printer listings that one sees, all too often containing only a few abbreviated captions, the techniques and problems of displaying information have not come to the notice of as many computer programmers as they might have. It is not just a question of pampering and coddling the users; serious misinterpretation of computer output can be a grave risk. There is also a risk of dismaying and perplexing users to the point at which they reject the computer altogether.

Our first paper on information display, by Preece, discusses the difficulties that school children meet in interpreting graphical information displays. Especially with the improved graphical displays on present-day micro-computers,

it is too often tempting to present a graph instead of a
table of figures and assume that no further thought is needed.
Preece firmly disposes of such attitudes, listing varieties
of misinterpretations made by children and attempting to
trace their origins. While some of the problems are not surprising (at least with the help of hindsight), such as difficulties in interpreting multiple interdependent curves and
discovering the causal relations between many phenomena all
displayed at once, other problems are unexpected; for
instance Preece finds several different sources of difficulty
in the interpretation of gradients on graphs. Even cues
intended to assist graph-reading, such as helpful arrows, can
turn out to be distractors setting up strong conflicts in
interpretation. This is important reading for anyone dealing with educational computing.

Senach's concerns are with workers in the Paris Metro,
where complex problems arise from rescheduling trains after
incidents that put the driver, the train, or both out of
commission. He shows how analysing possible incidents, and
the information needed to resolve them, reveals shortcomings
in the present form of information display used to resched-
ule the time-table. A redesigned display neatly corrected
the problem and showed that by applying our present understanding of the processes of problem-solving, it is at least
sometimes possible to pin-point sources of difficulty.
Senach also points out another lesson of his work. In conventional job analysis, skilled operators with several years'
experience are usually treated as experts, and ergonomists
rely on them for knowledge of the best strategies; but in
this study it was clear that the poor information display
was degrading their problem-solving performance quite
severely - for instance, they were unable to spot the res-
emblance between formally identical incidents, and treated
each one as a separate case. We should beware of using
"expert" information, it appears, unless it can be shown that
all the information needed for the task is properly displayed
for their use.

The last topic in this section is the design of command
languages - the instructions used to control the software
packages which, in the opinion of many, will take a larger
and larger share of computer usage at the expense of "real"
programming. Early command languages gave every impression
of having been pieced together. Today there is far more
concern for the user, and designers go to some trouble to
avoid arbitrary, illogical, unmemorable designs. Or do
they? Jørgensen *et al.* report a large study in which professional software designers chose names for the twelve functions of a simple software package. In this, the only such

broad comparison in the literature, designers varied enorm-
ously in the helpfulness and systematicity of the names they
chose. They also produced, between them, an astonishing variety of different names, but Jørgensen *et al.* were able to
find a degree of underlying order and to show that designers
frequently adopted similar strategies in choosing names; software functions of particular types were given names chosen
to reveal particular aspects.

In the second section we turn to the problems of programming, and more generally of supporting the activities of
software engineering. Here perhaps we meet the diversity of
viewpoint most strongly. For instance, in the first group
of papers, dealing with the design of programming languages,
we have papers describing armchair design based on a theory
of program comprehension, individual differences in relation
to language constructs, and mental models of novice programmers.

Sengler's design for a programming language is extremely
interesting. He starts with an analysis of the process of
comprehension, adopting recent work in the psychology of
information-processing and experiments on the relative com-
prehensibility of programming languages, and then offers one
realisation of the requirements, the language GRADE. This
language makes extensive use of graphical notations to con-
vey its information, since perceptually coded information is
more easily understood than symbolic, and makes efforts to
reduce the complexity of interactions possible between program components.

Van der Veer and van de Wolde present an experimentalist's
paper, in which they extend previous research on the design
of conditional constructions in programming languages.
Their work is the first to treat individual differences in
cognitive style and other learner characteristics systematically and successfully, and also the first to report com-
parisions between abstract and realistic scenarios. They
recorded the success of their subjects in writing a variety
of short programs in different miniature programming languages, dealing with deeper levels of nesting than have pre-
vously been used and also including "non-hierarchical"
problems. Although, like previous researchers, they found
some languages better than others, the pattern was not simply
that "nest" styles are always better than "jump" styles.
They conclude that we should not over-dramatise differences
between languages; a programming language that looks exceed-
ingly difficult may yet be successful because it maps onto
the learner's experience well. This paper is one of several
in this volume in which some of the more didactic utterances
of the structured programming school are brought into question.

   Rather than trying to isolate good and bad features of language design, Kahney attempts to characterise the "mental
model" of programming in the mind of the novice. Unlike van
der Veer and van de Wolde, who used traditional experimental
and statistical techniques, Kahney made extensive use of detailed verbal reports, or "thinking aloud", from people trying
to write programs. Classifying their utterances into types
revealed common strategies, and Kahney reached the conclusion
that one of the major differences between novice and expert
was in the underlying conception, the "mental model": the
novices' models of recursion were inaccurate or even super-
stitious. However, Kahney found a small number of talented
novices who were indistinguishable from experts (and, inter-
estingly, also found them in other published comparisons of
experts and novices) which suggests that our previous con-
ceptions of how the learning process applies to programming
may be over-simple.
   Next come two papers dealing with the methodology of structured programming, one of the most significant forces in the
software engineering revolution. In the methods advocated
for creating well-structured programs there are two important
components. Problems are attacked top-down, dividing them
into smaller sub-problems and then if necessary dividing those
in turn into sub-sub-problems, until a level is reached at
which program code can be written. The final design is then
rigorously checked to ensure that the code for each component
performs the intended task, and that the components taken
together add up to the intended whole. There are many ways
of doing each, some more heavy-handed, authoritarian, and
Levitical, others more relaxed and intuitive.
   Hoc reports briefly a series of experiments which bear on
the first component. For his first study he recorded the
progress of trainee programmers longitudinally during a three-
month intensive training course which taught the Warnier
method of program design, a method in which the steps to be
performed are laid out rather exactly and the programmer is
allowed very little variation. Some of the five steps in the
Warnier method are supposed to be completely determined by
the problem given - for instance, the structure of the input
data file and the output results file determine together the
structure of the program; other steps are supposed to be completely determined by the previous steps - for instance, when
the flow-chart stage is reached, its conversion to program
code is supposed to be mechanical. Hoc found that, quite
the contrary, even at the end of the training period his subjects still made a new analysis of the problem at each step
of the method, and were heavily guided by executing the program in their heads, so that they programmed parts of their

solution in the order in which they encountered them during
their mental execution rather than in the order specified by
the Warnier method. Further studies in which beginners
attempted to solve simple programming problems showed that
subjects found it very hard to perform some of the mental
operations required by structured programming methods; it was
difficult for them to approach the problems except by taking
previously-known procedures and adapting them to computer
operation, and once they had chosen a basic program structure
they found it difficult to change it, although they could
tinker with the details readily enough.

The second component of the structured programming methodology, verifying that the program design is correct, forms
the subject of Naur's paper, based not on experimental method
but on careful observation of a single expert programmer -
himself. Naur has described for us the process of writing
and testing a program of moderate length. During this process he kept a careful diary or day-book, recording progress,
calculations, important details, etc. The solution process
as recorded in the diary diverged strikingly from some of
the more extreme suggestions of methodological enthusiasts.
Although meticulous planning and well-judged decisions were
clearly vital to the success of the programming project, the
order of working was not rigidly laid down (in contrast to
the training course studied by Hoc); moreover the justification for each step was simply that the author could see that
it was correct, using formalisms only as and when necessary,
whereas some writers have recommended rigid and highly formal
techniques for justifying each step in program development.
Naur concludes that keeping the diary was a significant help
in accurate, well-planned programming and recommends it as a
standard practice. He also points out that studying programming diaries makes a useful supplement to more standard
methods of psychological investigation, helping to find what
hypotheses about the program development process might be
worth investigation for validity.

The last papers in the book deal with the support environment for programmers. Programming is not carried out in iso-
lation; it requires text editors, cross references, "pretty-
printers" to format the program text in a consistent and useful style, etc. Contemporary program development requires
very complex support environments, in which the programming
tools and their inter-relationships can become very complex.

Hägglund and Tibell describe one kind of tool, a system
for rapidly constructing draft versions (prototypes) of programs requiring interactive dialogue. Frequently about two-
thirds of an interactive program is taken up with dialogue
management, they point out, which argues very strongly for

their notion of "control independence" - separating the dialogue management from the real purpose of the program. Their
system models dialogues in terms of messages, contexts, and
context transitions, and is sufficiently powerful to allow
the same dialogue to be carried out in different styles, such
as menu-selection, command languages, or VDU forms, with minimal modification; a significant step for the goal of systems
easily adapted to individual preferences and easily trimmed
to changing requirements.

The last paper, by Arblaster, describes the evaluation of
a proposed environment for software engineering under human
factors criteria. This project is both unusual and important,
both for tackling such a large system and for coming to grips
with the new programming language Ada. Although a number of
empirical studies on small programming problems have been
reported there has been little well-informed treatment of
large systems; only suggestions (based on what Arblaster
calls "armchair musings") for avoiding user difficulties. It
is not hard to see why. Arblaster and his colleagues used a
number of methods. Starting from a survey of the state of
knowledge of human factors as applicable to programming support environments they developed checklists to be used
against design features of each part of the environment.
They then made a detailed evaluation of the UK design for a
support environment for Ada and finished with two "rapid
prototyping" exercises during which the proposed facilities
were tried out. The particular conclusions reached during
this exercise included a large number of detailed findings,
not contained in the present paper, and a number of general
findings about inter-relationships between different programming tools in the same software environment. Most important,
however, is the demonstration that a serious human factors
evaluation of a large software project is feasible, and that
at least one commercial organisation is prepared to carry it
out.

INTO THE FUTURE

As it happens, we have not touched on some important issues.
Computing scientists have recently spent much effort on designing systems incorporating concurrent processes, which can
take place either genuinely simultaneously or else in any
convenient order. Finding notations that are readable,
powerful, and secure has not been easy, and the results have
not yet filtered down into common use. We have no contribution in this book that deals with the problems of concurrent
programming; nor with program generators, which supposedly
turn English-language problem statements into working pro-

grams; the effect of networks of computers, of electronic
mail systems, and of small, powerful, battery-operated portable computers; or the future of "expert systems" and "knowledge engineering", computer programs which can perhaps en-
capsulate the knowledge of expert clinicians or gardeners
and provide advice to laymen.

As that list shows, there are exciting times ahead. But
most of the issues we have not covered will affect how we
use computers and how our lives are altered by them, without
changing in any fundamental way the nature of the difficulties we meet in using them. So let us try and sum up, very
briefly, what the state of research suggests at present.

First we take a look at computer education, since very
large numbers of people of all ages will have to learn about
computing over the next few years. Our contributors seem to
agree that the highly structured approach to programming has
drawbacks as well as rewards. Both Hoc and Naur raise doubts
about rigid programming methods, and although van der Veer
and van de Wolde found that the modern, "structured" programming languages were on the whole better in the design of
some of their syntactic constructions, the advantages were
not as overwhelmingly impressive as they could have been.
Evolutionary, plastic programming - or hacking - seems to
have a future for novices.

More attention will need to be given to how programs are
understood. Kahney's paper shows very clearly that the programming of novices is controlled by their mental model of
how the system works, and it will be necessary to design
languages for novices taking into account underlying models.
It will also be necessary to simplify drastically the mental
operations needed to make sense of a program. Sengler's
unusual graphical programming language shows that there are
still many paths we can explore, and that language design
could be influenced much more by cognitive psychology than
it has been so far.

Turning to professionals, the evidence suggests that at
present it is hard to get as close to their difficulties as
we can to the difficulties of learners. Nevertheless,
Arblaster's paper shows that the study of human factors in
programming has generated enough applicable knowledge to
make it feasible to evaluate large systems at the prototype
stage. We can also look forward to a time when it will be
easier to take psychologists' evaluations into account.
Where today it is impossible to get adequate guidance on
whether a system will be hard to use before it is so near
completion that little can be changed, with tools like
Hägglund and Tibell's system, the structure of the user inter-

face can easily be trimmed in the light of assessment and experience.

The users of packages of various sorts will eventually be able to benefit from improved and more systematic approaches to both their input and their output, although our contributors have found more problems than answers, as yet. Jørgensen *et al.* have been able to shed some light on the apparently haphazard process of naming commands. With some idea of what approaches designers can choose between, we may be able to take steps towards showing how different repertoires of names help to elucidate different types of information and to give suggestions as to when particular choices might be appropriate. At the output end, the dangers of casual assumptions are revealed by Preece; making a computer draw a graph is by no means the easy solution to displaying information comprehensibly that one might well think. Here again, care will have to be taken to avoid those features of graphs that confuse their less expert users. As Senach demonstrates, the successful approach to information display is to analyse the task performed by users and to discover what information they need, and then to design the display so that that information is clearly revealed. Probably it will take time to build a tradition of careful work of this sort.

Lastly we return to the fascinating comparison between the interaction of people with each other and the interaction of people with machines. The contributions of psycholinguists and their kin will be needed before we can make much headway, perhaps, yet the need to do so is demonstrated by Pinsky's reports of the difficulties met even by experienced operators as they grapple with the inflexibilities of machine "dialogue". Can we see how to improve matters? Perhaps we are beginning to; Maass offers one type of formal analysis, and continued efforts may help to make it clearer how to match the expectations of users.

We began this introduction with the claim that many of the problems of using computers were psychological, unlike the problems of using most other devices born of technology. By now it will be clear that effective solutions depend on the joint contribution of psychologists and computer scientists. The contributors to this book illustrate some of the possible routes of progress.

Psychology of Using Computers

WHY SYSTEMS TRANSPARENCY ?

SUSANNE MAASS

Universitaet Hamburg
Hamburg, Germany

1) INTRODUCTION

User friendliness, ergonomic systems design, systems flexibility, ease of use, systems transparency - these are some of
the increasingly well-known catchwords in computer human factors discussions of the last five years (cf. Dehning, Essig
and Maass, 1981). This paper will concentrate on the issue of
systems transparency. It characterises the computer not any
more as a number crunching machine but as a communication
medium, even as a virtual communication partner programmed
for the performance of certain roles. The analogy with human
communication provides concepts for a new understanding of
the users' situation in their interaction with a computer
system. It will become obvious that systems transparency
should be a central issue in the discussion of human factors
and user friendly systems design.

Systems transparency can be defined in different ways.

a) - A transparent system does not hide any of its functions
     and mechanisms from the user (you can "look inside").
b) - A transparent system does not obscure the user's view on
     the problems he wants to solve with the computer (com-
     parable to a well cleaned window).
c) - A transparent system appears well structured, consistent
     and comprehensible to its users; the users can easily
     build up an internal model of the relevant parts of the
     system.
d) - Transparency is the degree to which the logical user
     interface conforms with the user's prior knowledge or
     human intuition. (Notice the reference to the individual
     user!)

Our later definition will integrate b, c and d.

PSYCHOLOGY OF COMPUTER USE
ISBN 0-12-297420-4

2) WORK WITH COMPUTERS

Computers are said to be universal machines which can be specialised by programming. A specific characteristic of these
machines is that we manipulate them by language: By means of
words we indicate the functions to be performed and (in most
cases) we see the effects that have been achieved displayed
verbally on the screen. Especially important is the fact that
the computer can comment on its own functioning; it can tell
the user how to handle it in what situations and for what purposes. So the notions "human-computer dialog" and "human-computer communication" have grown up to characterise the resulting particular system-user relationship.

The implicitly suggested analogy to natural interpersonal
communication has already often been criticised as misleading:
the anthropomorphisation of computer systems might induce
people to over-estimate the machine facilities. It also con-
tributes to the unnecessarily high status of interactive work
with computers.

But how do people work with computers? Let's take the
example of office computers.

In most cases computers - as other technologies before
them - are being introduced for rationalisation purposes;
nearly every application program aims at the substitution of
human work (cf. Briefs, 1980). The permanent standardisation
and formalisation of work processes in the past and the reor-
ganisation of work by increased division of labour have prepared the ground for the advent of computers.

Instead of using documents, reports, filing cards and
forms the office worker now sits at his VDU screen entering
data, following programmed procedures and watching the results.
For this he has to learn how to handle the system, i.e. the
dialog commands and data formats. A great part of the experience he had with the office procedures he performed before
is not important any more. The procedures are incorporated in
the programs he's now working with. The remaining work processes of data preparation and interpretation get further
standardised and formalised.

The system's behaviour and through it the surrounding
work organisation is thus determined by the systems designers
and programmers. Users normally only get some minimal information about the system. In many companies it is common to
give them a short introduction in a training session of 2 -
3 hours at the terminal. After that they certainly do not
understand how it works or how to recover from problematic
situations in dialog. Their own role has been defined without
them being able to exercise much influence, but nevertheless
they have to conform to it.

This short description of people's working conditions in the computerised office should have made clear that in many applications users do not perceive the computer just as a handy tool. (They possibly rather get the feeling of themselves being tools for running the machine). And how could they - additionally considering the fact that the system may permanently monitor their performance data at the terminal: their reaction times, their mistakes, their preferred function sequences, their break times ... as common management information systems do.

In our opinion the situation could be partially improved by transparent systems design, which helps the user to understand the machine and make use of it. Of course the control of users by management cannot be removed by systems transparency as it will be defined later on.

In spite of the criticism mentioned above we will stick to the expression "human-computer communication". We will compare human interaction with computers to an extremely restricted kind of communication, namely that of formal or even algorithmic communication. This analogy will explain the vital importance of systems transparency.

3) NATURAL VERSUS FORMAL COMMUNICATION

The study of psycholinguistic literature (see e.g. Laing et al., 1966; Lewis, 1969; Gloy and Presch, 1975) has led us to a rough model of natural communication. For representation we use channel/agency and means/activity nets, which are special kinds of Petri nets (see Oberquelle, 1980).

* Clearly this feeling of importance is a bad thing, but is the solution to make the system more understandable, or to make it seem to be more understandable?

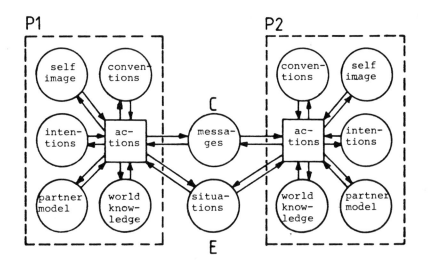

(channel/agency and means/activity net
representations combined as indicated below)

Communication is seen as a complex of social actions for the
purpose of understanding and of allowing coordinated actions.
It takes place by means of a *medium*, the communication channel (C), and involves at least two communicating *agents* (P1
and P2). In the model we separate the communication medium
from the rest of reality (the *environment* E) which surrounds
the partners.

   Several factors are supposed to influence people's communicating behaviour.*

   In communication the *sender* wants to achieve some effect
in the recipient, i.e., he has some underlying *intentions*
which guide the planning process for his messages. In order
to be comprehensible to the partner he orients along certain
common *conventions* and a *partner model*. In natural communication social norms of conduct and social roles are reflected

---

*Of course this kind of formal model cannot deal with all
aspects of the complicated phenomenon of communication. However, it already suffices to provide new insights.

in the applied syntactic, semantic and pragmatic linguistic
conventions. Partner models help to predict the partner's
behaviour and expectations. The statement planning process
is also influenced by the sender's *self image*, i.e. his self
confidence, his conscious habits, the role he considers himself to be in... As well as knowledge about conventions the
sender uses his *world knowledge*.

The *recipient* tries to reconstruct the planning process of
the message to understand it. To comprehend its meaning he
has to find out the factors that influenced the partner in
formulating his statement. This understanding process and the
subsequent actions of the recipient of the message in turn
depend on his set of conventions, self image, intentions,
partner model and world knowledge.

An essential feature of human communication is the permanent possibility of making the dialog itself and the relationship between the participants a topic of communication (in so-
called "*metacommunication*"). Partner models, intentions, conventions etc. can be discussed and mutually modified explicitly. (In our model this is indicated by the double arrows
between all the components).

An agent is said to show *formal communicating behaviour* if
all the components relevant to his behaviour can be described
by mathematical models. Sometimes only a subset of the model
components might be at all relevant. *Formal communication*
takes place if at least one of the participants shows formal
communicating behaviour. By this he indirectly forces the
other participants to adapt themselves and communicate formally as well: if they do not consider the partner's restricted interpretation facilities they run the risk of being
misunderstood or just rejected. Strictly formal communicating
behaviour often does not allow any questioning, not to speak
of modification by the partner.

In many cases formal communicating behaviour of people can
be explained by the fact that they act in certain *roles* which
may have been *delegated* to them and by which they feel restricted: think, e.g., of an inflexible clerk. (For further
details see Kupka, Maass and Oberquelle, 1981). Delegation
usually covers the handling of standard cases only. In exceptional cases it must be clear who identifies them as such
and what has to be done. This is no problem in human communication, where people play roles consciously and normally are
able to leave their roles temporarily to cope with unexpected
situations.

4) HUMAN - COMPUTER COMMUNICATION

The programming of computer systems can be considered as an

extreme form of delegation. Here the relation between behavior and its preconditions is not just formally but even algo-
rithmically described. The delegation of tasks to computers
requires the previous formalisation of the delegated work
processes.

Designers and programmers of interactive systems do not
only delegate functional behaviour (problem solving functions)
but also communicating behaviour (how to handle the virtual
problem solving machine by means of dialog functions). They
design *virtual communication partners* for the users. This is
why we propose a new paradigm which characterises *computers
as communication media with formal communicating behaviour*
(see Kupka, Maass and Oberquelle, 1981 and Maass, Oberquelle
and Kupka, 1982).

In the normal systems design process the designers assume
certain user characteristics, i.e. they have certain - at
times not extremely realistic - *user models* in their minds:
What problem solving functions will the users want to be
carried out by the system? Which technical terms do they use?
What kind of screen layout would they prefer? Would they like
to be led through the dialog or formulate commands without
any prompting? Have they already worked with computers? What
kinds of input errors are they likely to make? According to
their user model certain formal dialog strategies and conventions are chosen and implemented. Altogether they define a
scope of possible user actions and thus: *the system's "partner model"* of the user. Very rarely a system gets a detailed
and comprehensive *"self image"*, which means that it has access to explicit information about its own functioning in
order to give explanations to the user. HELP-functions and
computer-guided dialog forms are steps in this direction.

The designers' intentions concerning the users' behaviour
may be various: they may, for example, want to hurry the user
or to teach him system handling step by step and minimise his
errors, to reduce his actions to data input only or to leave
him a wide scope of actions. Through the dialog conventions
these intentions underlying system design will be perceptible
during system use and the users will attribute them to the
system itself. So we can speak of *"virtual intentions" of a
system*.

The programmed communicating behaviour of the system is
formal and restricted by its nature. The "naive" non-pro-
gramming user has to put up with it. In his dialog with the
interactive system he must *adapt* to the formal models which
do not necessarily match his real needs and expectations and
must follow the conventions. Even if there are alternative
dialog modes to choose between it should be clear that the
user is restricted by the implemented set of options.

Only those users who are able to re-program the machine can theoretically modify the implemented user model to their own liking. In practice, however, this kind of machine adaptation will hardly ever be done because of the complexity of computer systems.

We conclude that computer systems are extremely inflexible virtual communications partners. They force the human user to a strictly formal communicating behaviour. For this purpose the user has to build up a suitable system model in his mind which helps to predict and explain the system's behaviour.

5) SYSTEMS TRANSPARENCY

In our opinion transparent systems design can help the user in this situation of compulsory adaptation.
We define *transparency* as follows:

A transparent system makes it easy for users to build up an internal model of the functions the system can perform for them. This includes the problem solving functions as well as the dialog functions.

Its logical interface conforms with the users' prior knowledge about the problem domain and with human intuition (i.e. how they are used to coping with certain situations in communication). The effort of handling the system (by dialog functions) must not disturb the users' problem solving processes.

This definition is confined to the users' immediate tasks. A user understands the virtual machine he's working with, but he does not necessarily see through the other functions it has, for instance, for his manager or for the personnel division of his company.

So, what makes a system transparent to its users? Obviously, a system which is transparent to one user need not necessarily be transparent to others as well. The ability to understand the system depends on the user's knowledge and experience. (We can thus make a given system transparent even without modifying it - just by extensive training of its users).

However, referring back to the components of our communication model we can derive some general guidelines for transparent design of human-computer communication. (See also Dehning, Essig and Maass, 1981). "Natural" is a function of expectations.

Dialog conventions (syntactic, semantic and pragmatic) should appear as natural as possible to the user:

- For problem solving functions use the language of the application field or technical terms that are common to the user.

- Allow, but do not insist on, abbreviated codes for all kinds
  of functions.
- Avoid artificial expressions that are "natural" only to the
  designers (e.g. in error messages, but also for the required
  commands).
- Allow underdetermined commands (incomplete parameter specification) and let the system ask back.
- Allow metacommunication, e.g. questions for available functions and obligatory formats, choice of different interaction modes, modification of defaults, definition of complex commands (procedures). So, the user can decide which
  dialog conventions he prefers or modify the conventions set
  by the designers within the implemented framework.
- In particular, allow questions at any time, so that the user
  can explore the conventions currently in operation.

A special problem is caused by the fact that the user is rarely confronted with one *consistent interface:* Computer systems
consist of a number of different programs - like operating
systems, editors, compilers, application packages etc.. These
subsystems have been designed independently by different
people who have each implemented their own rather individual
conventions.

- Provide a consistent user interface: similar user commands
  for similar functions, consistent conventions concerning
  abbreviations etc., consistent reactions to user mistakes...

The system should have a *"self image"* to be able to give
explanations about itself to the user.

- Provide context-sensitive HELP-functions that can explain
  the current input alternatives and the expected formats to
  the user; different levels of detail should be available on
  demand.

Apart from systems transparency there are also other requirements for better systems design that can be explained by the
presented concept of formal human-computer communication. For
example, the need for *participative systems design,* or even
"users' design" (cf. Eason and Damodaran, 1981). In our terminology it means that the users get the opportunity of
designing the system's user model themselves, and of making
the system use their own conventions.

 User participation is now beginning to be realised and if
it is practised the right way it has undeniable advantages for
the users. But there are also serious fundamental disadvan-
tages in that systems designers profit from the worker's job
experience to computerise work processes as far as possible
with the effect that the worker's qualification may largely

become superfluous and with it the whole job.

Obviously, user friendly design and user involvement alone are not sufficent to guarantee humane jobs, and cannot reduce the function of computer systems to being simple tools for their users. Their introduction affects the working conditions of the persons concerned too significantly.

6) CONCLUSIONS

The foregoing discussion of human-computer communication should have shown that there is no way of avoiding formal communication for computer users. They cannot but conform to the implemented user model.

The least a designer can do to facilitate the users' compulsory adaptation is to strive for systems transparency so that the users get a chance of understanding the virtual machine they are working with. Nevertheless the system's rigid and formal communicating behaviour will seriously affect the users' work and satisfaction.

This paper was not intended to provide new recommendations to ensure systems transparency. It rather gives a framework of concepts to describe human-computer dialog and to understand its problems; by so doing it also supplies a framework for the many existing design guidelines.

REFERENCES

Briefs, U. (1980). "Arbeiten ohne Sinn und Perspektive? Gewerkschaften und 'Neue Technologien'". Pahl-Rugenstein, Koeln.

Dehning, W., Essig, H. and Maass, S. (1981). "The Adaptation of Virtual Man-computer Interfaces to User Requirements in Dialogs". Lecture Notes in Computer Science, No.110. Springer, Berlin, Heidelberg, New York.

Eason, K.D. and Damodaran, L. (1981). Design procedures for user involvement and user support. In "Computing Skills and the User Interface". (Eds M.J. Coombs and J.L. Alty), pp. 373-388. Academic Press, London.

Gloy, K. and Presch, G. (1975). "Sprachnormen". Vol. 1 - 3. Frommann-Holzboog, Stuttgart.

Kupka, I., Maass, S. and Oberquelle, H. (1981). Kommunikation - ein Grundbegriff fuer die Informatik. Universitaet Hamburg, Fachbereich Informatik. Mitteilung Nr. 91, IFI-HH-M-91/81.

Laing, R.D., Phillipson, H. and Lee, A.R. (1966). "Interpersonal Perception". Tavistock, London, New York.

Lewis, D. (1969). "Convention - A Philosophical Study". Cambridge, Mass.

Maass, S., Oberquelle, H. and Kupka, I. (1982). Human-computer communication: Towards a new understanding. *In* "Office Information Systems". (Ed. Najah Naffah), pp. 551-561. North-Holland, Amsterdam.

Oberquelle, H. (1980). Nets as a tool in teaching and terminology work. *In* " Net Theory and Applications". Lecture Notes in Computer Science. No. 84, pp. 481-506. Springer, Berlin, Heidelberg, New York.

WHAT KIND OF "DIALOGUE" IS IT WHEN WORKING WITH A COMPUTER

LEONARDO PINSKY

Laboratoire de Physiologie du Travail et d'Ergonomie.
Conservatoire National des Arts et Métiers
Paris, France

1) INTRODUCTION

What is one to call the interaction between a computer and
its operator? Considering the range of tasks and the wide
assortment of users that perform them, the answer to this
question is not immediately apparent. Nevertheless, the term
"dialogue", evoking a characteristically human mode of
communication, discourse between two people, is very wide-
spread. Is it a useful or a confusing term?

From the prescriptive point of view Smith (1980) has urged
many serious objections to the argument that natural language
ought to be the model for the design of interactive systems.
Nevertheless, some systems must deal with information in a
natural language; and to enable operators with little or no
formal training to use computers, some interaction facilities
must be very similar to a natural language. So that
interacting with computer systems often has something to do
with natural language. Then one may wonder from the descriptive point of view how appropriate "dialogue" is for the
actual interactions between users and computers?

I will consider this question in the context of a
particular working situation, on-line data entry and coding.
Research on that situation was conducted in two stages:

1. an analysis of operators' work using a first system
   (Pinsky *et al.*, 1979) and
2. experimentations with a group of operators during the
   design of a new system.

The whole research will not be discussed here but only the
point concerning the characterization of the interaction

between the operators and the computer.

2) PRINCIPLES OF THE DATA ENTRY-CODING SYSTEM

The system under consideration was the building of a coded data-base of industrial and occupation information. In a previous investigation people had filled out a printed form (Fig. 1.) containing "closed" questions (like 15 in Fig. 1.) and "open" ones (like 12 and 14) concerning their profession, the name, economic activity and address of the organisation where they work, and so forth.

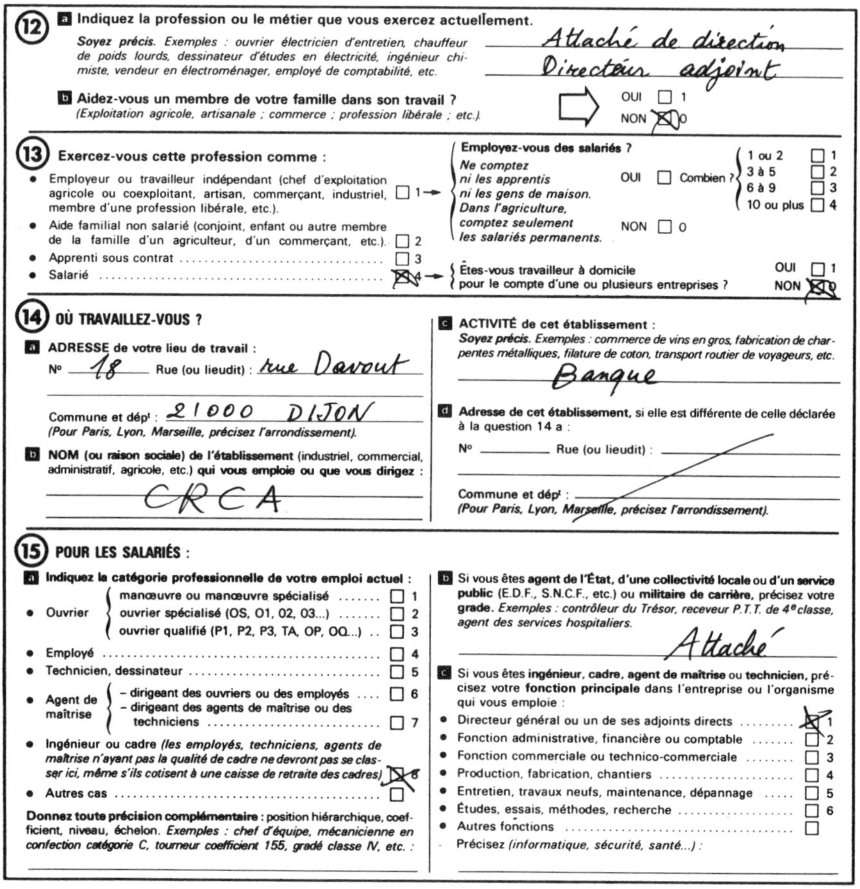

(12) **a Indiquez la profession ou le métier que vous exercez actuellement.**
Soyez précis. Exemples : ouvrier électricien d'entretien, chauffeur de poids lourds, dessinateur d'études en électricité, ingénieur chimiste, vendeur en électroménager, employé de comptabilité, etc. — Attaché de direction / Directeur adjoint

b Aidez-vous un membre de votre famille dans son travail ? *(Exploitation agricole, artisanale ; commerce ; profession libérale ; etc.)* OUI 1 / NON 0 [X]

(13) **Exercez-vous cette profession comme :**
- Employeur ou travailleur indépendant (chef d'exploitation agricole ou coexploitant, artisan, commerçant, industriel, membre d'une profession libérale, etc.). 1 →
- Aide familial non salarié (conjoint, enfant ou autre membre de la famille d'un agriculteur, d'un commerçant, etc.). 2
- Apprenti sous contrat 3
- Salarié 4 [X] →

Employez-vous des salariés ? *Ne comptez ni les apprentis ni les gens de maison. Dans l'agriculture, comptez seulement les salariés permanents.* OUI — Combien ? 1 ou 2 (1), 3 à 5 (2), 6 à 9 (3), 10 ou plus (4); NON 0

Êtes-vous travailleur à domicile pour le compte d'une ou plusieurs entreprises ? OUI 1 / NON 0 [X]

(14) **OÙ TRAVAILLEZ-VOUS ?**

a ADRESSE de votre lieu de travail : N° 18 Rue (ou lieudit) : rue Davout
Commune et dép^t : 21000 DIJON
(Pour Paris, Lyon, Marseille, précisez l'arrondissement).

b NOM (ou raison sociale) de l'établissement (industriel, commercial, administratif, agricole, etc.) **qui vous emploie ou que vous dirigez :** CRCA

c ACTIVITÉ de cet établissement : *Soyez précis. Exemples : commerce de vins en gros, fabrication de charpentes métalliques, filature de coton, transport routier de voyageurs, etc.* — Banque

d Adresse de cet établissement, si elle est différente de celle déclarée à la question 14 a : N° Rue (ou lieudit) : Commune et dép^t : *(Pour Paris, Lyon, Marseille, précisez l'arrondissement).*

(15) **POUR LES SALARIÉS :**

a Indiquez la catégorie professionnelle de votre emploi actuel :
- Ouvrier: manœuvre ou manœuvre spécialisé 1; ouvrier spécialisé (OS, O1, O2, O3...) 2; ouvrier qualifié (P1, P2, P3, TA, OP, OQ...) 3
- Employé 4
- Technicien, dessinateur 5
- Agent de maîtrise: – dirigeant des ouvriers ou des employés 6; – dirigeant des agents de maîtrise ou des techniciens 7
- Ingénieur ou cadre *(les employés, techniciens, agents de maîtrise n'ayant pas la qualité de cadre ne devront pas se classer ici, même s'ils cotisent à une caisse de retraite des cadres)* 8 [X]
- Autres cas

Donnez toute précision complémentaire : position hiérarchique, coefficient, niveau, échelon. *Exemples : chef d'équipe, mécanicienne en confection catégorie C, tourneur coefficient 155, gradé classe IV, etc. :*

b Si vous êtes **agent de l'État, d'une collectivité locale ou d'un service public** (E.D.F., S.N.C.F., etc.) ou **militaire de carrière,** précisez votre **grade.** *Exemples : contrôleur du Trésor, receveur P.T.T. de 4e classe, agent des services hospitaliers.* — Attaché

c Si vous êtes **ingénieur, cadre, agent de maîtrise** ou **technicien,** précisez votre **fonction principale** dans l'entreprise ou l'organisme qui vous emploie :
- Directeur général ou un de ses adjoints directs 1 [X]
- Fonction administrative, financière ou comptable 2
- Fonction commerciale ou technico-commerciale 3
- Production, fabrication, chantiers 4
- Entretien, travaux neufs, maintenance, dépannage 5
- Études, essais, méthodes, recherche 6
- Autres fonctions

Précisez *(informatique, sécurité, santé...) :*

FIG. 1

The task of the computer operators is to transmit a coded version of all the answers to the data base. The first stage in the interaction is to fill in the blanks in a version of

the form which is on the screen (Fig. 2.). Some answers will
have been precoded allowing the operator to enter the code
directly; for others the operator must first enter the answer
in natural language and later engage in interaction with the
computer to ascertain the correct code. When the screen-form
has been completed the operator transmits it to the computer
and awaits the responses.

```
0221 SUI        FOR    MODE O  MAJ     RECH
ECH 20    -D- 59      -C- 178 DST  AH05      IMM 001 LOG 04 CP-   NO- 0009 TA-
PROFESSION DIRECTEUR ADJOINT                                      13-ST 4C
14A-ADRESSE LT:NO- 18                14A-RUE R DAVOUT
14A-COM DIJON                        14A-DEP 21
 14B-RS CAISSE REGIONALE CREDIT AGRICOLE
 14C-AE BANQUE
14D-ADRESSE ET:NO-                   14D-RUE
14D-COM                              14D-DEP
15A-CPF 8      15C-FONC 1    P75 9916          SAU      OPA   PUB   -T-

01   CAISSE   REGION   CREDIT   AGRICOLE   018 R   DAVOUT     8903   03
02   CAISSE   REGION   CREDIT   AGRICOLE   110 AV  EIFFEL     8903   05
03   CAISSE   REGION   CREDIT   AGRICOLE       BD  BACHELAR   8903   03
04   CAISSE   REGION   CREDIT   AGRICOLE   103 AV  DRAPEAU    8903   04
05   CAISSE   REGION   CREDIT   AGRICOLE   089 AV  HUGO       8903   06
06   CAISSE   REGION   CREDIT   AGRICOLE   013 PL  DARCY      8903   12
07   CAISSE   REGION   CREDIT   AGRICOLE       R   JOLY       8903   07
08   CAISSE   REGION   CREDIT   AGRICOLE   004 PL  BANQUE     8903   15
09   CAISSE   REGION   CREDIT   AGRICOLE   060 R   AUXONNE    8903   06
10   COMMISSI REGIONAL AGRICOLE           005 R   RENAUD     9102   02
```

FIG. 2

The computer treats the information on the form in a strict
order as follows:

1. It searches for the name of the organisation in a
   catalogue.
2. If the organisation is found its economic activity, legal
   status, size and address are automatically coded, and the
   sequence jumps to step 5.
3. If the organisation is not found the computer searches for
   the organisation's economic activity as entered by the
   operator in a file of pre-established designations (about
   4000). If found, it is coded; otherwise menus of designations containing recognised words or messages in natural
   language are sent back to the operator.
4. In the same way the computer searches for the organisation's
   address.
5. To code the profession the computer uses the description
   entered by the operator as well as other pieces of
   information (e.g. economic activity, wage earning status,

professional category, duties, size of organisation etc.).
It searches first in a file of pre-established designations
(about 9000) but in contrast to the situation with respect
to economic activities, the match between the description
entered by the operator and the designation in the computer
file need not be complete. For example the computer may
classify all repair-men under the same category, so that
any entry containing the word 'repair-man' (electrical
repair-man, washing machine repair-man etc.) would be
matched against the same designation: 'repair-man'. The
other pieces of information are then used as variables for
decision tables. Which ones will be used in a given case
depends upon the profession in question. If the combination
of the designation and the decision algorithms is successful a code is assigned; otherwise messages are sent back
to the operator requesting further information.

During this complete coding sequence, whenever a code is
finally assigned a brief description of the category is sent
back to the operator for approval.

To clarify the interaction procedure I shall itemise an
extract from an ideal example sequence before going on (in
the next section) to present an analysis of some actual
interactions. Please note all natural language items have
been translated from the original French.

On the printed form is written:

Profession: Certified Nurse
Name of firm: Centre for the Struggle against Cancer
Address: ....
Economic activity: Hospital

The operator enters these data on the screen-form.

The organisation is not found, so the computer searches
for the economic activity. "Hospital" is not coded
automatically so the computer sends a menu of possible designations together with the corresponding codes (see step 3
above):

                8402   SURGICAL HOSPITAL
                8402   GENERAL HOSPITAL
                8402   MATERNITY HOSPITAL
                8402   PUBLIC HOSPITAL
                8404   ALCOHOLIC HOSPITAL
                8404   CANCER HOSPITAL
                8404   PSYCHIATRIC HOSPITAL
                9035   MILITARY HOSPITAL

The operator enters the code corresponding to the designation
he judges appropriate (8404 in this case) and the computer

responds with a brief description of the 8404 category:

8404   SPECIALISED HOSPITAL

If the operator agrees with this category he transmits a
confirmation and the coding process for profession begins.
If however he disagrees he must re-enter the activity
(hospital) whereupon he will again be given a menu and should
choose a different code.

The coding process for the profession will follow very
similar lines.

3) INTERACTION ANALYSIS FROM THE OPERATOR'S POINT OF VIEW

I shall now present some evidence that the interaction
procedure is not always as smooth and easy as the description
above may lead us to believe.

The analysis is based on two types of record:

- observable behaviour: video tapes were made of the operator's
  actions (filling in or modifying the screen-form), his eye
  movements (to determine when he was looking at the screen,
  the printed form, or the keyboard), and the computer's
  responses.
- verbal protocol: tape recordings were made of the operator's
  remarks on his reasoning both while executing the task and
  afterward.

The interpretation of the data so collected requires extensive
discussion with the operators. Close cooperation between
researchers and operators, then, is an essential feature of
our method.

In what follows, I seek only to sketch a framework for the
analysis. By examining the circumstances in which something
goes wrong during the interaction, we may hope to learn more
about the interaction and the operator's cognitive activities.

It often happens that the operator does not understand the
computer's response or thinks it is improper or even is lost.
This is especially evident when considering the verbal
protocol. In the examples that follow I shall first outline
the scenario, that is the stage of the interaction procedure
that is being considered, together with relevant information
concerning the case in hand. Then the computer's most recent
response will be given, as it appears on the screen, followed
by the operators remarks.

A.

    Scenario: The transmitted screen-form contained:

            profession = Doctor of Urology
            economic activity = Hospital

The economic activity has already been coded.

The computer's response is:

DOCTOR OF MEDICINE..., DOCTOR... (WITHOUT A PRIVATE
PRACTICE)

-SPECIALIST	
(SURGEON, OPTHALMOLOGIST)	ENTER THE SPECIALITY
-HOSPITAL STAFF DOCTOR	
(ARMY DOCTORS EXCLUDED)	ENTER C-SA01
-NON-HOSPITAL, STAFF DOCTOR	
(ARMY DOCTORS EXCLUDED):	
COMPANY DOCTOR, SCHOOL DOCTOR,	
CONSULTING DOCTOR...	ENTER C-SA02
-INTERN	ENTER C-SA23
-ATTENTION: DOCTORS OF DENTAL	
SURGERY AND ORTHODONTISTS ARE	
DENTISTS	ENTER C-PL23

Verbal protocol: "One has to 'enter the speciality'...
I'll type 'hospital staff doctor'
(Researcher: Didn't you enter the speciality?)
"I did but they didn't accept it."

B.

Scenario: The transmitted screen-form contained:

profession = inspector
economic activity = tax administration

The economic activity has been coded and confirmed as:
'9004 external administrative services other than economic
or financial.'

The computer's response is:

PIVOT WORD 'INSPECTOR', SECTION SUPERVISOR (PUBLIC DUTIES)

-INSPECTORS, POSTAL	ENTER C-FP21
-INSPECTORS, TREASURY, CUSTOMS, TAX	ENTER C-FP22
-INSPECTORS, STATE (VERY RARE)	ENTER C-FP11
-INSPECTORS, CIVIL AVIATION	ENTER C-TD02
-OTHERS	ENTER C-FP24

Verbal protocol: " I think it ought to take the economic
activity code into account because it has returned
'inspectors, treasury customs, tax,' when that is part of
the entry."

C.

Scenario: The transmitted screen-form contained:

economic activity = food manufacturing

The computer's response is:

            6101 SUPERMARKET
            6102 GROCERY STORE
            6103 SUPERMARKET COMPLEX
            6111 INDEPENDENT RETAIL GROCERY STORE
            6211 FRANCHISED RETAIL GROCERY STORE
            6212 SMALL INDEPENDENT SUPERMARKET
            6222 SMALL FRANCHISED SUPERMARKET

COMMERCE, WHOLESALE: CLASS 57, CERTAIN AGENTS... (BROKER,
COMMISSIONER) ARE IN CLASS 60
COMMERCE, RETAIL: CLASS 61 FOR THE LARGE STORES... AND
CLASS 62 FOR SMALL AND SPECIALIZED STORES.
*** End of this designation.

Verbal protocol: "This is for... commerce?!
One would have expected something about production...
strange!
If I enter 'production' will it be the same?!"

D.

Scenario: Exactly as in example (A) above.

The computer's response is:

DOCTOR OF MEDICINE..., DOCTOR... (WITHOUT A PRIVATE
PRACTICE)

-SPECIALIST
  (SURGEON, OPTHALMOLOGIST)   ENTER THE SPECIALITY
-HOSPITAL STAFF DOCTOR
  (ARMY DOCTORS EXCLUDED)   ENTER C-SA01
-NON-HOSPITAL, STAFF DOCTOR
  (ARMY DOCTORS EXCLUDED):
  COMPANY DOCTOR, SCHOOL DOCTOR,
  CONSULTING DOCTOR...   ENTER C-SA02
-INTERN   ENTER C-SA23
-ATTENTION: DOCTORS OF DENTAL
  SURGERY AND ORTHODONTISTS ARE
  DENTISTS   ENTER C-PL23

Verbal protocol: "I suppose he's a specialist since he's a
doctor of 'urology'. And it tells me to enter the speciality (laughs). I'll key in 'urologist'.

Operator keys in: profession = urologist

The computer's response is:

SA01 HOSPITAL STAFF DOCTORS (HAVING NO PRIVATE PRACTICE:
ARMY DOCTORS EXCLUDED)

Verbal protocol: "It's strange that it doesn't respond
with 'specialists'. I don't understand."

E.

Scenario: The transmitted screen-form contained:

profession = professor of textile design
economic activity = technical instruction

The computer's response is:

9214 POST SECONDARY, NON-UNIVERSITY INSTRUCTION JUNIOR
COLLEGE, TECHNICAL COLLEGE, TRADE SCHOOL, AGRICULTURAL
COLLEGE...
THE ECONOMIC ACTIVITY CODE IS INSUFFICIENT TO DETERMINE THE
INSTITUTION IN QUESTION
-JUNIOR COLLEGE; EXCEPT INDUSTRIAL
 ARTS COLLEGE (IAC)   ENTER C-EN09
-IAC AND OTHER TEACHING INSTITUTIONS   ENTER C-EN07

Verbal protocol: "I am going to enter 'and other teaching
institutions'. The respondent [who filled in the original
form] didn't specify whether it is a junior college."

Operator keys in: economic activity = EN07

The computer's response is:

UNKNOWN ECONOMIC ACTIVITY CODE

Verbal protocol: "Was I supposed to enter it under the
organization's name?"
(Researcher: No... the confusion comes from the fact that
your message pertains to the profession.)
"Should I enter it there, then? [he puts it in the profession zone] But it's not a profession, is it? I don't
understand."

F.

Scenario: The transmitted screen-form contained:

profession = inspector, business frauds

The economic activity has already been coded as:
'9004 external administrative services other than economic or financial'.

The computer's response is:

PIVOT WORD 'INSPECTOR', SECTION SUPERVISOR (PUBLIC DUTIES)

-INSPECTORS, POSTAL   ENTER C-FP21
-INSPECTORS, TREASURY, CUSTOMS, TAX   ENTER C-FP22
-INSPECTORS, STATE (VERY RARE)   ENTER C-FP11

```
-INSPECTORS, CIVIL AVIATION         ENTER C-TD02
-OTHERS                             ENTER C-FP24
```

Verbal protocol: "Ah! It's 'others'".

Operator keys in: profession = FP24

The computer's response is:

FP24 OTHER PERSONNEL UNDER CATEGORY B OF PUBLIC OFFICE
(ADMINISTRATIVE SECRETARIES; INSPECTORS, WORK, TRADE...)

Verbal protocol: ...... (silence)
(Researcher: Does that surprise you?)
"No... but, after all! A moment ago it said 'others' and
then... Still, if that's the way it works! One has to read
it in relationship with the message just received. Is that
it? No, because read like that it is 'other personnel under
category B'. One asks oneself 'What's going on here!' Still,
one must remember that... (others?) Exactly!"

I shall not enter into a detailed analysis of these exchanges.
It is easily seen, however, that the following conclusion may
be drawn: if the operator is troubled by the responses of the
computer, it is because he expects it to follow a principle
of exchange that one might call, borrowing an idea from Grice
(1975), the "cooperative principle". I would suggest some
rules that the operator appears to assume the computer
respects:

a. Take account of all the information transmitted.
   Violations: (case A) some information is not taken into
   account; (case B) information already transmitted is
   requested again.
b. Be pertinent.
   Violation: (case C) a response is given which has little
   bearing on what has been transmitted.
c. Be logical.
   Violation: (case D) a failure to take the preceding step
   into consideration.
d. Give all the information necessary in the exchange.
   Violations: (cases A, B, and E) failures to indicate that
   all the information has not been used.
e. Be clear
   Violation: (case F) no reference for the word "others".

These rules are very similar to those that apply to human
communication. I can connect this fact to other features of
the interaction:

-The result of the operator's action (i.e. the computer's
 response to the transmission of a display form) is unknown

to him. As a matter of fact, he does not know the contents of the files consulted by the computer. For the operator, therefore, it is not as if he were simply giving orders to a machine. He is faced with a kind of interlocutor.
-The computer's responses are utterances, either explicit ("The economic activity code is insufficient to determine the institution in question", case E) or elliptical (as when, for example, it produces lists of designations, case C). Moreover, these utterances were initially composed by real interlocutors for the operator (i.e. those who developed the economic activity and profession classifications in order to transmit information to him and to compel a certain action).

From this connection it follows that operator-computer interaction shares several characteristics with human conversation. But if the interaction resembles a conversation in some respects, it is quite different in others: the computer's responses are fixed and sometimes are not well suited to the situation; they are produced in a mechanical way; the means available for interrogating the computer are poor (consisting only of an ability to modify the content of the zones). The operator, indeed, confronts a machine which responds to his orders. Even so, the operator expects the machine to be reliable, regular, systematic.

The interaction then has an ineradicably double nature: it is at once both conversational and mechanical.

It is with this reservation that I would use the term "dialogue". Notwithstanding the reservation, one must not overlook the fact that the operator supposes or seeks rules or, at least, regularities, in order to define his conduct. When the rules are violated:
-either the dialogue malfunctions (in ways ranging from the *"pathological dialogue"*, when the anomaly is serious (case E) to a simple *incongruity ("irregular dialogue")* when the breach of rules is slight.
-or the operator, taking it for granted that the response is consonant with the rules, will seek to discover something implicit in the response which gives meaning to it (case F).

On the basis of this analysis, I conclude that the interpretative activities of the operator are not only of a semantic character, but equally of a pragmatic nature. The computer's response is not a simple transmission of information, because it takes place in the context of what one can call, following Wittgenstein (1961), a language game of a particular kind.

4) WORK LOAD AND SYSTEM DESIGN

Pathological or irregular dialogues lead to an increase in
work load, as one sees by looking at certain indices that
we are able to operationalise: parasitical supplementary
activities, misleading induced reasoning, increasing
burdening of the memory etc. An analysis of the sort that I
have sketched enables one to make certain prescriptions. I
will call that feature of the system which leads to these
effects *conversational incompetence*. For the system that we
have studied we can define precisely the elements of this
incompetence and seek ways to reduce it.
These latter can take several forms:

a. editing and presentation of the responses (this would help
   in cases E and F).
b. modification of the files of pre-established designations
   (cases A and D).
c. modification of the search algorithm for the file (case B).
d. modification of the way in which the lists are constructed
   (case C).
e. introduction of a marking operation for the screen-form
   of words and zones used by the computer in its search
   (case B).

5) CONCLUSION

I have examined here only one aspect of the operator's
activity, that concerning the dialogue with the computer. This
dialogue is only a means for realizing the codification of
information. As demonstrated in a previous study (Pinsky *et
al.*, 1979), this codification is not a simple categorization;
it is an authentic problem-solving process. The question
arises as to what kind of connection exists between this
problem-solving activity and the dialogue with the computer.
The classical studies of problem-solving (from Piaget to
Newell and Simon) have only considered what one might call
the operating logic of the subject and not the interaction
phenomena with the other participant of the dialogue. On the
other hand, studies of human communication have been little
concerned with the pursuit of a cognitive objective or the
solution of problems introduced by constraints other than
those of the dialogue.
    As in every work situation, the one we have considered
above is not "psychologically pure", and its analysis requires
that one have recourse to several scientific disciplines. In
the field of computer design considerations of the problem
solving activity suggests the need to build a second type of

competence into computer systems: a competence which aids the
operator in solving problems. But this is another subject,
Which I must leave for another occasion.

REFERENCES

Grice, H.P. (1975). Logic and conversation. *In* "Syntax and
    Semantics". (Eds P. Cole and J.L. Morgan), Vol. 3, Speech
    Acts. Academic Press, London.
Pinsky, L. Kandaroun, R. and Lantin G. (1979). Le travail
    de saisiechiffrement sur terminal d'ordinateur, Coll.
    Physiologie du travail et d'Ergonomie du C.N.A.M. No. 65.
Smith, H.T. (1980) Human-computer communication. *In* "Human
    Interaction with Computers". (Eds H.T. Smith and
    T.R.G. Green), Academic Press, London.
Wittgenstein, L. (1961). "Investigations Philosophiques".
    Gallimard, Paris.

GRAPHS ARE NOT STRAIGHTFORWARD

JENNY PREECE

Open University
Milton Keynes, England

1) INTRODUCTION

Many extraordinary and unsubstantiated claims are made about
the educational potential of computer generated cartesian
graphs.

Consider Fig. 1 which shows a simplified screen display
from a computer simulation called POND (Tranter and Leveridge,
1978). The program has been designed to be used by pupils of
14 years and upwards to investigate changes in populations of
pond organisms. Using different versions of the program, the
pupils can set the initial population and pollution levels
and the intensity of fishing. The program then produces a
variety of different graphs. Figure 1 is the simplest type
of graph; in some of the other graphs considerably more
information is shown. Pupils are expected to interpret these
interdependent curves in relation to each other. This
involves suggesting and testing hypotheses in order to
explain what is happening in the simulated pond. In theory
this activity appears to be well designed but we should ask
"how much of the information presented in the graph, can
pupils interpret in practice". My research indicates that the
answer to this question is "very little".

Of course, it is not just graphs from computer simulations
that are difficult for pupils to interpret. Authors of text
books have assumed for years that data could be interpreted
more easily from graphs. Look at the graph in Fig. 2 and the
accompanying questions, for example. You could not be blamed
for suspecting that it appears in a research paper. In this
instance, however, it has actually been copied from an
ordinary level examination school text book. Pupils aged
14-16 are expected to interpret this graph, after some

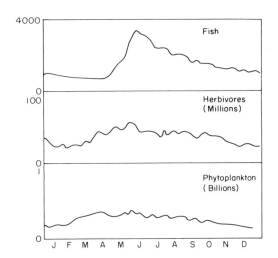

FIG. 1 *A simplified version of a screen display produced by the POND program. (Data from Tranter and Leveridge, 1978.)*

discussion about the key biological issues. It is not my intention that you should interpret Fig. 2, but let us consider what interpreting this graph involves. There are many issues including:

1) Domain specific concepts about fresh water ecology.
2) Graph concepts (e.g. gradients, discontinuity of some curves etc).
3) The number of graphs.
4) The number and grouping of the curves.
5) The number and type of dependent variables.
6) The absence of scales on axes.
7) The vertical axis – what does it represent?
8) The arrow – what does it indicate?
9) The actual syntax of the graph (e.g. the representation of the curves as lines, dots and dashes).

I shall examine some of these factors in more detail later in the paper, but mentioning them at this point indicates the complexity of this kind of interpretation task. Of course, not all graphs are as difficult to interpret as Figs 1 and 2 but research (Janvier, 1978; Hart, 1980; Preece, 1981) and empirical evidence from examination reports (Dudley, 1977) indicates that many pupils cannot interpret similar displays involving only one or two independent curves. The ways that students deal with the fundamental concepts required to

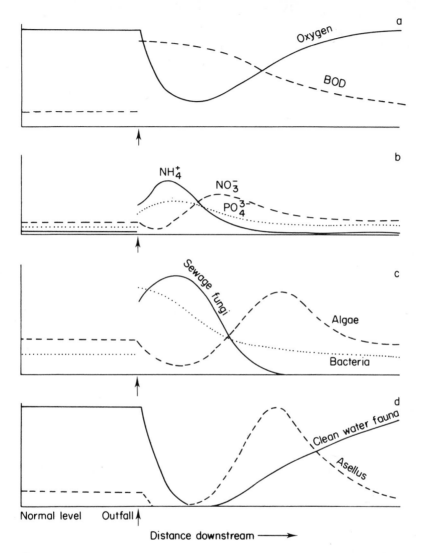

Distance downstream ⟶

Note

Asellus is a small animal commonly found in rivers and streams. It is a scavenger on dead plant and animal remains and does not have high oxygen requirements. Algae are green plants and the clean water fauna includes fish and other animals.

► Relate the changes in graphs a and b to the changes in graphs c and d. In doing this make clear the cause of each change and the interactions involved.◄ Comment on the complexity of the series of changes illustrated by this data and their causes.

FIG. 2 *Exercise from a SCISP Ordinary Biology Text. (From Mowl et al., 1974, with permission.)*

interpret these kinds of graphs must be identified and
explained before displays can be designed which will
capitalize on the potential offered by the interactive
facilities, speed of delivery and colour available in today's
microcomputers. In this paper I shall:

1) Present empirical evidence of the kinds of interpretation
   errors that pupils make; suggest reasons for the occurence
   of the errors; and describe when they occur;
2) discuss evidence for the kinds of interpretation strategies
   that pupils develop to interpret multiple curve graphs;
3) outline plans for future research; and
4) present some conclusions and guidelines for authors of CAL
   materials.

2) AN EMPIRICAL STUDY OF GRAPH INTERPRETATION ERRORS

A cartesian graph is made up of 2 axes which each represent a
variable, and the curve of the graph which shows how one variable changes in relation to the other. In this research I examined how pupils interpreted single curve and multiple curve
graphs of independent and dependent variables with either simple linear scales as in Fig. 1 or with no scales as in Fig. 2.
   Interpreting these kinds of complex cartesian graphs
requires more than just reading points; the pupil has to
deduce the story contained in the graph. This involves a
translation process in which information presented in a
condensed visual format is interpreted in relation to the
pupil's knowledge of the graph domain, the subject domain and
her world knowledge. Concepts which are purely graphical in
nature (e.g. a point, maximum and minimum points, intervals
over which variables change, gradients etc.) must be understood and so must concepts which are concerned with the
situation represented in the graph. Sometimes these concepts
will be present in the labelling of the graph (e.g. the title,
names of the variables, scales etc.), but they may also arise
from the relationship of 2 variables (e.g. speed in a
distance-time graph). Possibly the most difficult concepts of
all are those which do not appear on the graph in any obvious
form. For example, in Fig. 2, the concept of photosynthesis
is essential to interpret the display. Graph reading skills
are also important. Janvier (1978) reported observing 2 styles
of graph reading. The first and simplest style involves
reading points using co-ordinates, whilst the second requires
pupils to continually relate the 2 variables to each other.
This latter, relative reading is more descriptive and is
necessary to describe trends such as those shown in Figs 1
and 2. My research shows that many pupils have poor graph

interpretation skills because they either do not understand
the relevant concepts or have inadequate graph reading skills.

I conducted a survey to investigate the performance of 122
pupils aged 14 and 15 years on specific graph interpretation
tasks. These tasks were designed to isolate the kinds of
errors that pupils make when there is no interaction with the
computer. I also collected protocols of a few of the pupils
to provide more detailed information about the pupils' errors.
When I analysed my results I found 12 different sources of
errors and I shall briefly describe each in turn and suggest
explanations of their sources.

(i) Reading and Plotting Points

A few pupils were unable to read and plot points except when
the values were integers. Some pupils read the axes the wrong
way around and some did not seem to understand the fundamental
concept of graph representation.

(ii) Relative Reading

Inability to read relative values was particularly common when
scales were present on the display. Many pupils tried to read
exact points and acquired too much specific information to
cope with. They seemed to be unable to relate variables to
each other, especially when abstract and unfamiliar variables
were used. Use of familiar variables such as time resulted in
an improvement in some pupils' relative reading performance.

(iii) An Interval is Interpreted as a Point

This error occurred most frequently when the wording of the
task was ambiguous. Consider, for example, the following
questions which were asked about Fig. 3.

"When is Susan heavier than Paul?"
"When is Susan growing faster than Paul?"

"When" is ambiguous and weak pupils normally took the easiest
option and gave a single point as the answer.

(iv) Concepts Arising from the Variables were not Understood

Some pupils were not able to answer questions about concepts
which arose from the variables but which were not actually
mentioned in the display, e.g. speed in distance-time graphs.

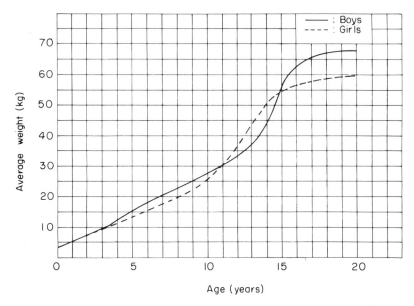

FIG. 3 *Growth curves. (From Swan, 1980, with permission.)*

(v) World Knowledge Interferes

Sometimes pupils thought that the answer was so obvious that
they did not need to refer to the graph. Consider, for
example, the following question which was asked about a
simplified version of Fig. 2. "Which type of animals
disappear first when the stream is polluted?" Some pupils
said "clean water fauna" without looking at the graph.

(vi) A Pronounced Graphical Feature Distracts the Pupil

Some pupils seemed to focus their attention upon a pronounced
graphical feature such as a sudden rise or fall or a
discontinous curve. These features appeared to be so
distracting that pupils failed to consider the rest of the
display.

(vii) Misinterpretation of a Symbol

The point at which sewage is tipped into a stream is indicated
by the small upward arrow in Fig. 2. A few pupils interpreted
this arrow according to its everyday symbolic meaning and
said that it indicated that the sewage was rising.

(viii) Confusion Caused by too many Variables

Less able pupils found it very difficult to select the
relevant parts of multiple curve graph displays. Several
pupils did not attempt the task and others gave up part way
through as they were confused by the number of variables.
Long questions also cause pupils to behave in this way.

(ix) Only One Curve on a Multiple Curve Display is Interpreted

Sometimes pupils would interpret only one curve from a
multiple curve display. These pupils seemed to be unable to
relate more than 2 variables so they opted for the strategy
of interpreting a single curve and ignored the other curves.

(x) Failure to Transfer Information between Graphs

Several pupils were unable to read information from one graph
and use this information to interpret a graph with different
variables.

(xi) Gradients are Confused with Maximum and Minimum

Many pupils answered questions which referred to gradients by
giving maximum and minimum points. Consider, for example, the
responses of the pupils to the following questions which were
asked about Fig. 4.

Question: Which car is going faster after:

(i) 4 seconds?
(ii) 6 seconds?

Answers: (i)

	Black	Blue	Red	Can't tell
Frequency of pupils' responses	7	4	92	8

(ii)

	Black	Blue	Red	Can't tell
Frequency of pupils' responses	29	10	67	4

Some pupils seem to associate *fastest* with *highest*. These
pupils look for a high value and not for the line with the
steepest gradient or even for an interval. Notice that fewer
pupils were misled by the red car's line in the second

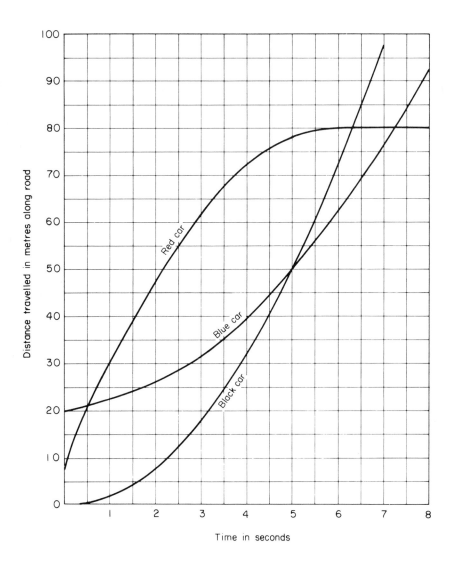

FIG. 4 *Graph of three cars travelling along a road. (From Swan, 1980, with permission.)*

question. This is probably because all the lines are closer
to the top of the graph after 6 seconds than after 4 seconds.
In fact, the line representing the black car is highest at 6½
seconds, indicating again that fastest is answered as highest.

(xii) The Graph is Interpreted Iconically

Graphs which appear to represent a familiar iconic form are
often interpreted iconically. Kerslake (1977) observed this
phenomenon with younger children, who interpreted distance-
time graphs as though they were pictures of hills or maps.
She called graphs which elicit this kind of response, visual
distractors. Some of the pupils in my survey described a
simplified version of part of Fig. 2 as though it were a
cross-section of a stream. Clearly they had seen several
cross-sections and this kind of representation made more
sense to them than the graph. Similar kinds of responses were
given by pupils as answers to questions about Fig. 4. The
following excerpts from my protocol data clearly indicate that
these pupils are interpreting the graph as though it is a road
or a car.

Question:		What happens to the red car? (Does it speed up, slow down or what?)
Pupils'	JS:	It turns off to the right.
answers:	CH:	It crashes.
Question:		Does black overtake blue, or does blue overtake black? How can you tell?
Pupils'	DV:	Black overtakes blue. You can tell because
answers:		the black car went a different route.

In collecting, describing and analysing these errors I have
been looking for information which would help me to answer the
questions:

1) what is the translation process that is needed to interpret
a complex cartesian graph; and
2) at what point in the process do these errors occur?

I shall now describe how my data relates to these questions.

Question ⟶ Graph ⟶ Answer
(language)   (diagrammatic)   (language)

FIG. 5 *Simplified model of the translation process*

Figure 5 shows a very simplified model of the translation
process required to interpret a graph. A question is asked
and the pupil must decide what the question means and which
part of the display it relates to. At some point the pupil
translates the information presented in language form into

diagrammatic graphical form and then back to language in order
to give the answer.

In reality the pupil refers backwards and forwards between
the different types of information (language and diagrammatic)
several times. Of course the process is not quite as simple
as it sounds and the task and the labels on the graph may
contain many concepts which are specific to the domain
represented in the graph. Similarly the graph itself contains
concepts. In Piagetian terms, assimilation and accommodation
must take place; the pupil has to relate the task to her
already existing knowledge of the domain and then translate
the curves in the graph in relation to this knowledge, and
to her knowledge about graphs. In other words, having worked
out what she thinks the task actually is, she must then find
and translate the relevant part of the graph. I have observed
some errors which indicate that pupils may be very susceptible
to different types of cues at this stage. Pronounced graphical
features and visual distractors, for example, will focus
pupils' attention in specific ways. Similarly, as in most
kinds of educational activity, the language used in the task
will influence how pupils interpret the graph (Preece, 1981).
(For example: "fastest" may cue some pupils for a gradient
question and others to seek for the highest or furthest point.)

After deciding where to look on the graph, the pupil needs
to have reading skills in order to extract the information
contained in the curves. Ideally she will be able to read
both point-wise and relatively. At this stage she will have
to interpret the information contained in the curves and this
requires an integration of concepts. Figure 6 summarizes these
stages diagrammatically.

FIG. 6 *Stages in the translation process*

If we reconsider the 12 errors that I have just described,
it is apparent that they can be grouped into 3 categories
depending upon their nature and source. These categories arise
from:

1) Cues - errors caused by either the language of the task or
   the appearance of the graph.
2) Reading - errors resulting from poor reading skills.
3) Conceptual - errors due to incorrect or insufficient understanding of graphical, domain-related, or symbolic
   concepts.

Figure 7 shows when the 12 errors appear to occur during the process. Notice that some of the errors are italicized which indicates that they either occur more than once or that it is not clear when they do occur.

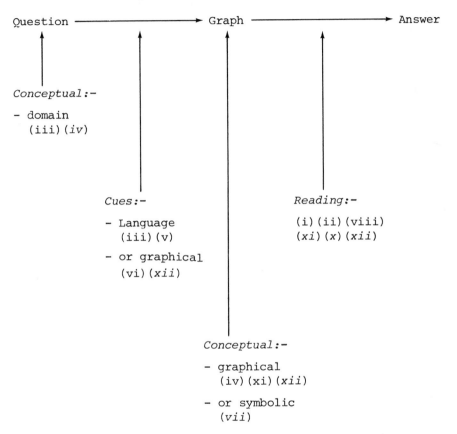

FIG. 7 *The occurrence of pupils' errors in the translation process. Errors: (i) Reading and plotting points.*
(ii) Relative reading. (iii) An interval is interpreted as a point. (iv) Concepts arising from variables are not understood.
(v) World knowledge interferes. (vi) A pronounced graphical feature distracts the pupil. (vii) Misinterpretation of a symbol. (viii) Confusion caused by too many variables.
(ix) Only one curve on a multiple curve display is interpreted.
(x) Failure to transfer information between graphs.
(xi) Gradients are confused with maximum and minimum.
(xii) The graph is interpreted iconically.

Figure 8 shows when the cueing errors occur in more detail and their sources.

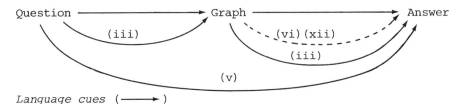

Language cues (———➤)

(iii) Instance given instead of a point due to ambiguous language.
(v)   World knowledge interferes.

Graphical cues (- - - -➤)

(vi) Pronounced graphical features distract.
(xii) Graph interpreted as though it is another iconic form.

FIG. 8 *Cueing errors*

In the next section I shall discuss the kinds of strategies that pupils use to answer open-ended questions about multiple curve displays. Errors such as those which I have just described tend to be less frequent in these tasks, because pupils are able to avoid them by giving general answers and avoiding features and concepts which they find difficult. The protocols collected from this task illustrate the kind of reading skills and interpretation strategies that pupils use. This information complements the data collected from the survey and it also illustrates how pupils cope with displays like the POND diagram shown in Fig. 1.

3) STRATEGIES FOR INTERPRETING MULTIPLE CURVE GRAPHS

I conducted a pilot experiment in which I gave a simplified version of Fig. 2, to 6 subjects from the same population as the survey. The pupils were asked to interpret the graphs by describing the information that they contain. If the pupils were silent for more than 30 seconds I prompted them in unstructured interview style. I collected the pupils' protocols on an audio cassette tape and later transcribed them. In previous lessons the pupils had been taught the biological concepts required to interpret the graphs, and as the purpose of this study was to explore the kinds of responses pupils gave and to develop a method of qualitative data analysis, I did not check their grasp of these concepts. Their teacher said that 3 of the pupils were well above average ability and 3 were average, but analysis of the

transcripts revealed a range of competence. My general
impression was that none of the pupils were confident at the
task because they had had very little experience of this kind
of graph work. They were not used to qualitative interpretation
and the absence of scales on the axes was unnerving for them.
Weak pupils were worried by the apparent complexity of the
displays and were confused by the number of variables. The
able pupils looked for dependent and independent relationships
between the variables, but none of the pupils suggested
hypotheses to explain what they saw.

Analysis of the transcripts revealed that by the end of the
interview each pupil seemed to attain a particular level of
competence. The pupils also exhibited different starting
levels of competence and during the interview gradually
progressed to the final level. This progression appeared to
go through several identifiable stages as the pupil became
more and more familiar with the graphical concepts embedded
in the displays and the biological concepts of the subject
domain. In the following discussion I shall describe these
levels of competence and illustrate them with extracts from
the protocols. I shall also describe the reading and interpretation strategies that the pupils used.

Despite the absence of scales one pupil tried to read
absolute points along a single curve and paid little attention
to the variable that the curve represented and consequently
made no reference to the biological situation depicted.
After some prompting the pupil described the curve relationally
but still made no reference to the situation. (Notice particularly the italicized words.)

HB: It (points at curve for oxygen) starts off *high*
             and then *it* goes *low* (points to minimum point) and
             then *it* goes *high* (points to crest of curve).
Researcher: Fine, now I want you to look at the curve a bit
             more carefully and describe in a little more detail
             what is happening.
HB: Well, *it* goes *sharply* down and then *it* goes
             gradually up (there is no pointing this time).

A more advanced strategy involved referring to the curves
by name and describing gradients and different sections of
each curve relationally. No attempt was made to relate the
curves to each other, but a causal relationship between the
introduction of the sewage and the curve for oxygen was made.

SR: *When* the *sewage* is put in the *oxygen decreases*
             quickly and *gradually* it seems to *increase again*.
             The plants *decrease at first then* they *increase*
             to *more than* they were *before*.

In the next stage the curves are related and cause and effect relationships are sought between the curves.

MD: After the sewage goes in the amount of oxygen in the water goes down. *This* then *causes* the small green plants to go down, no the amount of small green plants goes down *so* the amount of oxygen goes down.

Many intermediate stages could also be identified, but none of the pupils extrapolated the curves in order to suggest that they would return to their original levels. Nor did they look for cause and effect relationships at a deeper level than comparing 2 curves. Thus, no hypotheses were generated to suggest what was happening.

The results of this pilot study indicate that pupils perform poorly on this type of qualitative interpretation task and despite the lack of scales some pupils will still read the curves in an absolute point-wise manner. Most pupils start by selecting a single curve and gradually progress to inter-relating the curves. None of the pupils were proficient enough to obtain very much of the rich and detailed information contained in the display and it is very unlikely that they would perform differently with computer generated graphs, unless they received a lot of help from a teacher. The educational philosophy underlying many computer simulations such as POND is to provide pupils with an opportunity to devise and test hypotheses - the "what would happen if......" approach. This research suggests that the richness of this type of educational environment cannot be exploited by most pupils.

Many questions about the translation process involved in graph interpretation need to be answered. The study of specific errors is one way of examining the process, but we need to know more about how the errors are related, when they occur, whether the error detected is the only one or merely the last one, and what conditions cause the student to make the error. Questions involving gradients are a stumbling block for many pupils, and more research is also needed on multiple-curve displays of inter-related variables and on the effects of individual strategies of graph interpretation.

4) CONCLUSIONS: SUGGESTIONS FOR AUTHORS

The obvious conclusion from this work is that many pupils cannot interpret cartesian graphs adequately, and that multiple curve graphs are particularly difficult. More research is needed before displays can be designed to alleviate some of these problems. Teachers also need to pay attention to the

teaching of both the graph and contextual concepts. This
includes taking care to ensure that the wording of tasks is
unambiguous.

At this stage in my research the suggestions that I have
for CAL authors have to be seen as tentative. It does,
however, seem likely that pupils who are poor at graph
interpretation might benefit from tables being offered as an
alternative to graphs, if the number of items of data is
small and if only discrete information is required. Tables
are not a good format for displaying trends. A useful aid
for interpreting multiple curve graphs might be the facility
to select and superimpose curves. This would enable pupils
to thoroughly familiarize themselves with a single curve
before trying to relate it to other curves. This kind of
approach appears to correspond to the natural strategies used
by many pupils to interpret multiple curve displays. The
results of my next set of experiments should provide evidence
to refute or confirm this idea. Similarly my future research
should show whether displays with dynamic delivery help to
improve pupils understanding of gradients. The intuitions of
some program authors, researchers and teachers are that
microcomputers have great educational potential if used in
this way, but so far there is no empirical evidence (Avons
et al., 1981) to substantiate this claim.

The results of my current research indicate that symbols
are easy to misinterpret and that they should not be added
to displays unless absolutely necessary. Similarly, blinking
characters and colour are likely to be confusing if used
indiscriminately. Human factors research on PRESTEL displays
(Sutherland, 1980) suggests that blinking characters are
hard to read, distracting and fatiguing. This research report
also shows that viewers react to change in colour in a
display or text by looking for a reason for the change, and
are confused if no reason can be found.

Finally, it is worth mentioning that, although the subjects used in this research were 14 and 15 year olds, it is
likely that many adults would perform similarly. Certainly
my experience of working with students who have no scientific,
mathematical or technical training, on the British Open
University Science foundation course indicates that this is
true.

ACKNOWLEDGEMENTS

I would like to thank Marc Eisenstadt, Ann Jones and my
supervisor Tim O'Shea for their comments on drafts of this
paper.

REFERENCES

Avons, S.E., Beveridge, M.C., Hickman, A.T. and Hitch, G.J.
    (1981, undated). Teaching Journey Graphs with Microcomputer
    Animation: Effects of Spatial Correspondence and Degree of
    Interaction. An Experimental Study. Report No. 1 Micro-
    processors in Education Research Project. University of
    Manchester.
Dudley, B. (1977). The mathematics of school biology
    examination papers. *Journal of Biology,* 11, 41-48.
Hart, K.M. (1980). "Secondary School Children's Understanding
    of Mathematics". Mathematics Education, Centre for Science
    Education, Chelsea College, University of London.
Janvier, C. (1978). Interpretation of Complex Cartesian Graphs
    Representing Situations - Studies and Teaching Experiments.
    PhD Thesis, University of Nottingham.
Kerslake, D. (1977). The Concept of Graphs in Secondary School
    Pupils aged 12-14 years. M. Phil. Thesis, Chelsea College,
    University of London.
Mowl, B., Hall, W., and Bausor, J. (1974). "Patterns 4:
    Interactions and Change". Longman, London.
Preece, J. (1981). Investigating how Students Interpret
    Complex Cartesian Graphs. Open University CAL Research
    Group Technical Report No. 19.
Sutherland, G. (1980). PRESTEL and the User. Commissioned by
    COI Centre for Research on Perception and Cognition.
    University of Sussex, Brighton.
Swan, M. (1980). The Language of Graphs: a Collection of
    Teaching Materials for Interpretation of Graphs. Shell
    Centre for Mathematical Education, University of
    Nottingham.
Tranter, J.A. and Leveridge, M.E. (1978). Pond ecology. *In*
    "Computers in the Biology Curriculum," (Ed. M.E. Leveridge),
    Edward Arnold, London.

COMPUTER-AIDED PROBLEM SOLVING
WITH GRAPHICAL DISPLAY OF INFORMATION

BERNARD SENACH

Institut National de Recherche
d'Informatique et d'Automatique
Le Chesnay, France

1) INTRODUCTION

The main problem with human-machine communication has been
described as the compatibility between two representations:
the machine representation as an outcome of the designer's
choices and the operator's representation as a result of the
processing of the information displayed. According to this
perspective, one aim of ergonomics is to design the machine
in such a way that it fits with the user's cognitive representation (Bisseret *et al.*, 1979). In certain cases this
approach will prove fruitful (Falzon, 1982).

However, in many human-machine systems no systematic task
structure is apparent in advance and the operators have to
identify for themselves what are the problems to be solved
in the system. To design a computer-aided system it is important, therefore, to understand how the operators construct
their representation, and which are the problems that they
really process.

The studies reported here are part of a large human-machine
system design project. They aim to find out if the information
displayed can induce an inaccurate cognitive representation,
or inappropriate problem-structuring techniques. The studies
are analysed with reference to the information processing
concept of "problem space reduction" (Newell and Simon, 1972).

2) THE HUMAN-MACHINE SYSTEM

The system under study is the control room of the Paris Metro.
Each day the Metro carries two million people. According to

the time of day (rush hours or not) the trains' frequency is
different, and the interval between successive trains varies
from 2 minutes up to 20. Particular problems occur when a
train is immobilised, by a suicide or a breakdown for example.
The most important task of control room operators is to solve
such problems and minimise their repercussions. The operators
must maintain passenger transportation despite traffic inter-
ruptions. To assist in this task the trains' positions are
displayed in the control room on an analogical representation
of the line.

3) THE HUMAN-MACHINE SYSTEM ANALYSIS

The system analysis was conducted in three steps.

a. *Wholistic Approach*
   A first step was a wholistic approach including standard
   job analysis tools and techniques of observations, inter-
   views and critical incidents analysis. This paper is not
   concerned with this phase of the project: the results are
   published elsewhere (Senach and Janet, 1979; Senach, 1980a).

b. *Formal definition of the problem structures*
   This step was centred on a critical issue for a computer-
   aided system: the problem solving activity. The objective
   of this phase was the identification of formal features
   that would distinguish problem classes and types of incidents, so that:
   - all incidents showing the same pattern features belong
     to the same problem class and define a single problem
     for the operators, whatever are the other differences
     in their surface description.
   - two incidents different according to a formal feature
     belong to two different problem classes, and conse-
     quently the operator cannot use the same procedure to
     resolve these two incidents.
   The difficulty in identifying these formal features concerns the system complexity; two incidents can be described by very different patterns (using different variables, or different values of the same variable). To
   assist with the analysis an experimental problem solving
   simulation was run, using a *withheld information* technique.
   Subjects had to resolve incidents by asking the experimenter for information; each question asked by the subject
   was recorded. Eight skilled operators solved six problems
   each. It should be noted that the main concern here is
   with the problem analysis phase of the total problem-
   solving activity, which will be referred to as 'diagnosis'.

This investigation showed that the controlled objects are bi-dimensional:
- one dimension is the future plan for train movement,
- the other dimension is the future plan for driver assignment.

These two dimensions are independent: a driver does not always stay with the same train all day long.

The consequences, and thus the problem complexity, of any particular incident, vary with what has been planned for the driver and his train, and thus may be very different.

Here is an example in which *one* incident has two different consequences depending on the future plans for the train and the driver.

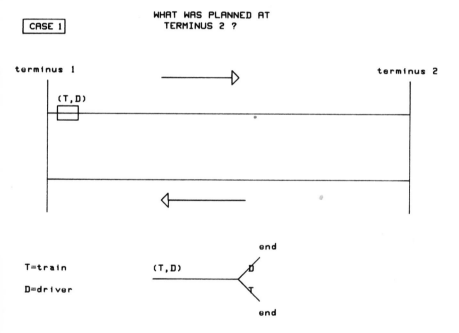

WHAT WAS PLANNED AT
TERMINUS 2 ?

CASE 1

terminus 1   terminus 2

(T,D)

T=train   (T,D)

D=driver

end

end

Fig. 1

In case 1 (illustrated in Fig. 1 above), the future plans are:

The train will go on a siding
The driver will go off duty.

There is no repercussion on the second line.

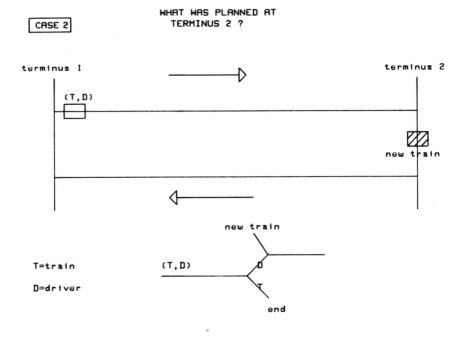

Fig. 2

In case 2 (illustrated in Fig. 2 above), the future plans
are:

> The train will go on a siding
> The driver will take a new train
> from terminus 2.

In this case the control room operator must find a new
driver for the new train, so the incident causes a delay
on the second line.

In summary, then, the problem classes can be defined
according to the structure of the train-driver pair regarding their future plans.

A second important outcome of the withheld-information
experiment is that subjects (experienced operators) did
not utilise all the information necessary for a correct
diagnosis of an incident. This important behavioural
observation is investigated further in the third step of
the analyis.

c. *Problem space reduction*
In problem solving literature the term problem space reduction has been applied to the general technique of
eliminating potential solutions so as to reduce the

number of alternatives. As such it is usually regarded as a part of skilled human problem solving behaviour, and an aid to effective problem solution.

For instance, Simon and Reed (1976) stress that when the problem constraints are well defined the problem solver has to evaluate few alternatives and the task environment tends then to reduce the space in which the search has to take place. The problem solver may even more reduce the space using a strategy: Elstein et al. (1978), pointed out that in complex systems - e.g. medical diagnosis - when the potential size of the problem space is important, the operators have to reduce it: early hypotheses are generated in the very first minutes of the meeting with the patient.

Problem space reduction is here given a different slant. Our concern is a reduction that occurs during the problem analysis phase (incident diagnosis). As will become clear, reduction at this stage becomes a hindrance rather than a help.

The general idea is that, even though skilled, a subject does not identify and use the relations contained in a problem structure which are necessary in order to solve the problem. In other words, the operator filters the displayed data and then may, in a complex system, process a problem simpler than (or different from) the real one.

An experiment intending to investigate this reduction phenomenon was carried out (Senach, 1982). More precisely we tried to show that the information about the drivers is not systematically processed by the operators. A problem solving simulation was used again.

Four incidents (structurally different according to our formal features) had to be solved under two experimental conditions:

1. Subjects solved the four problems using the existing tools; then,
2. The same subjects solved the same four problems with a new information display.

Five skilled operators took part in the experiment.

The new information display was, in structure, very similar to the existing tools. Among these, the document used by the operators is a very long graph (more than 5 metres long) showing the planned states of the process. An extract from this document is shown below.

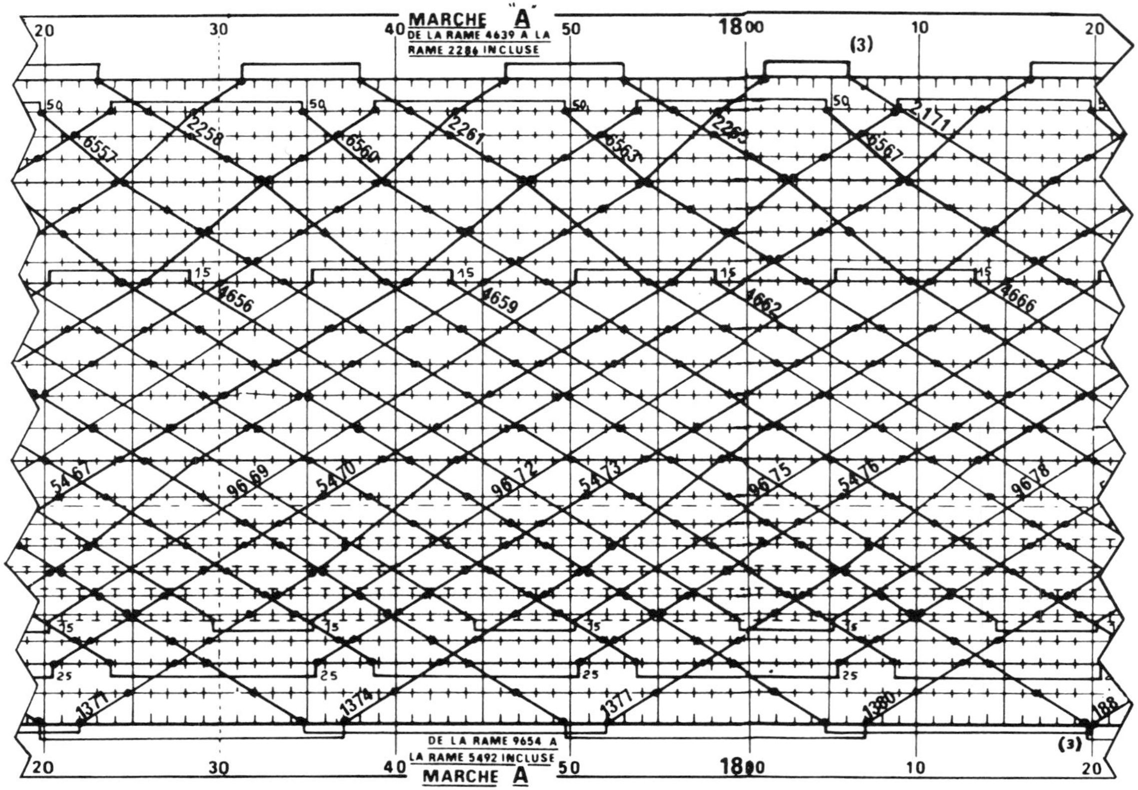
MARCHE "A"
DE LA RAME 4639 A LA RAME 2286 INCLUSE
DE LA RAME 9654 A LA RAME 5492 INCLUSE
MARCHE A
(3)
2258
2261
6557
6560
6563
6567
2171
4656
4659
4662
4666
5467
9669
5470
9672
5473
9675
5476
9678
1371
1374
1377

Fig. 3

In the new information display the only additional information concerned the drivers:

    - what was planned for a driver,
    - where did a driver come from.

The display of this information is a simple (though important) addition, as can be seen in Fig. 4, which represents
a simplified portion of the new display.

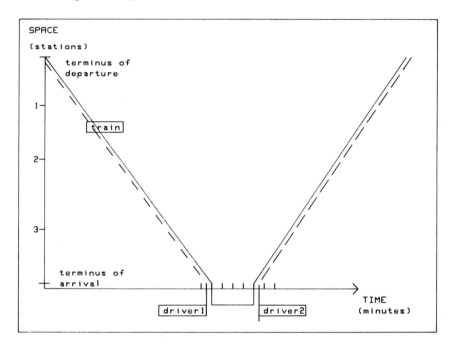

Fig. 4

In Fig. 4 the Y-axis is a space axis: the succession of
the stations between the terminus of departure and the
terminus of arrival. The X-axis is a time axis. The full
lines represent the successive theoretical train positions, and the dotted lines represent the drivers. In
this example there is a change of driver at the terminus
of arrival.
    The solutions produced by subjects using the two
different information displays clearly demonstrated that
the additional information in the new version illustrated
some critical properties of the problem not apparent on
the usual display. Let us illustrate this with one particular example of a diagnosis error which occurs when

operators are using the old display.

Figure 5 shows five separate "cases" or consequences
that can result from the same incident (compare with
Fig. 1 and 2 which illustrate the first two of these cases).
Case 1 and case 2 are treated by subjects using the old
information display in the same way. Thus in case 2 no
subjects produced an effective solution which would lessen
the delay of the new train. This diagnosis error disap-
peared when subjects were given the new information
display.

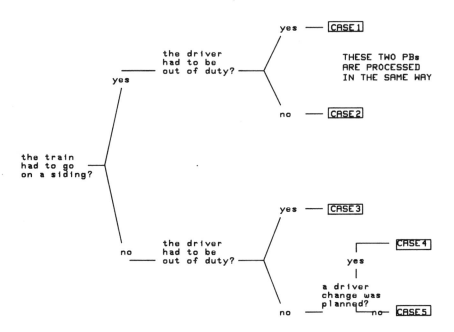

Fig. 5

It is this kind of error which perfectly exemplifies the
phenomenon of problem space reduction as we have introduced it above. In terms of information processing, the
problem space thus reduced can be seen as a decision tree
that has fewer branches than the theoretical one: some of
the branches are not used and might even not be known, and
some branches may not be completely processed.

It is possible to understand why this problem simplifi-
cation occurs by consideration of the following points:

Information displayed:
In the existing regulation system one of the two dimensions

appears more salient than the other. Trains' positions are
displayed in real time on the control panel and the most
important document is the graphical representation of the
process showing all the theoretical states and train
positions. Data about drivers are only supplied on an
alphanumeric list providing all the assignments for each
driver.

Information reliability:
The data are not organised as paired structures. Some of
the information is gathered by the operators: they write
it down but it is not always reliable, due to transcription
errors and/or to information not being updated.

Short-term memory limitations:
At the beginning of an incident the operators have to
diagnose and evaluate the repercussions, i.e. they have to
identify which operations were planned for both the train
and the driver and what are the consequences if these
operations are not fulfilled.

We could perhaps say that the origin of the difficulty
lies in short term memory limitations: it is difficult to
make inferences on bi-variate functions. This intrinsic
difficulty of the task is confounded by badly designed
information display.

    What is surprising here is that we are dealing with
skilled operators and if the diagnosis is defined as the
result of a categorisation process, the reduction means
that, in spite of their past experience, the operators
have not built the whole set of possible diagnoses, or
that the categories have somehow been defined in such a
way that two different problems can be processed in the
same way by an operator.

    Richard (1982) has suggested further clarification about
the reduction mechanism that could have taken place during
learning: during problem analysis, if a subject cannot
refer to any schemata guiding the identification of critical features he cannot use planning; as soon as an operational representation is reached analysis activity stops
and execution starts, prematurely.

    This description concerns what happens when the problem
is really new for the subject, but can be extended to
skilled operators by referring to the difficulties we have
described above.

4) CONCLUSIONS FROM THE ANALYSIS

a. An important outcome of this study is an indication that

the characteristic ergonomics approach to job analysis
may be flawed. Such an approach typically treats all
skilled operators as experts - then goes on to rely on the
knowledge, operations, procedures and strategies of these
"experts". But we have shown here that in complex systems,
skilled operators, having several years of experience, may
not have completely structured the problems.

b. A badly designed information display may induce poor
mental representations of the system in users. In particular it may lead to inappropriate "problem space reduction".
Our analysis also pointed to an important confounding rami-
fication of this effect: an incident which resulted directly from an inaccurate solution to an earlier incident may
be perceived as an entirely independent incident, even by
a skilled operator.

5) TOWARDS AN IMPROVED DESIGN

The computer-aided system we designed relies on the formal
features that have been identified. Up to now we have only
dealt with the problem analysis activity (diagnosis). In
problem *solving* the general structure of the solutions is a
substitution: the operators have to try and replace either
the trains or the drivers. The operators have then to
construct the possible substitution set with a combinatorial
activity.
     The new information display used in the second experiment
seems to provide in some cases a good diagnosis aid, but it
was not kept as an effective tool because there exists a more
convenient display, providing both diagnosis and problem
solving aiding. The rationale behind this improved design can
be described as follows. According to which problem class an
incident belongs, the information needed to solve it is not
the same: what are the available replacement trains and/or
drivers. It is possible to precisely define the meaning of
"available" from the analysis of experts' decision making.
The analysis of the choice criteria between several possible
substitution elements results in a solution hierarchy.
     Here is an illustration of the information needed in two
different cases:

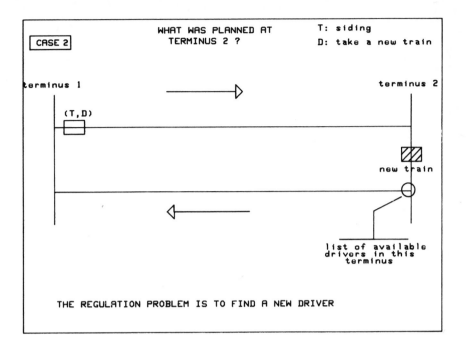

Fig. 6

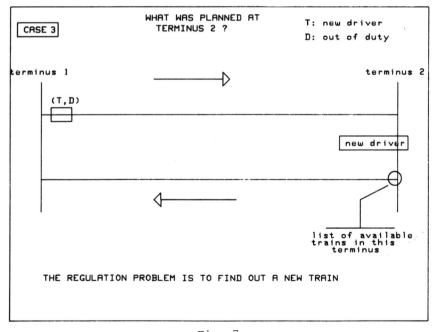

Fig. 7

Of course, having designed the basic structure of the information display, other decisions remain to be made. It is necessary to clarify the automation level. Several options are possible: from the simple information display of data, the combination into available candidate solutions, and up to an expert system.

REFERENCES

Bisseret, A., Michard and Boutin, P. (1979). Eléments Introductifs à l'Ergonomie des Systèmes Hommes-Machines. *Informatique et Sciences Humaines*. <u>44</u>.

Elstein, A.S., Shulman, L.S. and Sprafka, S.A. (1978). Medical Problem Solving, An Analysis of Clinical Reasoning. Harvard University Press. Cambridge, Massachusetts.

Falzon, P. (1982). Display Structures: Compatibility with the Operators' Mental Representation and Reasoning Process. Proceedings of the 2nd European Annual Conference on Human Decision Making and Manual Control June 2-4, Bonn.

Newell, A. and Simon, H.A. (1972). Human Problem Solving. Englewood Cliffs, Prentice-Hall.

Richard, J.F. (1982). Le Traitement Humain de l'Information: Sa Contribution aux Sciences Cognitives. Communication au Colloque de l'Association pour la Recherche Cognitive, Février 1982, Pont à Mousson.

Senach, B. and Janet, E. (1979). Propositions pour l'Aménagement du Poste de Commandes Centralisées de la Ligne de Sceaux. INRIA   RER 7910 R01.

Senach, B. (1980a). Analyse du Travail de Contrôle d'un Réseau Ferré: Recherche des Inadaptations du Système Homme-Machine. INRIA RER 8005 R02.

Senach, B. (1980b). Analyse du Travail de Régulation d'un Réseau Ferré: Résolution d'Incidents d'Exploitation. INRIA RER 8012 R05.

Senach, B. (1982). Aide à la Résolution de Problème par Présentation Graphique des Informations. INRIA Mars 1982, <u>13</u>.

Simon, H.A. and Reed, S.K. (1976). Modeling strategy shifts in a problem solving task. *Cognitive Psychology*. <u>8</u>, 86-97.

NAMING COMMANDS: AN ANALYSIS OF DESIGNERS' NAMING BEHAVIOUR

ANKER HELMS JØRGENSEN,[+] PHIL BARNARD,[*]
NICK HAMMOND[*] AND IAN CLARK[°]

[+]*Institute of Datalogy*
Copenhagen University
Copenhagen, Denmark.
[*]*MRC Applied Psychology Unit*
Cambridge, England.
[°]*Human Factors Laboratory*
IBM United Kingdom Laboratories
Winchester, England.

1) INTRODUCTION

In command-driven interactive systems, the command names, and argument structures associated with them, are a prominent aspect of the user interface. They form the basic communication link between the user and the functions provided by the system. Probably every user of an interactive system is familiar with the experience of having forgotten the function associated with a particular name or of having remembered the existence of a particular function but not the command name required to invoke it. Furthermore, users frequently complain not only of memory problems but also of confusion due to excessive use of jargon or computer-centric names, inconsistencies in namesets and their general unintelligibility (e.g. see Long *et al.*, 1983; Norman, 1981).

Such complaints, particularly those which concern the use of computer-oriented terminology, represent an illustration of the general problem of communication between people who possess specialist knowledge, in this case system designers, and those who do not, in this case the users of software packages. This potential mismatch in the use and understanding of terminology quite naturally leads to the question as to whether or not user-system communication would be better served by recruiting dialogue structures and vocabularies

PSYCHOLOGY OF COMPUTER USE
ISBN 0-12-297420-4

which are user-oriented rather than system-oriented.

A number of recent studies have attempted to evaluate
relationships between attributes of namesets and user
performance. The studies have included examinations of
attributes of names such as their suggestiveness (Rosenberg,
1982); their semantic specificity (Barnard *et al.*, 1982), use
of natural English words (Ledgard *et al.*, 1981) and the use of
system-oriented words (Scapin, 1981). Relationships between
the names within a command set have also been considered.
These include aspects such as the congruence and
hierarchicalness of naming schemes (Carroll, 1980); the
confusability or discriminability of names within a set
(Hammond *et al.*, 1980; Black and Moran, 1982); the structuring
of commands into noun-verb form (Scapin, 1982) and verb-
argument rule schemes (Barnard *et al.*, 1981).

Although many of the factors investigated have been shown
to influence user learning or memory, a casual reader of the
relevant literature might justifiably express some concern
over the somewhat complex and confusing set of apparent
implications. In the case of the choice of terminology and its
structure, different studies appear to have varying implications concerning the "naturalness" of dialogues. In one of the
studies Ledgard *et al.* (1981) report a finding implying that
a syntax employing "familiar descriptive everyday words and
well-formed English phrases" leads to better performance than
a more "notational" dialogue. Another finding (Scapin, 1981)
is interpreted as evidence that computer-oriented words used
as commands are better than more usual words for inexperienced
users. The same author examined memory for command names
(Scapin, 1982) and found that recall was better for names
invented by users themselves than for names which they had not
generated themselves. In contrast, Landauer *et al.* (1983)
compared "natural" names popularly generated by users with
names produced by system designers and with "random" names
like "ALLEGE". The fact that these manipulations did not
produce substantial main effects on the time taken to learn
the miniature editing system in question has been interpreted
by at least one third party as "it is not clear that it makes
much difference what the command names are" (Lesk, 1981).

Any potential confusion in the implications of these studies
is more apparent than real. From a technical viewpoint the
differences between the studies are more important than their
high level communal interest in terminologies for text-editing.
The studies quoted each addressed different specific issues,
manipulated variables defined in different ways for different
task environments and used different measures of human
performance. In consequence, the products of the studies are
not directly comparable and their implications for system

design are far from straightforward.

Two rather fundamental issues underlie the difficulties of establishing straightforward relationships between different types of command names and performance in actual interactive dialogue. The first issue concerns user performance. Some evidence (for example Barnard *et al.*, 1982) suggests that users will respond to different types of command names by adopting different strategies for learning. Hence, global measures such as time on task or errors may provide insufficient information to analyse the detailed cognitive consequences of name choices. Furthermore, the act of generating or selecting names may itself have properties which are different from critical properties required for comprehending or remembering them. For example, people may most readily generate high frequency general terms (see Black and Sebrechts, 1981) which may not define operations adequately or discriminate among them when it comes to comprehension and performance in interactive dialogue. Under these circumstances we cannot expect the intuitive selections of users or designers to be necessarily best.

The second fundamental issue concerns the difficulty in establishing what are the salient variables of naming. The "naturalness", semantic generality, suggestiveness or "computer orientedness" are variables which can be operationally defined but whose formal properties are difficult to elucidate. Underlying this difficulty is somewhat inadequate knowledge of what happens when people name things. Although this itself has long been of interest to linguists, philosophers and psychologists (for example see Carroll, 1978), we know very little about the pragmatics of the naming process. In addition, much of the speculation concerns how people name things rather than actions or functions and there is even less speculation concerning the construction of sets of names rather than the naming of individual referents.

In the specific case of generating names for the functions performed by computer software or for the "objects" referred to in the system some aspects of the pragmatics of naming processes are beginning to emerge with some degree of consistency. It is quite clear that a sample of users will generate an enormous diversity of names for the same function or object. For example, Furnas *et al.* (1982) report four studies in which the likelihood of any two people using the same main content word in their descriptions ranged from a meagre .07 to a mere .18. Similar diversity is apparent in the results obtained by Carroll for command names (1980) and filenames (1982). Although Carroll obtained considerable variability in naming behaviour it is clear from his work that users can and do impose structure on namesets (for example

by utilizing hierarchies or congruent name pairs) but it was
equally clear that people can be rather inconsistent in their
use of certain kinds of rule schemes and abbreviation
strategies (Carroll, 1980).

The fact that people independently generate many different
names for the same actions or objects and apply rule schemes
inconsistently is not surprising given the creative nature of
language use and the fact that "names" generally get introduced
into speech communities one by one on the basis of consensual
usage. In this respect generating complete namesets for
immediate use is a somewhat unusual demand. However, people
patently do not usually name things at random - by for example
calling a "create" operation by the name "delete". As such,
understanding how people go about constructing namesets could
help us to evaluate how problematic namesets arise and also
to go about the business of defining and evaluating naming
variables and their consequences for interactive dialogues
between users and systems. The purpose of the present study
was to investigate the naming strategies employed by computer
systems designers. There are, for instance, examples of
problematic names drawn from many different systems produced
by different designers but systematic evidence is lacking on
how a large sample of designers would name the commands in a
single system. Accordingly the specific objectives of the
present study involved seeking broad answers to questions
concerning designers' naming strategies. Specific questions
include: Do designers show the same kind of variability in
their naming as users or does their common knowledge of
computing restrict their choice of name? What structural rule
schemes, if any do they employ? What semantic features do
they emphasize? Are there any consistent semantic strategies
for naming?

2) METHOD AND PROCEDURE

A sample of computer system specialists (designers) were
asked to provide names and argument structures for an
interactive system designed for computer-naïve users to decode
secret messages. The system incorporated twelve operations.
Four of these operations manipulated tables of data required
to establish a particular code value determining how a message
was encyphered and eight operations manipulated the message
itself to transform it into normal English text. The
interactive system in question was that employed by Hammond
et al. (1980) to investigate the performance and consequences
of command name types and argument structures.

For the purposes of this naming study, a questionnaire
technique was developed for answering on an interactive

terminal. The basic naming task was straightforward. For each
operation the designers could view VDU frames representing
task states before and after the execution of a particular
operation. The designers were asked to name the operation and
assign a structure for the arguments associated with each one.
The present paper will focus only on the naming data, the
argument structure data will be presented elsewhere.

The Interactive Questionnaire

The questionnaire consisted of four sections: in the first
section the designers were asked six yes/no questions in order
to assess their experience with interactive systems. The
questions were graded so that endorsing each additional
question generally reflected increasing experience or
involvement in system design.

The second section consisted of a display frame introducing
the decyphering system and details of the naming task. The
designers were informed that users would be experts in
cryptography but would typically have no computer experience.
The designers were also told about the before-after frame
technique and that their task would be to provide names for
the functions illustrated and to define their argument
structure. No constraints were imposed concerning any features
of the required names – such as length, name type or
structuring principles. Thus the designers were given the
maximum possible freedom of choice.

In the third section the designers actually named the twelve
functions. The twelve functions were ordered in sequence and
the designers were to name them in that sequence. They were
allowed to flip freely between the "before" and "after" frames
for each function before deciding upon a name for it. After
each choice was made the system carried on to the next
operation to be named. Hence it was a strictly sequential
task-they could not preview the entire set of operations before
starting. They were, however, subsequently given the opportunity of reviewing and changing their name choice.

The twelve operations to be named were divided into two
phases. In phase 1 a "code value" was obtained by four table
manipulating operations. These were a prerequisite to the
second message manipulating phase and the table manipulating
operations were named first. Example before-after frames
for the third operation in this phase are given in Figs 1a
and 1b. The first operation enters information into the
"source" column of Table 10. The second operation fills in the
wavelengths in one row of Table 10. The third operation enters
a complete array of adjustment values in Table 11 and this is
indicated by the absence of the information in the before

A.H. JØRGENSEN *et al.*

```
BEFORE: This is what appears on the screen BEFORE the function is called:
------------------------------------------------------------------------
Zones:     1-Western Europe     2-North America     3-Communist block
Source: Washington  Day: Tuesday  Security: Confidential  Code value:
------------------------------------------------------------------------
        Table 10                  Table 11                  Table 12
  Transmission wavelengths      Adjustment values          Code values

 -----------------------    -----------------     -----------------
|Source Mo Tu Th Fr Sa Su| |Mo Tu Th Fr Sa Su|  |Mo Tu Th Fr Sa Su|
|1:Chic -  -  -  -  -  - | |-  -  -  -  -  - |  |19 84 10 66 31 27|
|2:LosA -  -  -  -  -  - | |-  -  -  -  -  - |  |41 60 45 76 34 57|
|3:NewY -  -  -  -  -  - | |-  -  -  -  -  - |  |15 62 97 71 04 79|
|4:Wash 12 78 33 19 83 41| |-  -  -  -  -  - |  |44 56 18 09 55 83|
------------------------------------------------------------------------

This operation will affect Table 11. The numbers which appear are used
later in the sequence for adjusting the codes in Table 12. The adjust-
ment table to be used depends on the wavelength for the source and day
(Washington and Tuesday here).

PF1 for instructions          PF8 to see the effect of the function
```

FIG. 1a *The "before" frame for function 3.*

AFTER: This is what appears on the screen AFTER the function is called:

Zones: 1-Western Europe   2-North America   3-Communist block

Source: Washington Day: Tuesday Security: Confidential Code value:

      Table 10   Table 11   Table 12

  Transmission wavelengths   Adjustment values   Code values

Source	Mo	Tu	Th	Fr	Sa	Su		Mo	Tu	Th	Fr	Sa	Su		Mo	Tu	Th	Fr	Sa	Su
1:Chic	-	-	-	-	-	-		33	52	86	20	07	21		19	84	10	66	31	27
2:LosA	-	-	-	-	-	-		49	22	78	43	93	17		41	60	45	76	34	57
3:NewY	-	-	-	-	-	-		66	22	86	02	57	48		15	62	97	71	04	79
4:Wash	18	78	33	19	83	41		40	69	41	61	50	06		44	38	18	09	55	83

Type the command you would use to call this function ==>

Now type 1 or 2 to select whichever argument order you think is best ==>

Orders are: 1 -- <Table number, Transmission Wavelength> viz. 11 78 here,

              2 -- <Transmission Wavelength, Table number> viz. 78 11 here.

PF1 for instructions   PF8 to see the previous screen once more

FIG. 1b *The "after" frame for function 3.*

frame of Fig. 1(a) and its presence in the after frame of
Fig. 1(b). The fourth operation changes the code values in
Table 12 as a function of the adjustment values established
by the prior operation.

In the second phase an encyphered message is gradually
transformed into English text. This is illustrated in Fig. 2
where a single after frame is shown. In this illustration
various operations are implicitly presented in their before
and after forms since each operation generated a new version
of the message and displayed it below the prior message state.
The first six functions either manipulated the structure or
content of the message whilst the remaining two operations
dealt with a security coding at the end of the message
(illustrated as **2** in line '27' of Fig. 2).

In the fourth section of the questionnaire the designers
were shown a full listing of the names they had generated. At
this stage they were invited to change any of the names if
they so wished. Only 55 names were changed (4%) and these are
not considered in the present report. Finally, the designers
were urged to state any principles or factors which had
governed their choice of names or their structure.

Administration of Questionnaire and Subject Population

The questionnaire was shipped on a major computer manufacturer'
internal communication network. This enabled the respondents
to answer the questions and name the operations working at
their own interactive terminals. For the naming task interactiv
presentation of the "before"/"after" displays for the operatio
enabled the respondents to imagine how the task would appear
to the anticipated end-user. Once completed the responses
were mailed back to the investigators over the same network.

The respondents ("designers") all had had experience of
interactive systems. Most of them had been involved in
designing new systems or in improving systems (84%).
Approximately half of the respondents (48%) had been involved
in some form of relevant teaching activity or had written
papers on the subject. Responses were actually received from
113 designers. Three of these were discarded from the analysis
because they had not followed the instructions.

3) DATA ANALYSIS

The names were initially tabulated into a matrix representing
the full set of 1320 names (110 designers by 12 operations).
This full corpus enabled examination of the properties of the
names (a) for individual operations and (b) for individual
designers. In relation to the analyses for individual

```
    AFTER:  This is what appears on the screen AFTER the function is called
    ----------------------------------------------------------------------------
    Security rating:    1-Secret    2-Confidential    3-Restricted
    Source: Washington  Day: Tuesday  Security: Confidential  Code value: 56
    ----------------------------------------------------------------------------
       <-------seg 1--------><--------seg 2---------><-------seg 3-------->
       <--e1--><--e2--><--e3--><--e4--><--e5--><--e6--><--e7--><--e8--><--e9-->


    20 LF        WBRLK  WVERM   7PUOLUE OIERJWB BWS      TLWXIBR LXRRYW ASLT
    21 AG        ENTAL  BERTZ   7QUPAIR PORTKEN NED      YATCONT ACTTUE SDAY
    22 AGENT     ALBERT Z7QIP   AIRPORT KENNEDY AT       CONTACT TU     ES    DAY
    23 AGENT     ALBERT AIRPORT KENNEDY AT      CONTACT TU      ES     DAY
    24 CONTACT AGENT    ALBERT  AIRPORT KENNEDY AT       TU      ES     DAY
    25 CONTACT AGENT    ALBERT  AT      KENNEDY AIRPORT TU      ES     DAY
    26 CONTACT AGENT    ALBERT  AT      KENNEDY AIRPORT TUESDAY
    27 CONTACT AGENT    ALBERT  AT      KENNEDY AIRPORT TUESDAY **2**
    ----------------------------------------------------------------------------
    Type the command name you would use to call this function ==>
    Now type 1 or 2 to select whichever argument order you think is best ==>
    Orders are: 1 -- <Message number, Security rating> viz. 26   2 here,
                2 -- <Security rating, Message number> viz.  2  26 here.


    PF1 for instructions            PF7 to see the previous screen once more
```

FIG. 2 *The "after" frame of function 11*

operations the names underwent a process of data reduction.

1) *Surface structure identity*: In order to establish the number of different superficial names, the frequency of different "surface" forms for each operation were counted. At this level all but the most minor differences (for example upper versus lower case) were binned separately. As such the full surface variation in names and their abbreviations could be examined.

2) *Lexical identity*: The purpose of this analysis was to establish how frequently the same root lexemes were employed in the names. This level of analysis involved interpretation on the part of the investigators. Some of the interpretation was relatively straightforward such as collapsing names differing only in suffices etc. However, in other cases interpretation was less straightforward. For example, abbreviations were often open to ambiguous expansion into a full surface form, for example *trans* could be either transform or translate. Likewise, the intended part of speech is frequently ambiguous - notably between noun forms and verb forms (for example *order*). These ambiguities were dealt with individually either by referring to the designer's comments, by attempting to resolve them on the basis of other choices made by the same designer, or by assessing the pragmatic plausibility of interpretations in the specific context of this naming task. Where ambiguities or abbreviations were not practically resolvable they were separately considered, and where names were totally uninterpretable for a particular purpose they were marked as such. In this respect the purpose of the analysis was exploratory with a view to capturing the broad characteristics of the names. As such, accurate characterization of all names on all possible features was not viewed as a practical possibility.

3) *Content*: The third analysis involved attempting to seek communalities in the content of the names in terms of their semantics and pragmatics. Here, names with synonymous or closely related meanings were treated together with a view to establishing the semantic features which designers were emphasizing in their choice of name. For example, the terms "gap" and "space" would be treated as expressing a similar conceptualization underlying the choice of name but which differed semantically and communicatively from a choice such as "apply#".

4) RESULTS AND DISCUSSION

In this paper we shall simply attempt to summarize some of
the major characteristics of the namesets generated. A fuller
and more detailed formal analysis of the data will be
presented elsewhere.

Word forms

Although the average number of different names for each
function was 51.75, ranging from 35 (function 11) to 62
(function 2), the distribution was sharply J-shaped. Many
forms occurred only once and a few occurred very frequently.

Number of different "surface" forms	51.75
Forms occurring only once	36%
Total of 3 most frequent forms	38%
Number of different lexical roots	38.3
Number in simple names	20.8
Number in compound names	17.5
Percentage of single-root name forms	76.4%
Percentage of compound name forms	23.6%

FIG. 3 *Basic Data on Surface Structure of Names. Entries are
averaged over all 12 functions.*

Even when the names are collapsed into those which share a
common composition in terms of their "root lexemes", the
average number of different constructions (including
unassignable and ambiguous forms) for each function is 38.3.
Of these constructions an average of 20.8 different forms
contain a single lexical root while 17.5 different forms
represent compound lexical roots (for example compound nouns,
verb phrases etc.). Although they are roughly equivalent in
terms of the number of different forms, the single-root name
forms are very much more popular for all functions, representing roughly three quarters of the names generated.

When single-root names were used only a very small
proportion (approx. 12%) were abbreviated, whereas almost two
thirds of the compound forms were subjected to abbreviation.
When abbreviation was used the names were usually truncated
(roughly 90% of the single-root name abbreviations and roughly
75% of the compound name abbreviations). Some form of mixture
of contraction and truncation was also common in the case of
compound names, representing about 20% of the instances of

abbreviated compound forms.

Not only was there relatively little consensus between designers, but individual designers were typically not using particular surface forms consistently across the twelve operations. For example, although single-root names were by far the most popular, only 31 designers used them consistently. Of the remaining 79 designers, a few came close to using compound names throughout but only one did so consistently for all twelve operations. The particular scheme involved was also rather idiosyncratic, all twelve names were prefixed with *ad* which was explained in the designer's comments as standing for A̲thene D̲ecoder - the "name" of the software package.

Inconsistency was also the rule rather than the exception with abbreviation schemes. Only one designer seemed to be using abbreviation in a straightforwardly consistent way. The abbreviations were:

$$e \quad s \quad w \quad a \quad b \quad g \quad f \quad e \quad p \quad s \quad t \quad \neg t$$

This designer's subsequent comments were equally abrupt: "After two days the names and what they stand for is irrelevant. I do not remember what the name of the black thing on the floor of my car is - but when you push it the car goes faster." This designer provided no inferred names and it proved impossible to disambiguate them with any degree of confidence.

A more typical example of the kind of inconsistencies observed is represented by the following set of names generated by another designer:

source	wave	adj	code	msg	gap
del	beg	ord	reduce	security	chgsec

In this case the maximum length is 8 characters. However, some of the inferred names (d̲e̲lete, b̲e̲g̲in, o̲r̲d̲er) would come under this length but are nevertheless abbreviated. When abbreviation is used it appears in the form of truncation (d̲e̲lete), contraction (m̲e̲s̲s̲ag̲e) and a mixed scheme (ch̲an̲g̲e s̲e̲curity).

In terms of the superficial aspects of the form and lexical content of the names there thus appears to be relatively little consensus among designers or internal consistency in the precise form of the names generated for each function. In terms of the variability in the number of discrete names generated for each function, the likelihood of any two designers coming up with the precisely the same name is about the same as that obtained by Landauer *et al.* (1983) for a sample of potential users naming text editing operations (Landauer and Furnas, personal communication). The observation that individual designers also tended to be inconsistent in their use of structural forms and abbreviation parallels earlier observations by Carroll (1980, Expt. III) for user-generated names in his robot manipulation task.

Functions 1-4:Nominal-Based Strategies

The substantial variabilities and inconsistencies visible in
the surface structure identity of the sets of command names
generated should not be taken to mean that the designers'
naming behaviour was entirely unsystematic. Analysis of the
content of the names indicated that there were a number of
systematic factors operating withing the designers'
underlying strategies for naming the functions. These are
best illustrated and discussed by reference to examples.

Designer	FUNCTION			
	1	2	3	4
*10	source	wl	adj	code
12	listsource	specsource	adjust	codeupdate
19	code	fillrow	filltable	filltable
*21	sources	wavelength	adjustments	codes
22	center	extend	matrix	adjust
*23	city	wave	adj	code
27	display	wavelengths???	adjustments	adjust
*33	source	wavelengths	adjust	code
35	origin	display	show	value
*37	cities	wavelengths	adjustments	codes
39	zone	source	adjust	code
*41	fromcity	length	adjust	code
42	tran	wavel	adjust	code
*46	list_sources	list_wavelengths	set_adjustment	set_code_values
47	tw	tw	av	av2
50	fromzone	fromcity	adjustwave	rekey
*54	adsource	adwave	adadj	adcode
57	city	day	adjust	apply
*58	source	wave	adjust	code
*61	defsrce	deftw	defadj	modcv
62	e	s	w	a
64	zone	source	length	adjust
68	sources	waves	adjustments	modify
*72	names	freq	adj	code
73	display	frequency	adj	decode

FIG. 4 *A small section of the names: 25 designers, functions
1-4 (Table manipulations). Starred designers consistently
chose names to refer to the displayed products of operations.*

Figure 4 illustrates the names provided for the first four
functions by a sample of 25 of the 110 designers. These
functions operated on the tables illustrated in Fig. 1. The
most striking aspect of this sample of names is the relatively
infrequent use of terms which appear to be being used as
simple verbs (for example "display, "modify"). A substantial
proportion of the terms are simple nominals (for example
"source", "wavelength", "adjustments", "codes") or compounds
including a nominal (for example deftw - define transmission
wavelength). In the case of function 3, the term "adjust" is
almost certainly a truncated form of the nominal "adjustment".
The function displays the entries in the table rather than
changing anything and the lengthier terms were those most
frequently abbreviated. Thus, in context it seems unlikely
that "adjust" is being used as verb form. Similar considerations would suggest that, for function 4, the ambiguous
"code" is also being used as a nominal representing "code
value". On this basis, it would appear that the designers are
most frequently naming not the operation performed, but the
products of the operation.

32 adjust	advalues	pickadj
13 adj	avcode	query-adjust
6 adjustments	buildaju	refer
5 adjustment	by	scramble
3 day	choseadjust	select
2 adjval	code	set-adjustment
2 av	defadj	setadjust
2 wave	execll	shoadj
adadj	fill	show
adjcode	filltable	show-data
adjstwvlngth	findadjust	tu
adjusts	fit	twladj
adjustnumbers	getadj	update
adjustwave	inadjval	variant
adjv	keyvalue	w
adjvals	length	waveadj
adjwave	linkadj	wave-adj
adval	matrix	

FIG. 5 *The names generated for function 3.*

Figure 5 shows the full listing of 110 names for function 3.
Of these names, 87 (79%) can be interpreted as representing
the term adjustment or as including it in a compound. The
vast majority of the designers are thus marking the nature of
the information displayed by the function. Similarly, with
function 1, 66 of the 84 simple names referred to the nature

of the information resulting from the action (source, zone, city, origin, location) and 21 of the 25 compound names included these terms as constituents. Included among the nominals for functions 2 and 4 were "wavelength" or "frequency" and "code" or "codevalue" respectively.

For these four functions, then, there was considerable consensus among designers. The majority were utilizing a strategy which involved referring to the information displayed as a consequence of the operations. They were also rather consistent in this respect. Nearly half (53) of the designers conformed almost exactly to the pattern outlined above for all four functions. Of the designers shown in Fig. 4, the eleven who conformed to this strategy are marked with an asterisk. A further 16 used nominal-based strategies for these functions but, for at least one function, marked some different feature of the information displayed (for example day), or used the same term for two operations. Only three designers consistently used simple verb forms (for example "read", "select", "refer", "use").

The basis for these nominal-based strategies is not difficult to establish. Some evidence (for example Olson, 1970) suggests that, for referring expressions, speakers will typically include sufficient information to distinguish an intended referent from other contextually available referents. In the present case it seems that, in the predominating strategy for the first four functions, the designers are seeking to discriminate one type of displayed information from other types of displayed information*. Under these circumstances the origins of the vocabulary used are easy to trace. The designers are not "creating" names, they are most often selecting their term from the vocabulary embodied in the system itself or are finding a close synonym. Frequently selected terms are drawn from the table headings, a column heading or from parameter descriptions. The designers' creativity and much of the superficial variation lies in the pragmatic basis of the selection, together with the construction rules and abbreviation strategies used to arrive at a final form.

*At least for the first three functions it is difficult to discriminate the 3 display operations. In the case of the fourth operation information present is in fact replaced and some of the mixed strategies involving a verb for function 4 can be accounted for on this basis.

Functions 5-10: Relational Strategies

Six of the remaining eight functions involved translating the
encyphered message into a comprehensible statement (functions
5-10). Functions 5 to 10 involved: (5) a letter-by-letter
substitution operation (Fig. 2, lines 20-21); (6) a systematic
resegmentation of the message in which sequence and character
identity are preserved (Fig. 2, lines 21-22); (7) a "deletion"
of an element (Fig. 2, lines 22-23); (8) the movement of a
particular element to the front of the message (Fig. 2,
lines 23-24); (9) the reordering of three elements within a
particular segment (Fig. 2, lines 24-25); and (10) the joining
of three elements within a segment (Fig. 2, lines 25-26). The
most popular terms (collapsed over different surface
realizations) for these operations are shown in Fig. 6.

Providing an unambiguous assignment in terms of intended
part of speech for a set of words such as those shown in Fig.
6 is an impossible task. Space also precludes a comprehensive
discussion of all the names produced. However, a number of
points are worth noting. The names shown in Fig. 6 contrast
with those generated for the first four functions. The bulk
of the names generated for functions 5-10 are most readily
interpretable, in context, as representing the operations
performed by the functions rather than their products. There
are some important exceptions to this (for example "gap",
"first", "front") but in the case of functions 5, 7, 9 and 10
most of the terms appear to be verb forms. In spite of this,
the sets generated by 59 of the designers involved at least
one word which was not readily interpretable as a verb form.
The sets generated by a further 48 designers could be
construed as consistently utilizing verb forms. The remaining
3 designer's namesets for these functions were not resolvable.

During operations 5-10, the information content of the
message is visible. Under these circumstances the
discriminating factors concern relationships between the two
successive versions represented by the before and after frames,
together with the scope of the operations (for example whether
they operate on elements, segments or the message as a whole).
Information concerning the version is a mandatory argument and
the scope of the operation is explicitly or implicitly carried
by the other argument. Thus, the predominant naming strategy
is to generate an appropriate relational term. For the most
part the designers appear to rely on their own mental thesaurus
and experience in selecting a term.

The selection process for the different functions is
clearly pragmatic. In the case of function 5, the domain of
cyphers provides obvious options (decode, encode, code). For
function 6 the resegmentation operation is most frequently

Function

5		6		7	
decode	34	gap	24	delete	31
translate	15	space	12	remove	12
change	5	format	6	drop	9
encode	5	regroup	6	discard	6
substitute	5	decode	5	ignore	4
tr(ans)	5	degap	5	eliminate	3
message	4	group	4	elide	2
code	3	shift	4	erase	2
transform	2	regap	3	omit	2
try	2	adjoin	2	tidy	2
others:		parse	2	zap	2
simple	16	split	2	others:	
compound	14	translate	2	simple	15
		others:		compound	20
		simple	17		
		compound	16		

8		9		10	
order	19	reorder	23	compress	22
first	16	order	17	concatenate	8
start	11	segment	5	join	6
begin	11	reverse	4	select	5
reorder	4	rotate	4	close	4
move	4	swap	4	combine	4
arrange	2	permute	3	condense	3
e	2	arrange	2	merge	3
front	2	flip	2	pack	3
others:		move	2	segment	3
simple	10	shuffle	2	s	2
compound	29	others:		squeeze	2
		simple	14	tidy	2
		compound	28	collect	2
				compact	2
				others:	
				simple	14
				compound	25

FIG. 6 *The more popular terms generated for Functions 5-10:*
(collapsed across abbreviations etc. except where unresolvable).

represented by "gap" and "space". In context both may be
construed as focussing on a spatial relationship between
constituents. The term "gap" and its variants (degap, regap)
were explicitly mentioned in the notes presented at the
bottom of the display frame for this function. The complete
set of terms for function 7 virtually exhausts the most
comprehensive thesaurus concerning deletion. The names for
function 8 divided between those which make explicit the
structural nature of the operation (for example order, arrange
move) and those which made explicit or marked the final
positional relationship of the element moved (first, start,
begin; or the compounds: first word, start element, message
start). The names for function 9 followed a similar pattern
to those for function 8, except that the alternative to a
general conceptualization of the structural nature of the
change (reorder, order) involved selecting a term which
marked the relative nature of the positional change (reverse,
rotate, permute, shuffle). The alternative conceptualizations
for function 10 appear somewhat different. Two conceptualizations predominate. One is represented by those terms which
focus on the process of linking elements (concatenate, join,
combine) and those which focus on the contraction of the
larger constituent (compress, condense, squeeze, compact).

Functions 11 and 12: Strategies Based on Domain Semantics

The names generated for functions 11 and 12 represented another
clear strategy shift. Function 11 had the effect of adding a
"security rating" at the end of the message (see Fig. 2). For
this operation the names generated were quite clearly based
on the information added. The root lexemes "secure(ity)";
"rate(ing)" and "classify" accounted for 82 of the 89 simple
names and were incorporated into 19 of the 21 compounds.
Terms such as "add" and "insert" only occurred in a handful of
compound names. The information added was referred to as the
"security rating" in notes on the before frame and as
"security" in the parameter field (see Fig. 2). As with
functions 1-4 the designers were clearly adopting a lexeme
present in the task environment or a close relative (classify)
Unlike functions 1-4 the designers divided between using verb
forms (secure, rate, classify) and nominal equivalents
(security, rating). The same pattern obtained with function 12
except that the relational aspect was marked using substantial
the same root lexemes - either in simple names (reclassify,
resecure, rerate) or in compound form (change security, rate
change, reset security etc.). Thus, for functions 11 and 12
the designers are predominantly referring to information or
describing a relationship but are consistently doing so using

a vocabulary reflecting the domain semantics of the information or relationship involved.

5) SUMMARY

As with other data on the naming of commands, the namesets generated by the designers showed considerable diversity in terms of the surface structure identity of the individual names. The designers were also not being consistent across their full namesets. However, in spite of the superficial diversity, there was rather more systematicity within and between designers as to the type of information "featured" in the names assigned to particular functions. Further analyses of these types of systematicities should facilitate definition of the factors involved in the naming process and studies of their implications for user comprehension.

ACKNOWLEDGEMENTS

The research reported in this paper was jointly funded by IBM and MRC. A.H. Jørgensen's participation in this work was supported by the Danish Natural Science Research Council, Egmont H. Petersens Fond and farvehandler L. Becks Legat.

REFERENCES

Barnard, P., Hammond, N., MacLean, A. and Morton, J. (1982). Learning and remembering interactive commands in a text-editing task. *Behaviour and Information Technology* 1, 4, 347-358.

Barnard, P., Hammond, N., Morton, J., Long, J. and Clark, I. (1981). Consistency and compatibility in human computer dialogue. *International Journal of Man-Machine Studies* 15, 87-134.

Black, J.B. and Moran, T.P. (1982). Learning and remembering command names. *Proceedings of Human Factors in Computer Systems,* Gaithersburg, Maryland; ACM, pp. 8-11.

Black, J. and Sebrechts, M. (1981). Facilitating human-computer communication. *Applied Psycholinguistics* 2, 146-177.

Carroll, J. (1978). Names and naming: an interdisciplinary review. *IBM RESEARCH REPORT RC 7370.*

Carroll, J. (1980). Learning, using and designing command paradigms. *IBM Research Report RC 8141.*

Carroll, J. (1982). Creating names for personal files in an interactive computing environment. *International Journal of Man-Machine Studies* 16, 405-438.

Furnas, G., Gomez, L., Landauer, T. and Dumais, S. (1982).
  Statistical semantics: how can a computer use what people
  name things to guess what things people mean when they name
  things? *In* "Proceedings of Human Factors in Computer
  Systems", Gaithersburg, Maryland, ACM, pp. 251-253.
Hammond, N., Barnard, P., Clark, I., Morton, J. and Long, J.
  (1980). Structure and content in interactive dialogue.
  IBM Hursley Human Factors Report HF 034, Oct. 1980.
Landauer, T., Gallotti, K. and Hartwel, S. (1983). Natural
  command names and initial learning: A study of text
  editing terms. (In press). *Communications of the Association
  for Computing Machinery.*
Ledgard, H. Singer, A. and Whiteside, J. (1981). Directions in
  human factors for interactive systems. *Lecture notes in
  Computer Science* 103, Springer-Verlag Berlin/Heidelberg/
  New York.
Lesk, M. (1981). Another view. *Datamation* 27, November issue,
  p. 146.
Long, J., Hammond, N., Barnard, P., Morton, J. and Clark, J.
  (1983). Introducing the interactive computer at work: the
  user's views. *Behaviour and Information Technology.*
  (In press).
Norman, D. (1981). The trouble with UNIX. *Datamation,*
  November issue, 27, 139-150.
Olson, D. (1970). Language and thought: aspects of a cognitive
  theory of semantics. *Psychological Review,* 257-273.
Rosenberg, J. (1982). Evaluating the suggestiveness of command
  names. *In* "Proceedings of Human Factors In Computer Systems",
  Gaithersburg, Maryland; ACM, pp. 12-16.
Scapin, D.L. (1981). Computer commands in restricted natural
  language: some aspects of memory of experience, *Human
  Factors* 23, 365-375.
Scapin, D.L. (1982). Computer commands labelled by users versus
  imposed commands and the effect of structuring rules on
  commands. *In* "Proceedings of Human Factors in Computer
  Systems", Gaithersburg, Maryland, ACM, pp. 17-19.

Psychology of Programming

A MODEL OF THE UNDERSTANDING OF A PROGRAM AND ITS IMPACT ON THE DESIGN OF THE PROGRAMMING LANGUAGE GRADE

H.E. SENGLER

URW-Unternehmensberatung
Hamburg, Germany

1) INTRODUCTION

The problem this paper addresses is the inability even of
experienced programmers to efficiently handle large programs.
The problem manifests itself in the huge efforts necessary to
maintain existing software and the impossibility of detecting
and removing all errors therein (c.f. the findings of Miller
(1979) and the recent description of the situation by Elshoff
and Marcotty (1982)).

The kernel of this problem is the understandability of
programs. "Understanding a program" can be defined as being
able:

1. to predict the effect of the execution of the program; and
2. to establish a causal relation between parts of the effect
   and those parts of the program that cause them.

Understanding a program in this sense, a programmer is at
least able to predict any undesired behaviour of the executing
computer (i.e. to detect the errors in the program) and to
trace it back to the part of the program causing it.

In their attempts to make programs easier to understand,
computer scientists lack deeper knowledge about what
properties of a program make it easy or hard to understand.
As a consequence, they often make decisions according to
their feeling of designs being "natural" or "simple". Such
arguments may be valid, yet they cannot be questioned or
sensibly applied to other design problems.

In recent years attempts therefore have been made to
acquire deeper insight into the understanding of programs.
One way is to perform statistical analysis based on assumptions of factors of understandability (see for example

Jørgensen (1980)); another way is to suggest models that describe the process of understanding (see Shneidermann and Mayer (1979) or Lukey (1980)).

This paper suggests a model of the process of understanding a program. The specific properties of this model are:

1. It assumes the experienced programmer, who is trained in using the respective programming language and programming system. As a consequence, problems of learning a programming language or learning how to program are not addressed, the programmer is assumed to be well-acquainted with both. Furthermore, programs are assumed to be syntactically correct.
2. The model assumes a "worst case situation": the programmer has no previous knowledge about the program, there is no additional documentation, there are no comments in the program and there is no way to execute the program in order to get sample outputs. Thus, the "formal" program is the programmer's only source of information.
3. The model describes the process of understanding as transformation of information, assuming a program to be interpreted by the programmer as a net of semantic components and relations (and not as text, which is just an interpretation of the net).

In the process of understanding, incoming information (symbols in the program) is related to existing information (knowledge of the semantics of the programming language) yielding new information (the semantics of program units) which is stored and can later be recalled. The end-result of this process is the semantics of the program, part of which is the effect of its execution.

In order to capture the characteristics of human information processing, the following assumptions are made about the process:

a. Limitation of the information processable at one time.
b. Associative access to stored information.
c. Five basic abilities (*find, associate, recall, evaluate* and *abstract*) and their characteristics.

The purpose of the model is not to describe real processes in the human brain (as for example the models of Newell and Simon (1972) or Anderson and Bower (1974) attempt to do), but to explain the difficulties programmers encounter when understanding large programs and to suggest improvements in the program design. The model is independent of a specific programming language, programming method and program representation. The suggested improvements are exemplified in the design of a programming language, an outline of which is given in section 3.

2) THE MODEL

The Internal Program

A human reading a text in a language familiar to him does not
analyse it characterwise but reads words and makes assumptions
about the words to follow. A corresponding behaviour is
assumed for a programmer reading a program. It can be interpreted as mapping the text into a new structure formed within
the human brain that represents all aspects of the text the
reader assumes to be essential. The structure formed when
reading a program will be called the "internal program". All
subsequent processes of understanding assumed in the model
are based on the internal program.

Independent of a specific programming language, the
properties of an internal program are as follows: an internal
program is a net; its nodes will be called "components", its
arcs will be called "relations". Basically, the components of
an internal program are the semantic units of the programming
language (i.e. symbols or combinations of symbols that are
given semantics by the language) as they are used in the
program, and the relations accordingly are the semantic
relations between them.

For example (all examples are from the programming language
Pascal, Jensen and Wirth (1976)), the character "+" will be
mapped into a component with the semantics "add the left and
right operands (when execution reaches this point)" with
relations to both operands and the previous and following
operation. The character "w" in the word "while" will not be
mapped into a component, nor would the word "while" alone
because only for the combination "while" .... "do" are the
semantics defined.

The actual mapping of a program text into an internal
program however is not determined by the language alone but
is additionally formed by the individual experiences a
programmer receives while learning the language and while
using it. In the attempt to reduce the amount of information
he has to cope with, the programmer may interpret subnets of
the internal program (as they would appear according to the
semantics of the language) as single components or relations,
if they often occur in the same combination.

Such a subnet mapping may be influenced by the kind of
programs the programmer works with, but it may also be
suggested by the language. For example, a variable, its type
and the read or write accesses to it are separate components
according to the semantics of the language, yet a programmer
may map them into a single component "variable" with a

property (type) and relations to operations (accesses). As
another example, a programmer may interpret a "goto"-statement
as a relation between the preceding statement and the one with
the goto's label.

As a consequence, one cannot assume for each programmer
the same mapping of a program text into an internal program
but rather a variety of similar mappings. (Note: the ability
to identify such subnets offers a nice explanation for the
better performance of experienced programmers as opposed to
beginners).

The Process of Understanding

At each moment the programmer is able to handle only a small
amount of information. This limitation determines the whole
process of understanding and characterizes his basic abilities.

When analysing a program the programmer is looking at it.
Due to his limited processing capabilities he cannot treat
the program as a whole but rather has to separate it into
portions, each of which is intellectually manageable by him.
Whenever he looks at a portion it is mapped into the
corresponding portion of the internal program (with the
qualification that he may have to search for or recall information not within his view). This portion of the internal
program is information that is directly accessible for
further processing.

In the process of understanding the programmer selects
portions according to different objectives. His primary
objective is to separate the program into a hierarchy of
portions. (A sequential slicing does not suffice because for
large programs it would yield too many slices.) In the
separation of portions the programmer is guided by the
syntactical separation of the program text into sections.
Examples of such sections are procedures ("procedure"....
"end"), blocks ("begin"...."end") or lines of text enclosed
by blank lines. The programmer chooses such a section as a
portion unless no such separation exists or a section
contains too much or too little information to be reasonably
processed. In that case he defines his own separation. The
separation of the program into a hierarchy of portions results
in what the programmer sees as the "structure of the program".

There are many secondary objectives according to which a
programmer may select portions. For simplicity, the model
assumes only one such objective: the understanding of
relations between components in different portions (see below).

The following is a description of the understanding of one
portion. As his first task the programmer has to *find* the

constituents of the portion. Its constituents are its components and relations as well as its inner portions (i.e.
portions inside the currently analysed portion) and its outer
relations (i.e. relations to components outside the currently
analysed portion, yielding the portion's interface).

The aim of the understanding is the semantics of the
portion. Before being able to evaluate its semantics, the
programmer must acquire (i.e. understand) the semantics of
the outer relations and inner portions that he does not know
yet (if there are any). This forces him to leave the current
portion and to look at other portions of the program. Because
of this switching between portions he has to memorize those
semantics he has already found out in order to be able to
recall them later.

The inner portions are understood in the same way as
described for the currently analysed portion. In order to
understand an outer relation the programmer selects a special
portion that includes the relation in question and the subnets
connected to it at both sides so far as they are relevant for
the semantics of the relation. He understands this portion as
he does every portion, concentrating here on the semantics of
the outer relation.

After he has understood all inner portions and outer
relations, the programmer has all the semantics of the
portion's constituents at his disposal. He can *associate* the
semantics of components and relations (from his knowledge of
the language and the system) and he can *recall* the previously
understood and memorized semantics of inner portions and
outer relations; thus he can evaluate the resulting semantics
of the portion. Evaluating the semantics in general does not
only mean a logical combination of the constituents' semantics
but also an imagining of the effect of the portion on the
program's state space. The state space includes all entities
that are explicitly or implicitly addressed in the program
and whose contents or existence may be changed during the
execution of the program.

The semantics resulting from evaluation in general is too
complex to allow further processing (i.e. memorizing and
recalling as well as constructions on higher levels of the
hierarchy of portions). The programmer therefore additionally
has to *abstract* it, i.e. develop a concept of the function
of the portion or of the subproblem the portion solves within
the surrounding program.

This description of the understanding of one portion
includes that of its inner portions. By viewing a program as
a portion too, the whole process of understanding a program
can be described in the following grammar-like form. (The
model does not imply a specific sequence of the operations

but only stresses their logical interdependences).

Understanding a program = understanding a portion.
Understanding a portion =
    Finding its components, relations, outer relations and
    inner portions;
    Understanding the outer relations and inner portions;
    Associating the semantics of components and relations;
    Recalling the semantics of outer relations and inner
    portions;
    Evaluating the resulting semantics of a portion;
    Abstracting the resulting semantics of a portion.
Understanding an outer relation =
    Finding the relevant portion;
    Understanding the relevant portion;
    Constructing the semantics of the relation;
    Abstracting the semantics of the relation.

(Memorizing is not included as a separate ability but it is
assumed to be performed implicitly after abstraction. Its
characteristics are covered by the recall ability).

The abilities of finding, associating, recalling,
constructing and abstracting are assumed to have the following
characteristics:

a. Finding includes searching (if necessary) and recognizing.
   It is easy if symbols representing components, relations
   and boundaries of sections are clearly visible and if
   symbols representing relations to components outside the
   current view are represented with an indication of where
   to find the related component.
b. Associating is easy if the semantics of components and
   relations of the language are clearly distinguishable
   from each other and if there is a correspondence between
   the kinds of semantics and kinds of symbolic representations. If the language offers a large number of components and relations they should be ordered hierarchically.
c. Recalling is easy if there are hints that identify or
   characterize the semantics to recall and if the semantics
   are not split into loosely coupled parts.
d. Evaluating semantics includes logical combination and
   imagining. Logical combination is easy if the number of
   details to include is low; imagining is easy if the
   entities to imagine are represented, if their structure
   is fixed and if changes occur in predictable succession.
e. Abstracting is easy only if there are clear indications as
   to what concept the resulting semantics of a section
   represent.

Conclusions

The model allows us to draw three kinds of conclusion:

1. The structure of the model allows us to identify those
   properties of a program that are relevant for its
   understandability.
2. The characteristics of the five basic abilities allow us
   to discuss requirements for the realization of the relevant
   properties.
3. The characteristics of the basic abilities further allow
   us to point out aspects where the mere formal program
   (as assumed in the model) does not offer enough information
   to simplify understanding, i.e. where additional information is needed (comments, documentation).

Properties Relevant for Understandability

The model makes two basic assumptions for the process of
understanding: the interpretation of a program as a net of
components and relations and the separation and portion-wise
processing of a program. From this, the following relevant
properties of a program can be deduced:

1. The syntax and semantics of components and relations.
2. The representation and composition of portions.

Implicitly or explicitly each program defines a state space,
changes of which must be imagined by the programmer as part
of the process of evaluating semantics. A third relevant
property therefore is:

3. The representation, structure and changeability of the
   program's state space.

Requirements for Realizations of the Relevant Properties

1. The syntax and semantics of components and relations
   affect the ease of finding, associating and evaluating.
   Components and relations are basically defined as language
   elements in the programming language, though a programmer
   may perform a simplifying mapping into his internal program.
      To simplify finding, the semantics of the language
   elements should be defined:
   - avoiding subnets that always occur in the same compo-
     sition (unless they are necessary for easy maintenance).
   To simplify association, the semantics of language elements
   should be:
   - unalterable at execution (preventing "self-modification");
   - context-free (for example no "overloading" of operators);

    - distinct from each other. If there are many language
      elements they should form a hierarchy of groups (for
      example operators - separated into logical and arithmetic).
  To simplify evaluation, the semantics of language elements
  should:
  - contain few bits of information (for example do not allow
    a language element for differentiating a function to
    integrate under certain conditions too);
  - not have to be related to many other elements (for example
    no long parameter lists for standard procedures);
  - not force the formation of long chains of relations
    (for example no "by name" parameter mechanism).
  The syntax of the language elements affects the ease of
  finding (i.e. searching and recognizing) and of associating.
  The syntax of the language elements should be:
  - distinct from each other and correspond to the grouping
    of the semantics (if there is one);
  - compact and conspicuous for components;
  - easy to follow for relations.
  The usual representation of language elements with text
  can hardly fulfil these requirements. There is a strong
  case for the use of a graphical representation, allowing
  more different symbols and especially a representation of
  relations by lines (as opposed to references to names or
  labels). Graphical representations are discussed for example
  by Green (1982) and Oberquelle (1981); Hoare (1975) rejects
  them because of the possible overloading of a picture with
  lines.
2. The representation and composition of portions affects
    the finding and evaluating. Representation and composition
    are determined mainly by the programming methods applied
    by the programmer when writing the program.
    The programming language and the programming system must
    provide the necessary means, however.
      As a prerequisite for easy understanding:
    - a program should be designed as a hierarchy of portions.
      To simplify finding:
    - the boundary;
    - the interface (i.e. its outer relations) and
    - the constituent components and relations;
    of each portion should be easy to recognize. Again, a
    representation using text causes problems, especially in
    representing the interface (for example accesses to global
    variables, side-effects). A better solution is the use of
    a line surrounding a portion or of shaded areas in which
    the portion's constituents are represented.
      Furthermore, to simply finding:
    - the constituents of a portion should not be widely

dispersed in the program (i.e. no deep nesting of blocks).
To simplify evaluation, a portion should:
- have few constituents and outer relations;
- be designed according to a well-pattern;
- fulfil a specific purpose.
These requirements apply mainly to programming methods and
are in accordance with the methods of "structured programming". Much can be done though to develop more standardized
patterns.
3. The representation, structure and changeability of a
program's state space affects evaluating, and within that,
imagining. A program's state space is predefined by the
programming language (the "address space" in machine
languages) or is defined and possibly modified in the
program (variables, files in higher programming languages).
The changeability of the state space includes the following
aspects:
- changes of states (for example contents of variables),
- changes of the structure of the state space (for example
  by generating variables using pointers),
- possible successions of changes (branches, sequential or
  parallel execution).
To simplify the imagining:
- the succession of changes should be sequential (if
  parallelism is needed it should be a cooperation of
  sequential processes),
- decisions about successors should be deterministic (if
  this is not forced by the language it should be ensured
  by the programming method),
- the state space should be represented in the program
  (for example no implicit declarations of variables),
- the state space should be structured corresponding to
  the program structure (not one large chunk of variables),
- the structure of the state space should be static (if
  dynamic alteration is needed, it should be localized,
  for example using stacks or queues).

Necessary Additional Information

Abstraction and recall are hard when there is only the formal
program. To support both, the purpose of a portion should
accompany the portion (as a comment), indicating the function
of the portion or the (sub)problem it solves.
    Graphical representation makes the strucure of a portion
visible to the programmer. If no such representation is used,
the programming method applied should be indicated as well.

3) THE PROGRAMMING LANGUAGE GRADE

Overview

In order to illustrate the impact of the model's conclusions,
a programming language GRADE has been defined. GRADE stands
for graphical description, indicating the most apparent
property of the language.

In this paper, only an outline of the language can be
given, emphasizing those properties of the language that are
of importance in relation to the model. A description of the
language and of a pilot implementation on a DEC PDP11 under
RSX can be found in Sengler (1982).

The application area of the language is scientific/
technical programming. The language is thus comparable to the
well-known high level languages. Many concepts of such
languages have been adopted, especially from Pascal.

Properties Relating to the Model

1. A GRADE program is a data processing machine, capable of
   performing a specific data processing task. It consists
   of parts that produce, transform or store data. These
   parts are connected by lines that allow the transport of
   data and lines that allow the transport of an activation
   pulse which controls the succession of processing. The
   composition of the machine is static, i.e. it cannot be
   changed during execution. The representation of a GRADE
   program on paper or screen therefore is a valid description
   of the program at all instants of its execution, simplifying the imagination of the effect of the execution.
   (This concept corresponds to Wirth's suggestion to see
   programming not as instructing a machine but as
   constructing one, Wirth (1976).
2. Only a few semantic concepts are included, in order to
   simplify association.
      A GRADE program consists of:
   - "Stores", which accept or produce data. The concept of
     a store covers that of variables, functions, data
     modules and I/O devices;
   - "Processors", which fetch, transform or send data. The
     concept of a processor covers that of operations,
     statements, blocks and procedures;
   - "Data lines", along which data can be transported
     between processors and stores. Datalines have a type
     (like the type in Pascal) and a direction;
   - "Activation lines", along which an activation pulse can
     be sent, transferring control between processors. At any

instant of execution there is only one activation pulse
in a program, ensuring strictly sequential processing.
Activation lines can contain branching points, offering
the semantics of Dijkstra's "guarded commands" IF and
DO (Dijkstra, 1975).

Stores and processors in a program can be language-defined,
implementation-specific or user-defined. A GRADE program
itself is a processor that can be activated from the
computing system. The duality of stores and processors as
well as their representation by rectangles and circles
(see below) is adopted from the concept of Petri nets
(Petri, 1980).

3. To simplify evaluation, the only relations between
   processors and stores that are relevant at execution are
   the data lines and activation lines. There is no "call"
   of a procedure; instead, any number of copies of each
   processor or store may be used in a program. Furthermore,
   there is no "parameter mechanism". Data can be fetched and
   sent by user-defined processors just as they can by
   language-defined processors (for example arithmetic
   operations).

4. In user-defined processors, inner processors can be
   activated explicitly via an activation line, yielding
   conventional control structures. In addition to that,
   processors within user user-defined stores are activated
   implicitly, on demand of a data transport from outside
   the store. The demand-driven activation simplifies the
   evaluation of semantics by reducing the number of
   relations, letting the programmer concentrate on the data
   to be transported and not worry about their preparation or
   acceptance in a store.

5. All processors, stores and lines are represented
   graphically:

   - a processor by a rectangle

   - a store by a circle

   - a data line by a solid line with
     an arrow to indicate the direction.

  - an activation line by a dashed
    line (the direction of the
    transport of the activation
    pulse is implicit)
  - branches within an activation
    line by a trapezoid

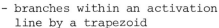

Additional information, indicating the kind of processor or
store, the type of data line and the conditions for a branch
is represented by text in the usual way. Colours can be used
to distinguish lines as well as shaded areas for processors
and stores but this is not part of the language (yet).

Examples

a. Language-defined processors and stores

An addition processor

Semantics: When an activation pulse reaches the processor
it fetches one value from each of the left side data
lines, adds them and sends the result on the right side
data line. Finally it sends an activation pulse back up
the top activation line.

A variable

Semantics: A value sent on the left side data line is
stored. When a value is requested on the right side data
line, a copy of the latest stored value is sent. "a" is
the initial value in the store.

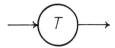

The user terminal

Semantics: Keys typed at the keyboard can be fetched as
characters on the right side data line. Characters sent
on the left side data line are displayed on the screen.

A sequential file

Semantics: Data sent on the "write" line are stored on
the file "FILENAME" and can be read on the "read" line.
The function of the store is a queue (indicated by the
swung arrow). On the "status" line the result of the last
access can be fetched. "Max" is the maximum length of the
file, or infinite.

"Write", "read" and "status" are the data types of the
respective data lines. "Status" must be integer or a subrange
thereof, "read" and "write" determine the type of data stored
in the file (and therefore must be compatible). Likewise, the
types of data lines leading to a variable determine the type
of the variable.

b. user-defined processor

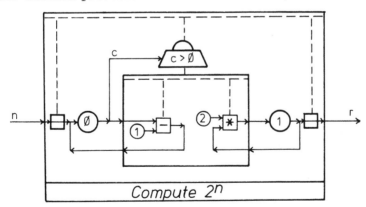

Semantics: This processor computes 2^n. It first fetches a
value from the left side dataline "n" and stores it in the
variable initialized with $\emptyset$. In a loop (indicated with the
trapezoid with the half-circle on top) this value is
repeatedly decremented by 1 and another variable multiplied
by 2. The loop terminates when the value on the "c" line
is less than or equal to zero. The result is then sent out
on the right side "r" line.

c. A constructed store

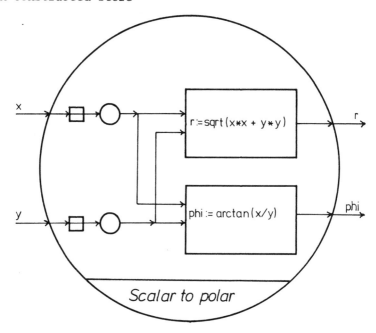

Semantics: This store converts scalar coordinates (x,y) to
polar (r,phi). Associated with each outside dataline is
one processor inside the store. This processor is
implicitly activated when a value is to be accepted or
prepared on the associated dataline. Both accepting
processors (x,y) simply store the sent values. Both
preparing processors (r,phi) compute the results from the
latest accepted x and y. Note that as an extension to the
language presented so far processors with expressions are
used.

d. A GRADE program (the uppermost layer)

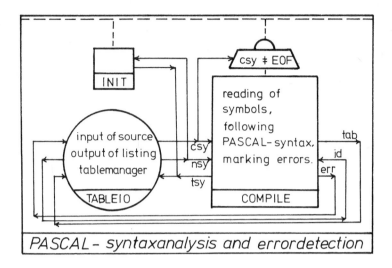

Semantics: The "INIT"-processor is activated, afterwards
"COMPILE" is activated repeatedly while the value on the
"csy" dataline is not EOF. The processors INIT, COMPILE
and the store TABLETO are defined in separate graphics.
Additionally, all types and constants used in the program
are defined in normal text.

First Observation

Using the GRADE language for programming, a few observations
have already been made (results from the implementation are
due at the end of 1983):

- it seems awkward to use GRADE on the low level of the
  program structure (which is the reason for introducing
  expressions in processors and stores),
- a program increases in size, but it is not clear by how
  much because no experience has been gained about the
  readability of small and compact GRADE-graphics,
- the programmer constructing a GRADE program is urged very
  much to develop a simple program structure through the
  visibility of the structure in the graphic representation.

ACKNOWLEDGEMENT

This work is sponsored by the West German government (BMFT/
GMD) under grant number 083 0214.

REFERENCES

Anderson, J.R. and Bower, G.H. (1974). "Human Associative
    Memory". John Wiley and Sons, New York.
Dijkstra, E.W. (1975). Guarded commands, nondeterminacy and
    formal derivation of programs, *Communications of the ACM,*
    18, 453-457.
Elshoff, J.L. and Marcotty, M. (1982). Improving computer
    program readability to aid modification, *Communications
    of the ACM,* 25, 512-521.
Green, T.R.G. (1982). Pictures of programs and other
    processes, or how to do things with lines. *Behaviour and
    Information Technology,* 1, 3-36.
Hoare, C.A.R. (1975). Data reliability, *ACM Sigplan,* 10,
    528-533.
Jensen, K. and Wirth, N. (1976). Pascal - User Manual and
    Jørgensen, A.H. (1980). A Methodology for Measuring the
    Readability and Modifiability of Computer Programs.
    BIT, 20, 394-405.
Lukey, F.J. (1980). Understanding and debugging programs.
    International Journal of Man-Machine Studies, 12, 189-202.
Miller, E.F. (1979). Some statistics from the software test
    factory, *ACM Software Engineering Notes,* 4, 8-11.
Newell, A. and Simon, H.A. (1972). "Human Problem Solving".
    Prentice-Hall, Englewood Cliffs.
Oberquelle, H. (1982). Communication by Graphic net Represen-
    tations. University of Hamburg, FB Informatik, Report
    75/81.
Petri, C.A. (1980). Introduction to general net theory. *In*
    "Net theory and Applications". (Ed. W. Brauer). Springer
    LNCS 84, Berlin.
Sengler, H.E. (1982). Programmieren mit graphischen Mitteln:
    Die Sprache GRADE und ihre Implementation. *In*
    "Programmiersprachen und Programmentwicklung." (Ed.
    H. Woessner). Springer IFB 53, Berlin.
Shneiderman, B. and Mayer, R. (1979). Syntactic/semantic
    interactions in programmer behaviour: A model and
    experimental results, *International Journal of Computer
    and Information Sciences,* 7, 219-239.
Wirth, N. (1976). Programming languages: What to Demand and
    How to Assess them. ETH Zuerich, Institut fuer Informatik.
    Report 17, March.

INDIVIDUAL DIFFERENCES AND ASPECTS OF CONTROL FLOW NOTATIONS

GERRIT C. VAN DER VEER AND G. JAN E. VAN DE WOLDE

*Vrije Universiteit
Amsterdam, Netherlands.*

1) INTRODUCTION

There has been quite some discussion recently about the urgency of incorporating computer literacy in our school curricula. An argument frequently adduced in support of such a development is the notion that the experiences of computer programming turn people into better problem solvers. Some authors claim that such a transfer is very general in nature, and applies to widely divergent domains of knowledge. A prominent advocate of this view is Seymour Papert (1980). His brainchild, the LOGO-project, springs from the idea that "doing" is a necessary condition for knowledge acquisition, and that problem solving performance will profit from the procedural approach stressed in computer programming. We should note however that the evidence for this hypothesis, provided by Papert, has not been very convincing up to now. Whether learning LOGO-programming, and elaborating its conditional branch statement, affects conditional reasoning ability in children has been the subject of a study by Seidman (1980). His experiments, more powerful than those of Papert, suggest that such effects, if present, are very limited in nature and strength. Less ambiguous positive transfer effects of computer programming have been reported by Soloway *et al.* (1982). The results of their experiments indicate that mathematical principles are handled more easily when they are to be expressed in program text rather than in plain algebraic terms. The authors warn against the danger that such an effect may be undone by the "current push in the direction of more *formality* in programming; programming languages are in danger of becoming like mathematics".

    The fact that notational formats play an important role in

understanding mathematical concepts also became clear to us a
couple of years ago, albeit in a rather odd way. In an experiment by Van der Veer and Ottevangers (1976), simple mathematical algorithms had to be developed in terms of a so-called
Pupils Programming Language. It appeared that those students
who were apt to avoid math as a study subject severely handicapped themselves by using meaningless identifiers and by ab-
breviating basic symbols, whereas mathematically minded subjects created maximum semantic transparency in the code. By
obscuring the code, the first group transformed the originally meaningful problems into a collection of incomprehensible
tricks.

It is evident, however, that the importance of computer-
literacy does not solely depend on transferability of skills.
Computing is useful for its own sake. It offers extra opportunities to organise and communicate knowledge, and may therefore augment human intelligence in problem solving and decision making. Moreover, we have to acknowledge the growing
social and economic needs for computer literate citizenship
in our modern society. Programming as a tool in education is
growing more and more popular. In Amsterdam at least 12 primary schools have a computer terminal in one of the class-
rooms at which a language is available that is especially
constructed for children of about 11 years of age. In a
growing number of secondary schools informatics is part of
the curriculum. At the moment this is only the case on a
voluntary basis, but it is to be expected that informatics
will be incorporated in the official curriculum within a few
years. In a growing number of university faculties informatics
or at least the use of computers, is becoming an integral part
of the study.

2) LEARNING A COMPUTER LANGUAGE

When somebody is introduced to computer programming for the
first time, there are at least four factors that affect the
learning process:

a. *learner characteristics*
   What are the learner's intuitions about computer program-
   ming?
   How are relevant concepts organised in his mind?
   What is style of representation?
   Here we distinguish between three sources of variation:
   - abilities; i.e. mental capacities like general intelli-
     gence, which are supposed to be relatvely stable over
     time;
   - educational background; e.g. previous training in math-

ematics or logic;
- cognitive style; the way a learner is apt to attack certain problem situations. The adequacy of a style will
  depend on the situation or the nature of the problem involved. Style as an operational mode is a product of
  past learning experiences, and may to a certain extent
  be influenced by directed training.

b. *characteristics of the problem solution,* i.e. the algorithm
to be constructed.
What kind of conceptual organisation is required in order
to solve the problem? E.g. the problem (solution) may ask
for some kind of hierarchical organisation, and some kind
of organisation may be suggested by the semantics that are
present in the wording of the problem definition.

c. *features of the programming language*
What kind of conceptual organisation may be expressed in
the code? What kinds of organisation are promoted by the
syntax? Being psychologists we do not pretend to be ex-
haustive in our analysis of language features. We will
deal one by one with syntactical aspects like flow of control, data structures or the vocabulary of basic symbols
and identifiers.

d. *didactics*
How do we attain a match between programming constructs
and routines of information processing present in the
learner's mind? This question concerns the use of modularisation techniques, top-down or bottom-up programming,
structured diagrams and the like.

From these factors, two have gained most of our attention up
till now, namely learner characteristics and aspects of control flow notation.

3) LEARNER CHARACTERISTICS

Our concern with learner characteristics stems from research
in our laboratory regarding individual differences in cognitive style.

Intelligence

About including intelligence in our set of relevant learner
characteristics we will be very short. Intelligence is a very
complex concept in which many aspects may be distinguished
(Guilford and Hoepfner, 1971). We all know that general intelligence, whatever operationalisation is being used, is a

strong predictor of very different kinds of problem solving
performance. In our experiments we felt content measuring
this factor by means of Raven's Progressive Matrices, and
then partialling it out from all effects of interest.

Educational background

One aspect of educational background, at least in the Dutch
school system, appears to be of great relevance when a computer language has to be learned. Students that leave secondary school show considerable differences in their apprehen-
sion of mathematics. Some students, to be called 'alphas',
are only exposed to very simple, introductory courses, and
often have deliberately avoided any continuation course, feeling no affiliation with the subject matter. Others, so-called
'betas', have received a substantial amount of practice in
dealing with formal notations, in symbolic manipulation, and
in applying algorithms (not so much in constructing these).
Both types of students share the same circumstances in higher
education, for instance in faculties like linguistics or social sciences. Their curricula often imply statistics and
several kinds of computer use. When we want to examine the
feasibility of programming constructs for an introductory
computer language, the difference in entry characteristics
between alphas and betas will have to be kept in mind.

Cognitive styles

Pask (1976) has developed some fruitful ideas in the field of
learning and teaching strategies. A guiding principle in his
work is the idea that educational methods are most efficient
when tailored to the individual competence of the student.
In view of this notion Pask is particularly referring to partly automatic, intelligent teaching systems. Basic to the
strategies are the individual learning styles or dimensions
of 'competence' as Pask calls them. These styles reflect
modes of organising the acquisition, storage and retrieval of
knowledge. Pask designed several devices to measure aspects
of these styles, some which have been translated and elaborated
in our laboratory. Most effort has been invested redesigning
and standardizing the Smuggler's Test. The plot of this test
is a story about a gang producing and trading narcotics. The
student is asked to imagine that he is embodied in some
international police organisation with the assignment of
rolling up this gang. From the way the student organises and
reconstructs or reproduces the data, we infer three learning
style factors (Van der Veer and Van de Wolde, 1982).

factor I   : inclination to learn and to put effort into memo-
              rizing. This factor does not reflect an ability.
              While the instructions do not necessarily suggest
              that the material should be memorized, some stu-
              dents do so spontaneously and consistently.
factor II : operation learning. This factor concerns the in-
              clination to deduce specific rules and procedural
              details. It results in the availability of mate-
              rials that may serve in the construction of pro-
              cedures, and it is expressed in consistency of
              references to related details of the knowledge
              domain.
factor III: comprehension learning. This style reflects the
              inclination to induce general rules and descrip-
              tions, and to record relations between different,
              or even remote parts of the domain. It is ex-
              pressed in the tendency to reconstruct lost de-
              tails by application of general rules and analo-
              gies.

4) CONTROL FLOW NOTATION

Our interest in different forms of control flow notation was
excited by the work of Sime, Green and Guest (1977) in
Sheffield concerning conditional branching. In a series of
experiments these researchers have compared a number of alternative branching devices as to their 'cognitive ergonomic'
properties. It concerned two familiar conditionals which were
called JUMP and NEST-BE and a prototypic construct called
NEST-INE designed in Sheffield. JUMP is a GOTO-branching
statement like the one we know from such languages as FORTRAN
and BASIC:

```
            IF ILL GOTO L1
            DO YOUR DAILY WORK STOP
    L1      STAY HOME AND RECOVER
```

NEST-BE (Begin-End) is a control structure like IF..THEN....
ELSE... in ALGOL-60, supplied with scope markers:

```
            IF ILL THEN
            BEGIN STAY  HOME AND RECOVER
            END
            ELSE
            BEGIN DO YOUR DAILY WORK
            END
```

NEST-INE is a related control structure but it provides more
redundant information about the conditions that have to be

met in order to have some action executed:

```
IF ILL STAY HOME AND RECOVER
NOT ILL DO YOUR DAILY WORK
END ILL
```

The usability of these structures was tested by comparing several aspects of programming performance when using a special-purpose 'microlanguage' featuring nothing but the construct in question. Summing up the results, the authors conclude that 'by and large' these experiments have favoured the NEST-INE dialect (Green, Sime and Fitter, 1981). Nevertheless there was some evidence in their data that raised doubts as to the limits of queuing decisions when parsing NEST structures. Sime *et al.* experimented up to a maximum of 3 levels of embedding and noticed a considerable decline in programming performance with increasing depth.

5) RESEARCH IN OUR LABORATORY

Design and procedure

Our experiments primarily aimed at examining the interactions between learner characteristics, language features and some relevant attributes of algorithmic structure. Furthermore we wanted to verify the queuing restrictions supposedly applying to NEST-structures. With regard to language features we decided not to compare all three control structures used in Sheffield, but to juxtapose JUMP with the most favourable nesting alternative, i.e. NEST-INE. The syntax of both languages was defined as follows:
The NEST-syntax:

```
<program>:: = <action>/IF <condition><program> IF NOT
              <condition><program> END <condition>
<action>:: = <simple action>/<simple action> AND <action>
<simple action>:: = A1/A2/A3/..../A10
<condition>:: = C1/C2/C3/..../C8
```

With the context-dependent restriction that <condition> at a certain level always points to the same identifier.
The JUMP-syntax:

```
<program>:: = <line>/<line><program>
<line>:: = <statement>/<label><statement>
<statement>:: = <action>/IF <condition> GOTO <label>
<action>:: = <simple action>/<simple action> AND <action>
<simple action>:: = A1/A2/A3/..../A10
<condition>:: = C1/C2/C3/..../C8
<label>:: = P1/P2/P3:..../P9
```

The basic symbols in both languages as well as the problem
defining elements were meaningful words in the native language of the subjects. In order to prevent typing speed bi-
assing any result we redefined the entries on the keyboard,
so that all language elements could be produced by pressing
single keys. By pressing a FORM-key the subject was able to
rearrange the format of his text automatically, providing
indentation in NEST, and label tabulation in JUMP. Another key
was used to submit the text to a syntax check. If the program
was shown to be syntactically correct, it could be run for a
semantic check by pressing a TEST-key. 63 subjects, young
adults of different occupations, all having completed secondary education, took part in the experiment. The programming
session was preceded by a test-session that supplied data for
the composition of a profile of learner characteristics
consisting of:

- the score on set II of Raven's Advanced Progressive matrices
  as an index of the general level of intelligence;
- the scores on the three learning style dimensions;
- information concerning the educational background. Here we
  classified our subjects in three categories:
  betas : 21 subjects who (according to themselves) were
           rather good at mathematics, and enjoyed it as well.
  alphas: 22 subjects who weren't good at mathematics and
           didn't like it either.
  ?   : 20 subjects who reported doing well in mathematics
           but did not enjoy it *and* those who weren't good at
           it, but enjoyed it all the same.

On the basis of previous findings it was predicted that on
the average the betas would make the best programmers, and
the alphas would make the poorest ones. The two groups in
the ? category, taken together because we were not able to
formulate separate hypotheses concerning either of these,
were supposed to perform somewhere in between. By making comparisons between test score profiles we were able to assign
two almost identical groups to both language-conditions. It
should be noted that our sample was rather heterogeneous.

The learning phase

At the programming session our subjects were introduced to
the apparatus, the procedure, and the secrets of programming
by means of self-instruction. Sitting behind a terminal they
followed instructions from a manual at a self paced rate.
Each significant action was followed by immediate feedback
on the screen. In order to stress the strict obedience ex-

pressed by the machine we used the metaphor of the computer as a modern, multi-purpose slave. In the first part of the programming session, the learning phase, our subjects could call for assistance from the experimenter whenever this was felt necessary. This phase terminated after completion of two programs. These programs, borrowed from Sime *et al.* (1977) were called Cook I and Cook II. To give an example, Cook II, more complex then Cook I, was specified by the following requirements:

> you have to program your slave in such a way that he will:
> grill - everything that is not big and not leafy,
> peel and fry - everything that is leafy and not hard,
> chop and grill - everything that is not leafy but big,
> chop and boil - everything that is both leafy and hard

Results of the learning phase

In our heterogeneous sample it appeared that the scores on learning style factors 2 and 3 correlated very highly (r =.68). For this reason we decided to combine these two scores, and to call the composite result a versatility-score. Pask reserves this label for an opportunistic learning style that includes both operation learning and comprehension learning. Versatile students may choose at will between the two ways of structuring learning material. They have a 'complete' repertoire of materials both for constructing particular rules and for creating general descriptions. Our criterion for versatility in this case was a combined score on factors 2 and 3 that was above median. Analyses of covariance on learning performance, eliminating the effect of intelligence, showed that beta-subjects indeed needed less time than alphas, $(F_{2,50}=3.63,$ p < 0.05) respectively 75 against 104 min. (all times quoted are mean times for subject in the particular groups). The subjects we could not label alpha or beta needed 92 min. The analysis also showed that learning NEST took less time than learning JUMP, respectively 79 and 99 min. $(F_{1,50}=5.28,$ p < 0.05). The final result of the analysis indicated that versatiles needed less time than non-versatiles, 75 and 105 min. respectively $(F_{1,50}=4.21,$p<0.05). Looking at the three competence factors separately, it appeared that all had significant *partial* correlations with the learning time.

```
factor 1 inclination to learn     -.50
       2 operation learning       -.40
       3 comprehension learning   -.36
```

In this first stage, we did not find any interaction between
language type, learning style and educational background.

Additional problems

After the learning phase the students were confronted with
four additional problems that had to be solved without any
further help from the experimenter. Designing the experiment
we argued that a comparison between language constructs should
be accompanied by an analysis of the structural features of
the algorithms to be coded in terms of these. The following
variables were considered:

a. The presence or absence of a hierarchy in the algorithm
   and the depth of embedding in such a hierarchy. We speak
   of hierarchy when a number of tests has to be carried
   out in some logical or preferred order. The 'depth of
   embedding' reflects the number of levels in this
   hierarchy.
b. The presence or absence of a semantic framework that
   suggests some kind of (hierarchical) structuring. Most
   algorithms are conceived in terms of meaningful identifiers which imply a tacit reference to some semantic
   framework, which may in itself suggest a certain order of
   tests. When it is absent (e.g. in the case of meaningless
   identifiers) such order only follows from the formal
   properties of the problem structure.

Biologist I is the label for a task to program a taxonomy
identifying animals (fish, worms, mammals etc.) by the presence or absence of certain unique features (feathers, fins
etc.) The presence of one feature excludes the presence of
all others and is a sufficient condition to identify the animal. Therefore there is no preferred or logical order of
tests, and the depth of embedding is zero (that is, from the
algorithmic point of view). The other three problems are
hierarchical in nature. Tourist Information Consultant is a
slave who advises tourists about means of transport (taxi,
bus etc.) on the basis of data about destination (far or
near), luggage (yes or no), budget (high or low) and time
available (in a hurry or not). Decision Maker is formally
identical to the former algorithm, but lacks any semantic
frame of reference, the antecedents being replaced by letters,
and the consequents being replaced by Action 1, Action 2 etc.
Biologist II shares the semantic domain of Biologist I, but
the decisions, more realistic, have to be made on the basis
of combinations of attributes which are not exclusive. Only

a few of the 'possible' combinations point to existing categories of animals. There are four levels of embedding in this
hierarchical taxonomy, as against three such levels in the
preceding algorithms.

Results with the additional problems

In solving the additional problems 8 subjects dropped out,
failing to complete their task within a reasonable amount of
time. None of them was a 'beta', and only one of them was a
'versatile'. Motivation was not the reason to fail here. Although the experimenter suggested leaving at the end of the
agreed time (three hours) five of these subjects continued the
experiment for one or two hours without extra payment. We
omitted the results of these eight subjects from the rest of
the analyses. The differences between the solution times for
the problem with four levels (Biologist II) and the average
results on the two problems with three levels (Tourist Information Consultant and Decision Maker) show a significant
interaction with type of language ($F_{1,41}=4.98$, < 0.05), illustrated in Fig. 1. This indeed suggests that some critical
value is passed as the number of levels increases from three
to four. With more levels NEST is inferior to JUMP. Regret-
tably we are unable to analyse these data in sufficient detail to ascribe the loss of time to either pure syntactical
problems, to a combination of syntactical and semantical
problems, or to mainly a short term memory problem. We should
definitely replicate this part of our study.

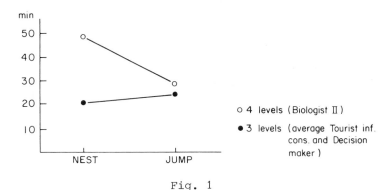

Fig. 1

There is another case in which JUMP is superior to NEST. For
the non-hierarchical problem, Biologist I, NEST takes significantly more time (38 min.) than JUMP (16 min.)
($F_{1,41}=5.59$, $p < 0.05$). Only in this case NEST invokes more
syntax errors than JUMP (72 against 37% in first runs). First,

one is apt to skip the IF NOT clauses in between the IF's
since they seem superfluous in this case. Second, NEST, as
opposed to JUMP, does not tolerate any redundant testing.
Redundant tests induce syntactical omissions since they leave
nothing to be specified in the IF NOT clause.
    The meaningful problem Tourist Information Consultant
takes less time than the subsequent Decision Maker, which is
formally identical, but framed in abstract terms ($F_{1,41}=9.94$,
$p < 0.05$). Here we also find a significant interaction with
versatility ($F_{1,41}=4.54$, $p < 0.05$). Figure 2 illustrates
this effect.

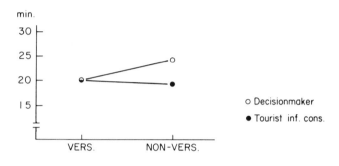

Fig. 2

Although the abstract problem followed after the meaningful
equivalent, non-versatiles met with considerable difficulties.
It seems that the availability of semantic connotations is
indispensable to them in order to cope with a complex, hierarchical structure. As the semantics are removed, their solution strategies are inferior to those of versatiles. Finally
we note some interesting results with learning style factor
I, inclination to learn. Controlling for effects of intelligence, the partial correlations with the solution times for
the Tourist Information Consultant and the complex algorithm
Biologist II are -.39 and -.52 respectively. In the case of
the abstract Decision Maker this correlation doesn't reach
significance. Here it is the versatility-style that is predictive for success.

6) FUTURE RESEARCH

At the moment we are preparing a series of experiments as a
follow up for the one reported here. In designing these, we
will take the following considerations into account:

Embedding

It appears that NEST is inferior to JUMP when there are too
many levels of embedding or when the algorithm proper does
not ask for a hierarchy at all. Both difficulties can supposedly be dealt with by the introduction of another
branching alternative presented by Atkinson (1979) as
NEST-PA (positive alternatives). According to Atkinson a programmer should be allowed to 'think positively' by avoiding
negative formulations. With the help of this construction,
which looks like the CASE-statement in PASCAL, we can cope
both with adjacent conditions (Biologist I) and with hierarchical tests. We will compare this alternative with NEST-INE.

Didactics

The present results suggest that we should not greatly
dramatize the differences between languages or language
features. Whether or not somebody will be successful in performing a programming task only partly depends on the qualities of the syntax. Much will depend on the combinations of
problem characteristics, and individual cognitive style factors or problem solving strategies. Furthermore, a language
that looks very hard to learn, nevertheless may easily map
into the learner's experience, depending on the metaphors
used to introduce the vitals of programming. In our future
experiments we will study the use of structural diagrams as
a didactical aid for the understanding of flow of control
principles.

"Tie"-structures

Until now we have not paid any special attention to problems
in which some partstructure is referred to from several
places in the algorithm, while there may be no question of
a hierarchy whatsoever, e.g.:

    Going on holiday, take with you

      - a caravan   : if driving licence and
                          same continent;
      - a hotelguide   : if no driving licence or
                          not same continent,
                          if winter and to inhabited
                          area;
      - a tent   : if no driving licence or
                          not same continent,
                          if summer or uninhabited
                          area, and not dry;

- a sleeping bag   : if no driving licence or
                       not same continent,
                       if summer or uninhabited
                       area, and dry.

Figure 3 indicates a diagram of the resulting algorithm.
Such problems that we tentatively call "tie"-problems ask
for special modularisation devices. We don't know yet what
precise form they will take, but our first prototype will be
parameter-free.

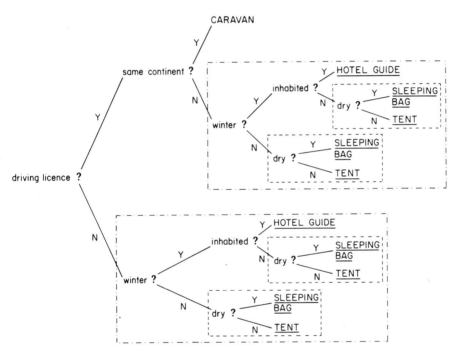

Fig. 3

REFERENCES

Atkinson, L.V. (1979). Should if...then...else...follow the
    dodo? *Software-Practice and Experience* 9, 693-700.
Green, T.R.G., Sime, M.E. and Fitter, M.J. (1981). The art
    of notation. *In* "Computing Skills and The User Interface".
    (Eds M.J. Coombs and J.L. Alty), pp. 221-251. Academic
    Press, London.
Guilford, J.P. and Hoepfner, R. (1971). *In* "The Analysis of
    Intelligence". (Ed. McGraw-Hill), New York.

Papert, S. (1980). "Mindstorms". The Harvester Press Ltd.,
    Brighton.
Pask, G. (1976). Styles and strategies of learning, *British
    Journal of Educational Psychology* 46, 128-148.
Seidman, R.H. (1980). "The Effects of Learning the Logo Com-
    puter Programming Language on Conditional Reasoning in
    School Children". (Ed. A. Arbor) University Microfilms
    International.
Sime, M.E., Green, T.R.G. and Guest, D.J. (1977). Scope
    marking in computer conditionals - a psychological evalu-
    ation, *International Journal of Man-Machine Studies* 9,
    107-118.
Soloway, E., Lockhead, J. and Clement, J. (1982). Does com-
    puter programming enhance problem-solving ability? Some
    positive evidence on algebra word problems. *In* "Computer
    Literacy", (Eds R.J. Seidel, R.E. Anderson and B. Hunter),
    Academic Press, New York.
Van der Veer, G.C. and Ottevangers, D.C. (1976). "Problem
    Solving by Programming". Proceedings of the Digital
    Equipment Users Society 3, no. 1, 345-351.
Van der Veer, G.C. and van de Wolde, J. (1982). De leerstijlen
    van Gordon Pask. Een Nederlandse bewerking van de Smokke-
    laarstest. *In* "Strategieën in Leren en Ontwikkeling",
    (Eds J.G.L.C. Lodewijk and P.R.J. Simons), Swets en
    Zeitlinger, Lisse.

PROBLEM SOLVING BY NOVICE PROGRAMMERS

HANK KAHNEY

Open University,
Milton Keynes, England

1) INTRODUCTION

In the pages that follow we present a model of the behavior
of novices who are learning artificial intelligence programming. Our novices are Open University students taking a third
level course in Cognitive Psychology. As this course is favor-
ably oriented to computer models of cognitive processes, the
students are given a course in artificial intelligence
programming early in the academic year. Their programming is
self-taught from a Programming Manual, although they are
given some help from course tutors during their early learning phase. A database-manipulation language, SOLO, has been
specially designed (Eisenstadt, 1978) for them and offers an
easy access route to high level programming concepts. We define a novice as a person who is not conversant with other
programming languages and who has read all of the SOLO programming manual and completed three 'course assignment' Study
Center Activities before setting out to perform experimental
tasks.
   A concise summary of one of these problems (to be discussed in some detail in Section 3 below) is:

Given a database describing objects piled up on one another
as follows:

```
          on           on           on          on           on
SANDWICH ----►PLATE ---►NEWSPAPER --►BOOK ---►TABLE ---► FLOOR
```

write a program which simulates the effect of someone firing
a very powerful pistol aimed downwards at the topmost object
(SANDWICH), yielding the final database shown below:

PSYCHOLOGY OF COMPUTER USE
ISBN 0-12-297420-4

The solution to the problem, in SOLO, involves writing only
two lines of code:

```
TO SHOOT /X/
1 NOTE /X/ HAS BULLETHOLE
2 CHECK /X/ ON ?                   if X is on something...
  2A If Present: SHOOT *; EXIT       then shoot that, and stop
  2B If Absent: EXIT               if X isn't on anything, stop
DONE
```

We have performed detailed studies of six Subjects (and other
Subjects in less detail) who were given this problem to solve.
The studies include concept rating, recall, and grouping
tasks, transcription tasks, program understanding tasks, ques-
tionnaires, and verbal protocols taken while they worked on a
specific problem. Of those we studied, only two produced an
adequate solution. There are obvious differences between expert programmers and novices, but there are also intriguing
differences among novices themselves. We distinguish 'talented'
from other novices, and in this paper we try to indicate a
couple of ways in which these two groups differ and ways in
which they are alike. But first, we place our research
in the context of other recent research into problem solving
behavior.

2) BACKGROUND AND RELATED MODELS

We are interested in providing a model of the mental processes which occur when novice programmers transform a verbal
statement of a problem into a programmed solution to the
problem. Problem solving in such a task involves understanding
what the problem is, finding or devising an algorithm, and
writing and debugging code. This is the usual concern of
anyone studying problem solving, and our model is in some respects an instance of what can be fairly described as the
'modal model' of problem solving.
    The modal model of problem solving exhibits the following

features. Firstly, there is a phase of 'problem understanding' during which the problem statement is transformed into a mental structure which represents those aspects of the problem which are critical to its solution. Secondly, there is a phase somewhere between problem understanding and the running of 'solution' processes, that is variously described as 'method finding', 'general solution approaches', 'schema activation', and so forth. It is during this stage that domain knowledge is accessed, knowledge which acts as a bridge between understanding and solution processes. For example, a problem statement in programming may contain information about database structures and alterations to be made to those structures but not mention recursion as an appropriate method for achieving the desired results. The person solving the problem must recognize the relevance of the particular method on the basis of the given features of the problem statement. Finally, there is the 'solution' phase itself. Often this stage is seen as somewhat less problematic than the other phases. Access to particular structures in the method-finding phase is often thought to provide direct information about the way the method should be used to transform the mental representation of the problem into a solution. That is, the method is often viewed as a solution framework into which elements of the problem are slotted, although other processes may then operate on the instantiated and filled framework.

The modal model has also been used to explain problem solving in areas in which there is no 'reading' phase - like go and chess. In these problems reading is replaced by 'board scanning', understanding is equivalent to 'recognizing meaningful patterns', and method finding involves selecting the best move from the alternative possibilities. Experts are described as having the ability to classify large numbers of meaningful patterns and large configurations of meaningful patterns whereas novices only know few and simple patterns.

Very often models of problem solving featuring these three phases are only really concerned with one of the phases in any detail. Below we discuss three such models - selected because they cover different phases of the process (understanding, schema activation, and solution) and because they are related to or differ in some important respect from our own model.

The Understanding Phase

A well known model of the understanding stage in problem solving is the UNDERSTAND program of Hayes and Simon (1976). In their model 'problem understanding' involves two subprocesses,

Language Understanding and Model Construction. The product of
these processes is a problem space containing the initial and
goal states of a problem, the problem objects and their properties and relations, and, finally, the operators for transforming the initial into the goal state, plus any restrictions
on the use of the operators. This final representation can
then be operated on by a special purpose problem solving mechanism. If the problem is not solved in this 'Solution' phase,
the problem understanding mechanisms are instantiated a second
time and the process begins again.

The UNDERSTAND program operates on 'well defined' problems.
These are problems that specify all the information a problem
solver needs to solve the problem. A problem with this model
from our point of view is that programming problems are not
well defined, in the sense that 'operators' are not usually
explicitly indicated in programming problem statements. Programmers have to recognize which operators are relevant from
an analysis of various features of the problem statement. If
the problem does not cue a known algorithm, then the programmer must devise one. Brooks (1977) makes much the same
observation and introduces the notion of 'method finding' to
account the programmer's need to determine a suitable algorithm, but he has nothing to say about method finding processes other than to indicate reflections of such processes
in the protocols he analyzed. Part of our goal is to demon-
strate such processes in operation.

Equally important, in UNDERSTAND, 'Solution Processes' do
not begin operating until enough is known about the problem
to get the processes going. Unfortunately, this 'enough' involves knowing everything. In 'well defined' problems solution processes cannot get started until the operators (and
the restrictions on their use) are known, and in the 'Tea
Ceremony' problem, which is used by Hayes and Simon to exemp-
lify the operation of the system, this information is not
finally given until the penultimate line of the problem statement. Thus, problem understanding processes necessarily pre-
cede any attempts at a solution to the problem.

In programming the solution process actually begins where
problem understanding begins: at the first line of a problem
statement. In our model Understanding and Solution processes
co-occur. Indeed, in many cases, it would be difficult to distinguish between 'understanding' a problem and knowing the
solution to the problem. If, while reading the problem statement, one of our Subjects states - "oh, this is going to be
like the 'Infect' program. I just have to insert these two
triples into that framework and that's it!", - and if the
Subject has a working model of the behavior of the Infect program, then he has solved as well as understood the problem in

the same moment. The novice may not have much knowledge of programming, but what little he has is brought to bear on understanding and solving the problem wherever opportunities arise.

Schema Activation

Chi, Feltovich and Glaser (1980) have undertaken extensive investigations of the cognitive structures which novices and experts have acquired in the domain of physics, and the manner in which this knowledge is indexed when these disparate groups set out to solve physics problems. They show that the expert's schemas are organized in terms of physics solution principles, while novice's schemas are based in 'object' categories with pointers to equation formulae for specific problems.

Chi, Feltovich and Glaser show that both experts and novices proceed in solving problems by first categorizing the current problem. This categorization makes available information which can be used to guide further understanding/solution processes. The major problem confronting the physics expert - the same problem confronting the chess expert - is in choosing amongst candidate schemas. Solution processes are more or less non-problematic once the correct schema has been selected from the candidate schemas.

Finally, Chi, Feltovich and Glaser conclude that novices are 'stimulus bound' - that they are influenced more by characteristics of the problem text (keywords) than by the principles of physics that underlie a wide range of such problems. The expert, on the other hand, is able to derive second order problem characteristics from the same textual features that influence novices and candidate schemas are then keyed by these second order representations. Another way of talking about the novices discussed by Chi, Feltovich and Glaser is to say that a novice can read through a problem statement and even develop a solution without ever discovering what the problem really is. This is the position which we take. Our view is that problem solving involves constructing and running a mental model of a problem, and that programming and world-knowledge interact to direct and constrain the mental models that are constructed. The notion will be elaborated below.

The Solution Phase

A model of the running of solution processes by experts in the writing of computer programs - given an adequate representation of the problem plus an appropriate mediating

algorithm - has been provided by Brooks(1977). In Brooks'
model the most complex processes are those concerned with
determining the effects of a piece of code, and updating the
problem model once a segment of code has been generated. Code
generation itself is a more or less straightforward translation process. Coding failures occur, of course, but this is
because the coding rules are inadequately specified or are
generated in 'circumstances for which [they are] not appropriate' (Brooks, 1977). In our studies we find that novices
have little difficulty with coding per se - other than minor
syntactic details, which are handled automatically by SOLO -
but there are large differences in novices in their ability to
evaluate a segment of code once it has been generated. A large
part of our investigation has been concerned with discovering
the evaluation rules used by novices once they have generated
a segment of code.

Although we are in essential agreement with the general
outline of this modal model of problem solving it has a number of weaknesses. Even in simple domains like puzzles there
is evidence that transfer of learning occurs easily only in
particular conditions (Reed, Ernst and Banerji, 1974; Hayes
and Simon, 1974; Luger and Bauer, 1978). In complex domains
like mathematics the problems of transfer are magnified
(Schoenfeld, 1980). Schoenfeld has shown that possession of a
relevant store of knowledge is not a sufficient basis for
solving mathematics problems. The development of skill in
this domain involves the construction of complex indexes to
that knowledge. Schoenfeld demonstrates that indexing is not
always a simple matter of 'keying' knowledge but may involve
applying heuristics to heuristics. That is, the novice must
be taught not only useful rules of thumb for accessing relevant information, but must also be taught heuristics for selecting amongst accessed concepts. We will show below that
even without 'indexing problems', that even when novice programmers are 'led by the nose' to a problem solution (a program that the Subject can 'imitate' or 'copy') problem
solving is often a laborious and problematic task that ends
in failure.

3) MENTAL MODELS

Novice programming behavior is only partially explainable in
terms of retrieval and direct application of schemas acquired
during a fairly brief training phase. As focus shifts away
from experts and onto novice and naive problem solvers, explanations based on domain specific knowledge tend to be sup-
plemented with general world knowledge. The processes through

which these different sources of knowledge are said to interact various, depending on the researcher, but they are often
now discussed in terms of the construction and evaluation of
mental models (Gentner, 1981; di Sessa, 1981; Eisenstadt,
Laubsch and Kahney, 1981; Norman, 1982; Kahney and Eisenstadt,
1982). The general notion behind mental models is that of a
cognitive structure that is constructed in working memory and
'run off' in order that its behavior might be observed. The
mental model that is constructed is presumed to be a function
of a large number of factors, such as the extent of conceptual knowledge, the number of concepts the person has mastered,
the rules for combining and evaluating models, and so forth.
We shall not discuss most of these issues in this paper.

To reiterate something that has already been said, there
are obvious differences between expert programmers and novices, but an equally important distinction is that between
'talented' and 'average' novices. That is, given the same
material to study, and an unlimited amount of time in which
to master the material, some newcomers to programming 'get
it' and some don't. Talented novices differ from the average
in the number of programming concepts with which they are
familiar and in the degree to which familiar concepts have
been understood (i.e., two novices may both be familiar with
the NOTE and PRINT primitives in SOLO, but one may think
they both serve the same function). Talented novices have
much in common with experts in terms of the way their knowledge is organized, and in the way in which it is brought to
bear in solving programming problems (Kahney, 1982). Unlike
average novices, much of the new knowledge of the talented
novice is organized in memory as 'plans' for achieving particular program-effects, such as 'Conditional-side-effect-
on-a-database', or 'Generate-next-object-and-side-effect-
each' (Eisenstadt, Laubsch and Kahney, 1981).

We have no evidence that 'talented' novices spend more
time or effort in understanding programming; we have evidence
that 'average' novices spend considerable time trying to come
to grips with concepts like recursion. But the talented novice is one who develops a model of 'the way recursion works'
(albeit, an incomplete model) while the average novice commits
a segment of code to memory with the rule that the segment
has a particular effect without having a model of the way
the effect is achieved. The model which talented novices
develop of recursion can be graphically described as shown
overleaf.

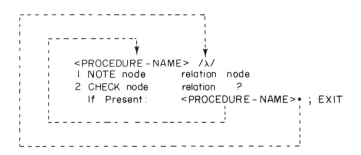

Recursion is seen as a kind of looping operation where successive nodes in a particular database structure are 'fed back'
to the 'top' of the procedure. The effect causes the program
to start up again and perform whatever action is indicated at
Line 1 of the program on the node delivered to the parameter
slot. We have derived this model from Subjects' performances
on various tasks, during one of which the Subject can be seen
on film indicating the loop with her pencil. The task involved understanding a program written by another novice.
When reading this segment of code:

```
CHECK /X/ WORKSFOR ?
If Present: IMPLICATE * ; EXIT
```

the Subject says: "Check X works for.... somebody. If so....
[at which point the Subject used her pencil to trace a loop
from the word IMPLICATE back up to the title line of the pro-
gram]"....back to the beginning." S8 uses the coding framework for writing her own recursion programs and also as a model which can be manipulated to determine its output. S8 produced the 'correct solution' program that is provided on page
1 of this paper and the following is a summary of the protocol produced by this Subject after the program had been typed
in at the computer terminal but before it was run:

> Right, so.... To Shootup X, let's say X is a sandwich..
> It notes in the database X has bullethole. It then
> checks whether X is 'on' anything. X is on plate, so it
> will do that to plate. So that should keep on doing
> that: plate's 'on', check, and so on and so on. If it's
> not 'on' anything it's okay to just exit. Right.

Up to this point S8's discussion and coding of the program
has been quite abstract in the sense that only programming

constructs are used or discussed. But when the program is
evaluated, variables are replaced by database objects like
'sandwich' and ' plate' and the recursive segment evaluated
to the depth of the second node ("X is on plate, so it will
do that to plate"). The next sentence indicates something
like "if it'll do it to the first two nodes, it'll do it to
all of them."

The average novice on the other hand writes recursion procedures without a model of the behavior of the program, and
therefore needs to use the computer to evaluate code. S5, who
is not untypical of the average novice in this approach to
writing programs, made several attempts to produce a procedure that would produce the required output. Since this Subject had no model of the behavior of the programs written on
successive attempts, all the Subject could do was type a program in at the terminal and 'wait for the computer to evaluate it'. If the desired output occurred the program worked
(and one of our novices did write a program which produced
the desired output - for the wrong reasons - but could not
say how the program achieved its effect) and if not, the program had to be debugged. The usual strategy adopted by novices without models of program behavior is to 'imitate' a
program found in the programming manual. These programs are
not hard to find as the first line of all our problem statements indicate where to look in the Programming Manual if
help is needed with the design of a program for the particular problem. Summarized extracts from the protocol of S5,
each taken after a different attempt to write a program, are
these:

Experimenter: What's going to happen when you run this
procedure?
S5: I hope it will go through that sequence and shoot
the floor. The database is in and I've copied that
program [from the Programming Manual] exactly.
This example in the book.... You've got one 'state'
and one 'relationship' and in my example we've got
three things. We've got two states and one relationship. And that's not fair. I·thought that following
the example in the book would lead through automatically, but I've decided the problem's got more, um,
states in it than the problem in the Unit.
Will it accept... Well, I can always type it in and
try.... And it will correct me won't it?
Meaningless example in the text.

The keywords and phrases in this protocol are 'hope',
'copied', 'following this example' and 'I can always try it

and see'. Trial and error, the last hope of a person with no other resources. Even so, this short extract is insufficient to indicate the grief experienced by many novices who find this problem beyond solution.

A Program Transcription Task

Differences between talented and average novices are found in the entire range of tasks they are asked to perform. Program transcription is a task in which programmers are simply required to copy a program which they are allowed to view five times for a period of ten seconds on each viewing. All Subjects are told that they should try to transcribe the program in as few attempts as necessary. Extraction of information is stressed; they are told to guess wherever possible, as they are allowed to cross out errors that are discovered on subsequent viewings.

The 'program language' used in the task derives from SOLO. The subjects are given five different colored pens and use a different color for each recall attempt. We are thus able to determine the amount and nature of the information extracted on each viewing. Figure 1 is a copy of the program we use for analysis. It is the last of three programs which Subjects are required to transcribe, so all subjects by this time have had practice in transcription and opportunity to learn the structural features of the language.

```
TEST flat has 2 bedrooms
  IF YES: looks promising ; CONTINUE
  IF NO: too bad ; EXIT
TEST rent less than £100
  IF YES: really looking good ; CONTINUE
  IF NO: too expensive ; EXIT
TEST neighbors are friendly
  IF YES: keep looking ; EXIT
  IF NO: take it ; EXIT
```

FIG. 1 *The program to be transcribed*

In Figs 2, 3, 4 and 5, the 'framework' is given of the first recall of the expert, the talented novice, S8, and two average novices, S5 and S10, respectively. The expert currently writes programs in ASSEMBLER (MACRO-20) and PASCAL and has considerable experience in writing FORTRAN and BASIC programs, and some experience in ALGOL 68.

```
TEST flat has 2 bedrooms
  IF YES:                ; EXIT
  IF NO:      CONTINUE
TEST
  IF YES:                ; EXIT
  IF NO:      CONTINUE
TEST
  IF YES:                ; EXIT
  IF NO:                         EXIT
```

FIG. 2 *Expert's first recall.*
The whole structure is present.

```
TEST flat has two bedrooms
  IF YES: looks promising; CONTINUE
  IF NO: too bad ; EXIT
TEST
  IF YES:
  IF NO:
TEST
  IF YES:
  IF NO:
```

FIG. 3 *Talented novice (S8)*

```
Test flat has 2 bedrooms
  IF YES: looks good ; CONTINUE
  IF NO: too bad
```

Fig. 4 *Average novice (S5);*
line-at-a-time recall

```
TEST flat has 2 bedrooms
  IF YES: looks promising : CONTINUE
  IF NO: too bad : EXIT
TEST
```

Fig. 5 *Average novice (S10)*

As can be seen (Figs 4 and 5), even after considerable practice at transcription, the typical novice is still extracting
information from the programs a line at a time. S5 needed all
five allowable viewings to transcribe the program perfectly.

The strategy used by S5 was to extract information from each 'TEST' block at a time, and to search for errors in the immediately previous recall attempt. S10 had a correct transcription after four viewings of the target program, and the recall strategy was essentially the same as that of S5.

Both S8 and the Expert (Figs 2 and 3) however extract the syntactical structure of the program plus the first few lines of program text on the first viewing. The expert extracted less text and more of the structure than S8 on this first viewing. The expert wrote and crossed out CONTINUE on the last line of his recall and replaced it with EXIT - presumably using his knowledge of programming to correct his recall. On the second recall the expert corrected the flow of control errors (he'd got them backwards on the first recall - an error he might have avoided then if he had extracted any of the textual information) and recalled four lines of text. Altogether the expert took four viewings before transcribing the entire program.

S8 also required four viewings to transcribe the entire program. On the second recall S8 extracted the rest of the text, although the last two lines of text were recalled in the wrong order. This was corrected on the third pass, and the final line of text was added on the fourth. The point is that the talented novice has extracted a model of the important characteristics of program structure, and the model is not unlike that of the Expert.

4) AN INTERPRETATION THEORY FOR PROTOCOL ANALYSIS

In this section we briefly discuss the behavior of novices from the point of view of the strategies they adopt when confronted with a problem statement. We argue that novices and experts are alike in bringing whatever programming knowledge they have to bear as early as possible in the reading of a problem statement. This is the same as to say that solution processes operate in parallel with understanding processes. Skilled novices have an advantage over unskilled novices in that they have program models, as discussed above, which can be brought into the service of understanding mechanisms. Thus, if subject S5 has a model of 'recursion' and this model is triggered early in the reading of the problem, then the model can be used to direct understanding processes to important aspects of text. We hypothesize that the programming problem solving behavior of a novice can be characterized in terms of the following types of behavior:

1) Method finding. The novice will attempt to classify the problem in terms of problem types with which he is already

familiar. This behavior is related, of course, to reading
a line or several lines from the problem statement.
2) Evaluation of candidate methods. This will involve a
   search for information which would instantiate a candidate
   method. A particular method might require a particular
   type of database structure, for example. If so, we would
   expect to see the problem solver actively search for such
   information if the method is selected as a candidate.
3) Instantiation of a method. The novice will begin thinking
   in terms of the way the problem can be realized in a program. When a method is instantiated the novice will assimilate what is already known about the problem to the instantiated schema, and will use the schema for problem
   solving - setting up expectations about what is to come,
   to detect conflicts between what is known and what is expected, and so forth.
4) Coding. This is self explanatory.
5) Evaluation of code. The novice will run a mental model of
   the behavior of his program. If evaluation indicates the
   code is successful the novice will go on to (6) below.
   Otherwise he will go through the previous steps in de-
   scending order (4,3,2,1).
6) Testing. The novice will type his program in at the terminal and run it.

We have formulated the theory as a set of rules for
scoring the verbal protocols provided by our Subjects while
they were writing programs. The smallest segment of protocol
used in our analyses is a sentence, or a clause if there is
a prominent pause in the Subject's speech. Each line of protocol is assigned to one of various behavior categories. A
simple example of a rule for scoring the protocols is in as-
signing a line of protocol to the READING category. A line of
protocol is scored as an instance of READING when the Subject
reads a line from the problem statement.

The program writing behavior of novices is not random, but
guided by various strategies. A strategy is a patterned sequence of behaviors all of which are related to a certain
goal. We need to be able to subsume larger segments of protocol than the single line if we claim that we have a 'theory'
of novice programming behavior, and in support of such a
claim we examine the 'derived' strategies of our Subjects by
applying the interpretation theory to the protocols and comparing the strategies with the theory outlined above.

Strategies are 'derived' by applying the scoring rules to
each segment of protocol. In the remainder of this paper we
shall be concerned only with one type of segmentation, involving the Reading phase. The Reading phase begins when the

Subject reads the first line of the problem statement and
ends when he has read all the problem statement. The Subjects
discussed below were asked to read the problem statement one
line at a time and to tell the experimenter everything they
knew at that point in time - what the problem was, how they
might tackle it, any predictions they had - before going on
to the next line of text. They could make notes, consult
notes or the programming manual, or any other source of
information, as and when they liked. The analysis below
concerns the scoring of the first segment of Reading
protocol - everything said between reading the first and
second lines of the problem statement - from Subjects S8 and
S5.

   In summary, we hypothesize that the primary strategy employed in program writing is finding a classification for the
current problem, and that attempts at classification will
occur early rather than late in problem understanding. When
a problem can be related to a class of problems for which
solution techniques are already known, a major part of problem solving has been circumvented. The 'Classification'
strategy involves RETRIEVAL of a candidate schema, REHEARSING
the schema, EVALUATING it with respect to the current problem.
If the result of the EVALUATION is positive then the schema
will be INSTANTIATED, which leads to PREDICTING the content
of the rest of the problem statement, or ASSIMILATING what
has already been read to the instantiated schema. ASSIMILA-
TION cannot occur after only the first line of the problem
statement, since the first lines of our problem statements
never contain anything that might be assimilated to a schema.
A strategy is initiated by READING of a line from the problem
statement. The category configuration of the Classification
strategy is shown below:

                    CLASSIFICATION:

            (A) READING-1
            (B) RETRIEVAL
            (C) REHEARSAL
            (D) EVALUATION
            (E) INSTANTIATION
            (F) PREDICTING or ASSIMILATING

Here are the protocol scoring rules for interpreting lines
of the protocol (Instantiation and Assimilating are not discussed, as the protocols do not contain instances of these
categories of behavior):

1) READING: A person reads a line from the problem text.
2) REREADING: A person rereads a line from the problem text,
   except the last line. That is, if a person has read lines

1, 2 and 3 and rereads either/both line 1 or 2, then
REREADING has occurred.

3) FOCUSSING: A person rereads the line of text last read.
That is, if a person has read lines 1 to 3 and rereads line
3, then FOCUSSING has occurred. The behavior is assumed to
be related to RETRIEVAL failure.

4) EXPERIMENTER-COMMENT: Any comment made by the experimenter.
The experimenter is indicated by 'E:' at the front of a
line of protocol.

5) RETRIEVAL: We consider that retrieval is equivalent to ac-
tivating some structure in LTM (Long Term Memory). Activation of a structure is sometimes signalled by Subject
statements such as "That reminds me of iteration". This
statement signals the activation of the 'iteration' schema.
RETRIEVAL is often a response to READING, REREADING, or
FOCUSSING, and a line of protocol immediately subsequent
to these processes should be examined for indications of
this process.

   RETRIEVAL may either be 'cued' or 'associative'. We regard responses to READING, REREADING, and FOCUSSING as cued
RETRIEVAL. The concepts that are used subsequently to cued
RETRIEVAL of a particular concept are considered to be as-
sociatively related to the particular concept, and made
available through an associative link. If a person READs
"On page 80 of [the Programming Manual] we look at a method
for making a particular inference 'keep on happening'".
and responds: "Is that 'iteration'? then 'iteration' is an
example of cued, or CUED-RETRIEVAL. If the Subject then
says, "Or maybe it's 'recursion'" then 'recursion' is an
example of associative, or ASSOC-RETRIEVAL.

6) PROBE: A person PROBEs what he knows about a concept by
explaining it to himself (aloud) or to the experimenter,
or when he provides a definition or makes an attempt to
construct a meaning for a particular concept, and so forth.
An example would be if a person thought the current problem had something to do with recursion (a RETRIEVAL) step,
but then had to determine what 'recursion' might be (e.g.,
"Is that where you use..... etc."). We know from pilot
studies that both talented and average novices 'probe'
their knowledge of a particular concept before trying to
apply what they know.

7) EVALUATION: This activity takes several forms. EVALUATION
occurs when a person determines the output for a segment
of code he has written. Also, EVALUATION occurs when a
person attempts to determine the appropriateness of a particular algorithm for the current problem. It may sometimes be difficult to distinguish EVALUATION from

REHEARSAL.

8) PREDICTION: The person states an expectation of some sort, generally about the type of program that is required, or about information that is yet to be given, and so on.

9) META-COMMENT: The person explains why he thinks some thing, or comments on the strategy being followed or in some way indicates the processes that are occurring in his quest for a solution to or understanding of the problem.

The first protocol below is that of S8, the talented novice. At the left of each line of protocol (the different lines are indicated by numbers in brackets) there is the category label which has been applied to that line. Lines 2, 5, 8 and 10 have been deleted from this protocol as have several lines from the protocol of S5. The deleted lines had been labelled 'UNACCOUNTED' as they could not be classified in terms of the categories indicated in the interpretation theory. Invariably these lines contained single words such as "Um..." or "Well.. ...". No account of this type of comment will be given in this paper.

(PROTOCOL, SEGMENT-1, S8)

READING   (1) "On page 80 of Units three to four we looked at a method for making a particular inference 'keep on happening'".

CUED-RETRIEVAL   (3) Is that called 'iteration'?

ASSOC-RETRIEVAL   (4) No, 'recursion'.

PROBING   (6) I can remember something about being told something about the distinction between iteration and recursion and one goes sort of like along a database and the other sort of going down.

META-COMMENT   (7) Well, that's how I sort of thought of it.

EXPERIMENTER-COMMENT   (9) E: Allright. Any further expectations or any....?

EXPERIMENTER-COMMENT   (11) E: I just want to know everything you, uh.... I mean as you read it......

PREDICTION   (12) So.....I think this is going to say something about what happens when you keep on applying a....

Figure 6 summarizes the derived strategy for this protocol segment.

S8:

READING
RETRIEVAL
PROBING
PREDICTION

FIG. 6 *Derived strategy for a talented novice, S8*

The structure of this first segment of S8's protocol is in
good agreement with the theory. The reading of the line results in the retrieval of relevant information at a fairly
high level of abstraction (recursion and iteration). And the
retrieval itself is followed by self probing. The exception
is the last category, PREDICTION. We associate this category
of behavior with an 'Instantiation' strategy (not further
discussed here) and we are led to infer that at this point S5
has already instantiated one of the candidate models mentioned
in lines 3 and 4. Subsequent lines in the protocol confirm
this inference (further details in Kahney and Eisenstadt,
1982).

(PROTOCOL, SEGMENT-1, S5)

READING-1	(1) "On page eighty of Units three to four we looked at a method for making a particular inference 'keep on happening'".
FOCUSSING	(2) Keep on happening
META-COMMENT	(4) I am very surprised, because I did not think it was going to be detailed like this.
FOCUSSING	(6) An inference keep on happening....
FOCUSSING	(9) Keep on happening.....
META-COMMENT	(11) That reminds me of something.
META-COMMENT	(12) I'm trying to remember what the words were that it reminds me of.
FOCUSSING	(14) Keep on happening....
CUED-RETRIEVAL	(16) For-Each-Case-Of, it reminds me of.
CUED-RETRIEVAL	(17) And then 'inference' is where you have, um....
PROBING	(18) Two statements, and the database is able to form, um....
PROBING	(19) Or the program is able to modify the database by, um....
PROBING	(20) Putting in a new relationship on the basis of relationships that were already in the database.
PROBING	(21) So you could have two triples and they would imply, or the....

PROBING	(22) The program has been made so that, um....
PROBING	(23) The existing two triples will form an inference which is formed....
PROBING	(24) Which is stated on....
PROBING	(25) ....the database as a third triple.
PROBING	(26) That's what an inference is.
FOCUSSING	(27) We looked at a method for making [an].... inference....
META-COMMENT	(28) I can't remember what it is.

Figure 7 summarizes the derived strategy for S5.

S5:

READING
FOCUSSING
META-COMMENT
FOCUSSING*
META-COMMENT*
FOCUSSING
CUED-RETRIEVAL*
PROBING*
FOCUSSING
META-COMMENT

FIG. 7 *Derived strategy for an average novice, S5 (Asterisks show that the behavior continued for several lines of protocol.)*

The structure of this segment of S5's protocol also is in good agreement with the theory. In this segment the Subject reads and focusses as an aid to retrieval, and continually probes what is retrieved.

The major difference between S5 and S8 in this segment is that S8 has an internalized model of recursion which has been indexed (presumably by a key phrase, such as 'a method for making an inference keep on happening) and instantiated, while S5 is left 'focussing'. The differences throughout the remainder of the two protocols are much more pronounced. S8's protocol indicates predictive understanding and a workable solution before the problem statement has been entirely read. S5 never really succeeds in understanding what the problem is, and all efforts at 'imitating' the solution indicated in the first sentence of the problem statement come to grief.

There are also counterexamples to the theory. Here is an extract from the first segment of protocol of S11:

(PROTOCOL, SEGMENT-1, S11)

READING	(1) "On page 80 of Units three to four.. ...."
META-COMMENT	(2) And then I looked at that again because I immediately tried to think of what page eighty might be like, and Units three to four.
META-COMMENT	(3) I couldn't remember.
READING	(4) "....we looked at a method for making a particular inference 'keep on happening."
META-COMMENT	(6) As I was reading that I started to think....
META-COMMENT	(7) About what I had read....
META-COMMENT	(8) And it rang a few bells, but.....
META-COMMENT	(9) I wasn't very clear about it.
META-COMMENT	(11) The procedure you need for that, so I decide to carry on reading.

Here is the structure of the derived strategy:

S11:

READING
META-COMMENT*
READING
META-COMMENT*

Essentially, this Subject is reporting that some of the words and phrases are recognizable - method, inference, 'keep on happening' - but the corresponding structures in memory are not activated. Each segment of the reading protocol for this Subject looks much the same as the segment provided here.

5) CONCLUSION

We believe that there is a useful distinction between two types of novice - those we have called talented, and the rest. We have studied 6 novices in considerable detail, and find that a talented novice is like an expert in many respects in which the average novice is quite unlike the expert. A good example is the behavior of novices on the transcription task by comparison with an expert. These differences hold across a variety of task situations that we have studied, most of which have not been discussed in this paper.

There is a great deal more to be said about mental models, about the theory of novice problem solving, about the interpretation theory, and about the various experimental methods used in studying novice programming behavior, than has been

indicated in this brief paper. We hoped simply to indicate
the direction our research has taken and give a very brief
account of some of our findings. We should have liked to present more detail about each of these matters, for the final
picture is far from simple. For example, a talented novice
may not only find his mental models an aid to understanding,
but a hindrance as well. S8, who believed that there were only two types of program you could write in SOLO - iteration
and recursion - began working on the second problem thinking
it would be a problem in iteration because a problem in recursion had previously been given. The preconception was mistaken, and the Subject's 'iteration model' led the Subject
astray for a considerable length of time in solving the second problem given. Mental models are more fully discussed in
Kahney and Eisenstadt (1982). A detailed discussion of all
the issues raised here can be found in Kahney (1982).

REFERENCES

Brooks, R. (1977). Towards a theory of the cognitive processes
    in computer programming. *Int. J. Man-Machine Studies* 9,
    737-751.
Chi, M.T.H., Feltovich, P.J. and Glaser, R. (1981). Catego-
    rization and Representation of Physics Problems by Experts
    and Novices. *Cognitive Science* 5, 121-152.
Di Sessa, A.A. (1981). The role of experience in models of the
    physical world. Proceedings of the Third Annual Cognitive
    Science Society Conference, Berkeley, California. (1975)
Eisenstadt, M. (1978). *Artificial Intelligence Project*. Units
    3/4 of "Cognitive Psychology: a third level course".
    Milton Keynes: Open University Press.
Eisenstadt, M., Laubsch, J. and Kahney, H. (1981). "Creating
    Pleasant Programming Environments for Cognitive Science
    Students". Proceedings of the Third Annual Cognitive
    Science Society Conference, Berkeley, California.
Gentner, D. (1981). "Generative Analogies of Mental Models".
    Proceedings of the Third Annual Cognitive Science Society
    Conference, Berkeley, California.
Hayes, J.R. and Simon, H. (1974). Understanding written prob-
    lem instructions. *In* "Knowledge and Cognition". (Ed.
    L.W. Gregg), Hillsdale, N.J.: Lawrence Erlbaum Associates.
Kahney, H. and Eisenstadt, M. (1982). "Programmers' Mental
    Models of their Programming Tasks: the Interaction of Real-
    world Knowledge and Programming Knowledge". Proceedings
    of the Fourth Annual Cognitive Science Society Conference,
    Ann Arbor, Michigan (In press).
Kahney, H. (1981). An In-depth Study of the Behavior of Novice

Programmers. Technical Report No. 82-9, Human Cognition
Research Group, The Open University, Milton Keynes,
England.
Luger, G. and Bauer, M. (1978). Transfer effects in isomorphic
problem situations. *Acta Psychologica* Vol. 42-2, 121-131.
Norman, D. (1982). Some Observations on Mental Models. CHIP
Technical Report No. 112, Center for Human Information
Processing, University of California, San Diego, California.
Reed, S.K., Ernst, G.W. and Banerji, R.B. (1974). The role of
analogy in transfer between similar problem states.
Cognitive Psychology 6, 436-450.
Schoenfeld, A.H. (1980). Can heuristics be taught? *In*
"Cognitive Process Instruction; Research on Teaching
Thinking Skills". (Eds J. Lockhead and J. Clement) The
Franklin Institute Press.

ANALYSIS OF BEGINNERS' PROBLEM-SOLVING STRATEGIES IN PROGRAMMING

JEAN-MICHEL HOC

Laboratoire de Psychologie du Travail de l'E.P.H.E.
Equipe de Recherche Associée au C.N.R.S.
Paris, France

1) INTRODUCTION

During the last decade, ergonomical studies on programming
have been widely developed, as one can see in recent syntheses
of works carried out in the field (Smith and Green, 1980;
Shneiderman, 1980). But these studies are also much criticized:
a methodological debate has recently been opened on this
problem (Sheil, 1981; Moher and Schneider, 1982). At the same
time these studies are criticized with being too much directed
by computer technology and also not giving enough methodological
precision.

It is true that the theoretical frameworks of cognitive
psychology do not permit us to derive very precise models of
the psychological mechanisms underlying programming. But these
models are, without doubt, more valuable than the implicit
frameworks which have directed a lot of studies on programming. Models are necessary to establish the relevance of the
experiments. When they cannot be entirely derived from a
theoretical approach, the role played by relatively open
observation of behavior, in order to obtain missing information, must not be neglected. Indeed, it is difficult to
generalize the results of such observational studies, but
they may lead to more relevant and economical experiments,
the aim of which is to be inductive.

This methodological option has directed my own works, as
well as those of authors such as Brooks (1977). Brooks tried
to model programming strategies at an expert level, while my
less formalized contribution related to beginners' strategies,
and with applications to views of training. The study of such
strategies was necessary for a better understanding of the

difficulties met in the acquisition of top-down programming
methods.

I shall restrict myself to reporting the main results of
my own works, published in French, hence less accessible.
Chronologically they are placed between two studies, published
in English, about which I shall not speak: an exploratory
study of strategies at diverse levels of expertise (Hoc, 1977)
and a comparative assessment of two top-down methods (Hoc,
1981a).

First, I shall present a longitudinal and observational
study (Hoc, 1978a) performed during a training course for a
business programming method, widely used in France: the
L.C.P.* method (Warnier, 1975). From it, I shall extract the
two essential research topics which directed the design of
subsequent experiments: the learning of the computer operation
and the mechanisms in expressing procedures.

2) A STUDY OF A TRAINING COURSE FOR A TOP DOWN PROGRAMMING METHOD

Program design strategies are not innate! They are learned by
training and professional practice. Training is not confined
to learning programming languages, as was the case in the
past: now programming methods are taught. In France, these
methods are in a large part inspired by structured programming. We tried to assess the learning of one of them, the
L.C.P. method (Hoc, 1978a). Afterwards an assessment of the
same type was done for another method (the Deductive method
of Pair, 1979) by a colleague (Kolmayer, 1979), leading to
similar psychological conclusions.

L.C.P. is a business programming method which consists at
first in structuring the results and the data, and then in
"deducing" (according to Warnier, its designer) the program
structure. Each structure is constructed by a top-down
(planning) method, in nesting and chaining two basic constructions: the conditional structure and the iterative structure.

I have chosen a familiar example, in order to show the use
of this method: the solving of a list of second degree
equations. I shall present the steps of the method, by following the order which is recommended by the author (J.D. Warnier),
though the subjects do not always operate like this (Fig. 1).

STEP 1: structuring the results (output file)

The levels of the structure (or the decomposition) are
indicated by the brackets. The conditional structures (only
tests with two exits, for this method) are coded by the

*"Logique de Construction des Programmes".

symbol "exclusive or" with the wording "0 or 1 times", the
iterative structures by the wording "x times" (here E times,
for example).

STEP 2: structuring the data (input file)

The method of structuring the input is the same as for the
output. The user of the method must then examine the
structural compatibility between the two constructions. He
must ask himself the following question: "are the identification criteria in the structure of the results also present
in the data structure?" Here, the answer is no, as early as
the second level (existence of root). Hence, one has to
introduce what is called "a run file" with an intermediary
variable: delta. Then the two files (output file and input
file) become compatible.

STEP 3: structuring the program (unit of processing)

One "deduces" (following the author) the program structure
(presented in the same form) from the input and run file.

STEP 4: flow charting

After that, one derives the flow-chart which must involve
all the tests. Of course, the flow-chart is isomorphic to
the unit of processing. But the flow-chart shows more clearly
the positions of the sequences of statements (in the boxes).

STEP 5: statements

Only after this, can the statements be introduced in the
boxes, by distributing the statements, type by type, among
them, but not by following the order of the execution:
first, all of the input statements are distributed, then
all the branching statements, all the computations, and all
the output statements (see Fig. 1).

In an intensive training centre, we have made a longitudinal
analysis of the acquisition of this method in twenty subjects.
Over three months I have analysed the draft copies of the
successive exercises, according to two principles:

- analysis of the *structural compatibility* between the steps
  (output file/input file, input file/unit of processing,
  unit of processing/flow chart, in order to see if the
  behavior of the subjects were consistent with the deduction
  rules of the method;
- analysis of the *success* of each step, in order to see if
  there were any difference in complexity between the steps.

Here I shall only cite the two main results:

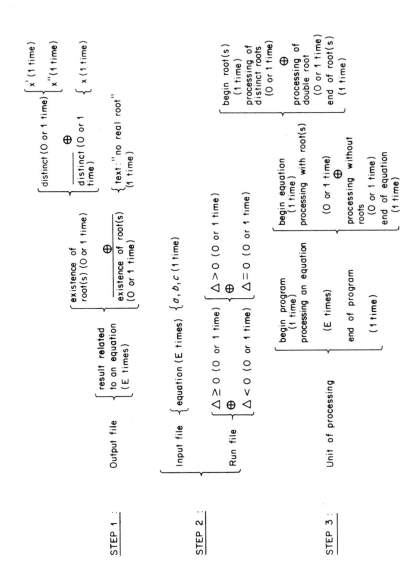

FIG. 1 L.C.P. analysis of a program for processing quadratic
equations (from Hoc, 1981a). The five steps of this analysis
specify: structure data; structure of program; flow-chart;
and detailed instructions. In steps 1 to 3 the symbol ⊕
signifies exclusive or. In step 1, the overline signifies
negation (thus distinct signifies "not distinct").

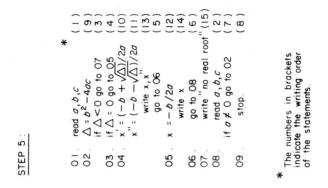

STEP 5 :

01. read a, b, c (1)
02. $\Delta = b^2 - 4ac$ (9)
03. if $\Delta < 0$ go to 07   (3)
    if $\Delta = 0$ go to 05   (4)
04. $x' = (-b + \sqrt{\Delta})/2a$ (10)
    $x'' = (-b - \sqrt{\Delta})/2a$ (11)
05. write x, x (13)
    go to 06   (5)
    $x = -b/2a$ (12)
06. write x (14)
    go to 08   (6)
07. write "no real root"   (15)
    read a, b, c (2)
08. if $a \neq 0$ go to 02   (7)
09. stop.   (8)

* The numbers in brackets indicate the writing order of the statements.

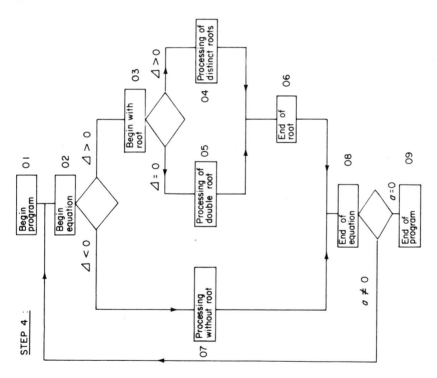

STEP 4 :

(Cont) *In step 5, the L.C.P. method requires instructions to be written down in the order: input statements; branching statements; computation statements; output statements. This order is shown in parentheses. However, subjects very frequently wrote instructions down in the order of their execution instead of the L.C.P. order.*

a. *The structural compatibility is not very good*. At the end
   of training:

   - 60 to 80 percent of the subjects show a structural
     compatibility between the output file and the input file,
     modified through the run file;
   - only 40 to 70 percent of the subjects show a structural
     compatibility between the input file and the unit of
     processing; this result contradicts the author's idea of
     a deduction;
   - and, more surprising, only 50 to 70 percent of the sub-
     jects show a structural compatibility between the unit
     of processing and the flow chart, though these two
     constructions are theoretically isomorphic!

   Even at the end of training, for each step, the subject
   carries out a new analysis of the problem, without clear
   coordination with the preceding step. There is no clear
   "deduction" of the program structure from the data
   structure.

b. *The performance improves when constructing the flow-chart
   of the program.*
   The preceding steps often contain errors. At the beginning
   of the training course these structure errors mainly come
   from data representations incompatible with the computer
   operation (for example: data access mode). These errors
   are corrected when writing the flow-chart. At the end of
   training:

   - only 40 to 50 percent of the subjects present correct
     output and input files;
   - but 80 percent of the subjects present a correct flow-
     chart.

   I interpreted these results by setting up two working
   hypotheses:

   1. The structure of the data and the results, hence their
      representations, are not independent from the processes
      the subject aims to apply to them. Some incorrect
      structures might be correct for other processing devices
      well known to the subject. Here, I shall return to the
      idea (Hoc, 1977) according to which the beginner uses
      representation and processing systems[*] based upon
      devices other than the computer, before having
      constructed an appropriate new system by differentiation.

---

[*]Systèmes de Représentation et de Traitement

A characteristic of beginners' strategies is perhaps a mechanism of adapting familiar procedures to the operation of the computer.

2. The improvement of the structure, in writing the flow-chart, might lead one to think that the beginner could not adapt a procedure, without access to the paths the machine will follow during the execution. Another characteristic of beginners' strategies could be seen as generating the statements by mental execution of the program.

The top-down and backwards programming methods that are taught run counter to these characteristics. For example:

- L.C.P., a top-down method, runs counter in deferring the introduction of the statements to the last step;
- the Deductive Method (Pair, 1979), that I am now studying on professional programmers, recommends a backwards strategy (from the results to the data) for generating statements, and, at the same time, a top-down strategy.

Following this observational study, I carried out two experiments with beginners according to a common paradigm, in order to study these hypotheses more closely. In this paradigm a problem is used for which it is certain the subject knows a procedure. At first this procedure is examined in all its details; after-wards, the subject is placed in a situation where, step by step, he commands a computer device simulated by a VDU. Constraints in the machine operation are gradually introduced. So, the subject can learn the computer operation by immediately obtaining knowledge of results, which is deferred in the usual programming situation (Hoc and Kerguelen, 1980). Mainly the errors and the response latencies are analysed. When the procedure is correct, the subject is asked to describe his procedure. This paradigm was used for two types of problems (an updating stock problem and a sorting problem), in two distinct experiments, with about twenty subjects in each case.

3) LEARNING THE COMPUTER OPERATION

Updating Stock Problem (Hoc, 1978b, 1981b, Fig. 2)

An old stock file must be updated from a transaction file. I simulated a simplified computer, "minimal" in regard to an optimal solution for this problem:

- a pair of memory cells for each type of record ("old stock" and "transaction") with the corresponding input operations: ENTER OLD STOCK RECORD and ENTER TRANSACTION RECORD;
- a summation operation (in the old stock cells): ADD;
- and an operation to output old stock cells: WRITE.

There were three stages in this first experiment:

Stage 1: The subject processes the data with the information in Fig. 2 visible. The display is modified after each command.
Stage 2: The subject sees only part of Fig. 2, the representation of the computer. In this situation it should be observed that it is necessary to input the transaction concerning a following item (in the old stock file) in order to establish the validity of outputting the current item (in the old stock cells).
Stage 3: The subject cannot see anything: he must use the the tests: "old stock = 99" (end of file), and "old stock = transaction" (does the transaction in the transaction cells correspond to the item in the old stock cells?).

The results can be summed up in the following way:

a. Very quickly the subject elaborates a sequence which I see

FIG. 2. (Facing) *Schematic of the updating device with its four operations: ENTER OS [old stock], ENTER T [transaction], ADD [OS = OS + T], and WRITE [to new stock file]; and its two tests, OS = 99? and OS = T?.*

The subject's task is to perform transactions as indicated by the transaction file: e.g. "3 13" means "add 13 to the quantity of item 3 in the old stock file". "3 -13" would signify that the quantity of item 3 should be decreased by 13. By the nature of the 'computer', files can only be traversed sequentially, and so all the transactions for a given item number must be done together. When all transactions for a given item are completed, the value of the old stock (OS) cell is sent to the new stock file.

Subjects performed the task under three conditions, in which they can see less and less of the "apparatus"; ultimately only the two windows, OS cell and T cell. (From Hoc, 1978b, 1981b.)

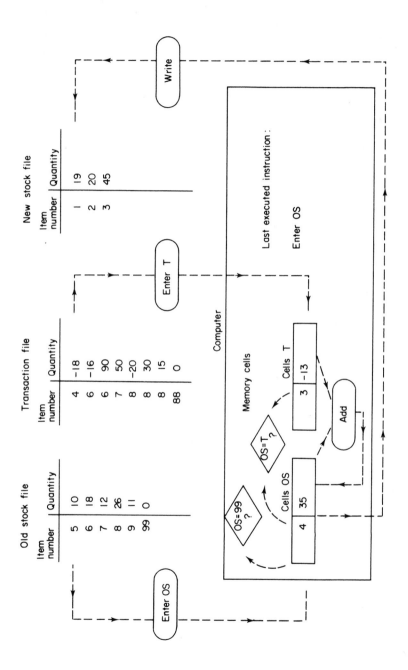

FIG. 2   For legend see facing page.

as prototypical (cf the 'typicality phenomenon' in semantic memory):

ENTER OLD STOCK RECORD
↓
ENTER TRANSACTION RECORD
↓
ADD
↓
WRITE

This sequence, or its overall structure, valid in processing an Old Stock record with only one transaction, will be transferred and adapted in order to process the records of another type without a transaction or with several transactions. This transfer persists up to the last stage.

b. In the first stage, the analysis of the response latencies shows that the subject concentrates on identifications just before the input of an Old Stock record (he counts the transactions to be processed, and afterwards he links up the operations very quickly. In subsequent stages *the prototypical sequence must be broken,* because identifications can only be done in the memory cells (transaction by transaction) and the two commands ENTER TRANSACTION RECORD and ADD must be reversed in the procedure.

The subject then operates less in terms of systematic identifications than of hypotheses on the number of transactions by record, in order to avoid breaking up the structure of the prototypical sequence. Although he puts up with seeing the hypotheses invalidated by error messages, he refuses to test these hypotheses for himself. This mechanism is still much used in the last stage, no matter in what way the subject is invited to command these tests explicitly.

Hence, in certain cases, the difficulty of the adaptation to the computer operation seems to lie less in the comprehension of the statements, than in destroying the structure of a procedure, by identification constraints in relation to the data access mode of the computer (or, in other cases, to the writing of results).

From a pedagogical point of view, it would be interesting to design such command situations, in order to facilitate the subject becoming aware of the effect of this type of constraint, upon the overall structure of programs. In order to do this, it is advisable that the operations should be rather those of a high level language than those of a low level one.

Sorting Problem (Nguyen-Xuan and Hoc, 1981)

The same experimental paradigm was used for a more complex
problem: sorting. I can only summarise the results of this
experiment, which clearly show the limits of learning by
doing, concerning the computer operation.

   Here, the command situation was less constraining. Several
procedures were possible. If the subject clearly transferred
his usual procedure (often an insertion algorithm), the
adaptation rarely led to an optimal procedure taking the best
advantage of the machine operation. This adaptation was
directed by a regulation of the mental load (especially the
memory load):

- the subjects stopped the adaptation as soon as the mental
  load was judged tolerable;
- the errors provoked by an overload were not sufficiently
  analysed, and the subjects made changes to "correct" the
  procedure, without these changes giving improvement.

   Learning by doing seems to be of interest only with simple
procedures and constraining devices, which direct the subject
towards an optimal procedure. It is of little interest when
the number of possible procedures is too large.

4) EXPRESSING THE PROCEDURES

At the end of the two experiments cited the subjects were
asked to explain the procedure which they had just used and
which was now correct. In the first case (updating), they
had to write a flow-chart, structured or otherwise, while in
the second case (sorting) they wrote up the procedure in
natural language. The aim was to examine formal and verbal
reports in situations where the processing device was well-
defined and the procedure already elaborated. Furthermore,
I wanted to study the role which could be played by a top-down
method, in constructing a flow-chart.

Flow-chart and Top-down Method (updating)

After having perfected a correct procedure of updating old
stock records with 0, 1 or several transactions, the subjects
had to construct three flow-charts in this order: the case
where the records have one and only one transaction, the
case where they have either zero or one transaction, and the
general case.

One group of subjects *(prescribed planning)* was constrained to:

- use only the two basic constructions of structured programming,
- and, after the first one, generate the flow-charts in a top-down mode, by transferring the overall structure (plan) of the preceding flow-chart (Fig. 3).

In prescribed planning, after solving the first problem (only one transaction for each item), the subject must solve the second problem (0 or 1 transaction for each item), by transferring the iterative structure. After solving the

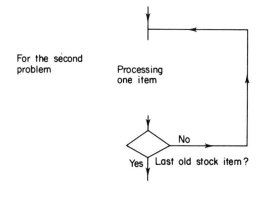

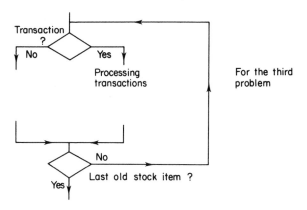

FIG. 3 *In the 'prescribed planning' group, each new problem was treated by refining the overall structure of the previous solution.*

second problem, he must solve the third problem (0, 1, or
several transactions for each item), by transferring the
iterative structure and nesting the conditional structure
within it.

Another group of subjects *(free expression)* had no
particular constraint. Here I shall present only the three
principal results (Hoc, 1979, 1981c):

a. In free expression, the subjects expressed the flow-charts
   following the order of execution: that is the mental
   execution of the program which is directing the expression,
   and not a representation of the program structure, which
   the subject discovers only at the end.
b. In prescribed planning, the order in which the instructions
   are written notably *deviates from the order of execution,*
   but the subjects refer to the production rules (condition
   → sequence of actions) used in the execution, by fitting
   them to the prescribed basic constructions.

   In order to evaluate the correlation between the
   writing order and the execution order, the sequence of
   writing was divided into production rules, and the two
   conditions were compared. For the last two problems, in
   free expression, 50 to 54 per cent of the transitions from
   one rule to another were the same in both the order of
   execution and the order of writing - i.e. rules were
   written down in the order of execution to a large degree;
   whereas in prescribed planning only 36 per cent of the
   transitions were the same in both orders.
c. Concerning the overall performance times (Fig. 4), we can
   see that, in prescribed planning, although the construction
   difficulties hamper the subject at the beginning, this
   handicap disappears as soon as the method becomes more
   familiar and the problem more complex. In free expression
   increasing complexity affects the subject far too much.

Expression in Natural Language (Sorting)

The analysis of the free expression of sorting procedures in
natural language led to the following results:

1. Before expressing the structure of the procedure, the
   subject for a long time can only express particular
   executions of this procedure. He defines particular cases,
   in order to express a sequential execution of the procedure
   without expressing its structure. This phenomenon is more
   especially obvious when the subject has attained a procedure with whose principle he is not familiar.
2. Afterwards, he expresses structures at first only as
   substructures; among the substructures iterations are

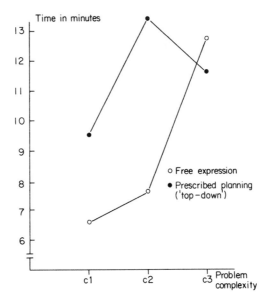

FIG. 4 *Mean time to write a flow-chart for three problems of increasing complexity. At higher levels of complexity there appears to be no clear advantage to either the free expression or the top-down methodology - while the less complex problems are evidently easiest using free expression.*

easiest, their written expression being obviously much closer to the sequence of execution than in conditionals.

5) CONCLUSION

These experiments bear out the hypotheses set up after the field study, but they show a larger complexity in the beginners' strategies. It is true that they are characterized by adapting known procedures to the computer operation, and by a mental execution of the program.

In relation to the learning of top-down programming methods by beginners, the results indicate the following points:

1. The subject must be aware of the effect of the computer operation on the overall structure of programs:
   - the difficulties are concentrated on identification constraints that lead to a representation of the data, and a structure of the procedure, different from those that are familiar to the subject;
   - these command situations must be sufficiently constraining, so that the subject takes the best advantage of the machine operation.

2. Although top-down programming is at first a handicap, afterwards it seems to be an aid for managing complexity.
3. Nevertheless, it seems necessary for the subject to express to himself an execution of the procedure, before he can grasp its control structure, form the substructures to the superstructures, and form the iterative structures to the conditional structures.

I suggest that a too early training of top-down programming methods should be avoided, before the subject has correctly learned the constraints of the computer operation on the overall structure (plan) of the procedures, and knows a wide range of concrete plans to be transferred. It has not been proved that these top-down methods are always feasible even at an expert level.

I have begun a research program with the aim of characterizing the components of experts' strategies and their conditions of implementation, and in particular those of top-down strategies. The practical problem is to contribute to the design of computerized aids in programming. The results of such research may permit a better setting up of training problems.

REFERENCES

Brooks, R. (1977). Towards a theory of the cognitive processes in computer programming, *International Journal of Man-Machine Studies*. 9, 737-751.
Hoc, J.M. (1977). Role of mental representation in learning a programming language, *International Journal of Man-Machine Studies*. 9, 87-105.
Hoc, J.M. (1978a). Etude de la formation à une méthode de programmation informatique, *Le Travail Humain*. 41, 111-126.
Hoc, J.M. (1978b). La programmation informatique comme situation de résolution de problème. Thèse de 3ème Cycle, Paris, Université René-Descartes.
Hoc, J.M. (1979). Le problème de la planification dans la construction d'un programme informatique, *Le Travail Humain*. 42, 245-260.
Hoc, J.M. (1981a). Planning and direction of problem-solving in structured programming: an empirical comparison between two methods, *International Journal of Man-Machine Studies*. 15, 363-383.
Hoc, J.M. (1981b). Une approche diachronique de la résolution de problème, *Psychologie Française*. 26, 182-192.
Hoc, J.M. (1981c). La planification dans la résolution de problème, *Le Travail Humain*. 44, 261-268.

Hoc, J.M. and Kerguelen, A. (1980). Un exemple de dispositif
    informatique expérimental pour la psycho-pédagogie de la
    programmation, *Informatique et Sciences Humaines*. <u>44</u>,
    67-86.
Kolmayer, E. (1979). Développement et Évaluation d'une
    Méthode de Programmation. Nancy, C.R.I.N., Report No.
    79RO74.
Moher, T. and Schneider, G.M. (1982). Methodology and
    experimental research in software engineering,
    International Journal of Man-Machine Studies. <u>16</u>, 65-87.
Nguyen-Xuan, A. and Hoc, J.M. (1981). "Adaptation d'une
    procédure connue aux règles de fonctionnement d'un
    ordinateur: la sériation". Paris, E.P.H.E.
Pair, C. (1979). La construction des programmes, *R.A.I.R.O.-
    informatique*. <u>13</u>, 113-137.
Sheil, B.A. (1981). The psychological study of programming,
    Computing Surveys. <u>13</u>, 101-120.
Shneiderman, B. (1980). "Software Psychology". Cambridge,
    Mass.: Winthrop.
Smith, H.T. and Green, T.R.G. (1980). "Human Interaction
    with Computers". Academic Press, London.
Warnier, J.D. (1975). "Les procédures de traitement et leurs
    données (L.C.P.)". Les Editions d' Organisation, Paris.

PROGRAM DEVELOPMENT STUDIES BASED ON DIARIES

PETER NAUR

Copenhagen University
Copenhagen, Denmark

1) INTRODUCTION

The purpose of the present paper is to discuss the use of
diary notes for illuminating the problems of program development. By diary notes will be understood here notes describing
problems considered and solved in the course of the development of programs, taken day by day as part of the development
process itself. The aspect of such notes considered here is
their recording of what actually goes on in the programmer's
mind during programming, in the sense of what the programmer
perceives to be the task to be done and the problems and
their solution. Upon subsequent analysis, diary notes may
contribute to an understanding of the problems of programming,
and to developing effective programming techniques. For
earlier experiments in this direction see Naur (1972) and
Naur (1975).

 The study of programming diaries is seen here as a
supplement to other kinds of studies of the programming
process, in particular group experiments in which the
behaviour of several individuals facing the same, constructed
programming task is studied (see for example Brooks, 1980).
While such experiments are indispensable in ascertaining the
general validity of relevant hypotheses, less structured
empirical work, such as studies of diaries, seems important
in finding what hypotheses might be worth investigating for
validity.

 An essential feature of the diary approach, as understood
here, is that the program development reported on in the
diary should be a true performance presenting, in some of
its aspects, new problems to the programmer. This requirement
is imposed so as to exclude from consideration such

160   P. NAUR

descriptions of program developments as appear to depict real
events, but in reality are for the most part constructed so as
to give credence to a given methodology. In the kind of diary
considered here one would expect to see displayed both
unfruitful attempts and unexpected successes.

It must be recognized that in the requirement that the
development presents new problems to the programmer lies a
deep problem of the approach, namely to identify that which
can be admitted as new. In principle the diary should start
with a complete enumeration of everything the programmer
knows already and that might be relevant to the problem at
hand, so as to make it quite clear to what extent the
problems encountered in the development can be solved by
means of techniques that are familiar to the programmer.

A complete enumeration is clearly practicably impossible.
In practice the background knowledge can only be stated to
some limited extent, while usually much of it will have to
be inferred indirectly from the description of the problems
encountered and their solution.

In the present notes the approach is illustrated by only
a single instance of a diary. This happened to be available
for study, having been produced by the author for a different
purpose, and thus describes a program development as it
proceeded without regard to any subsequent analysis.

2) PROGRAMMING OF A WELL-KNOWN TASK

As illustration of the use of a diary in programming studies,
this section will review some results obtained in a concrete,
modest programming task. The outlines of the task are as
follows:

1. Purpose of programming task: to develop and document a
   simulator, expressed in Fortran, for the INTEL 8080
   microcomputer. The ultimate purpose was to establish a
   model solution of the problem for use in university
   teaching.
2. Background of programming task: in addition to the specifications of the computers and programming languages
   involved, of the format of the simulator input language,
   and of the essential requirements on the simulator output,
   it was required that the simulator should be designed
   around a table controlling the analysis and simulated
   execution of the microcomputer instruction words. The
   relevant programming techniques were very well known to
   the author from several earlier similar program development tasks.

3. Program development: as the most unusual feature of the development process, all substantial design considerations and decisions were recorded as the work progressed as a typed problem analysis report. In this manner the basis of each part of the program was established in writing before the actual programming was done. Within the total development three subphases can be distinguished, although they overlap to some extent: (1) design of instruction word analysis and central simulator actions; (2) design of control by table; (3) design of output format.
4. Program punching, testing, and correction: the interface to the computer executing the simulator was given as a conventional batch-oriented operating system, with a turn-around time of the order of 15 minutes, and with primary input from punched cards.
5. Design and verification of tests: a properly documented test of the simulator was a vital part of the task. For testing, a series of 16 INTEL 8080 test programs was designed and their correct execution in the simulator verified. The development of the test programs and the testing and correction of errors of the simulator itself were done hand in hand. In this manner each run with the computer would usually include many independent test executions, corresponding to the various test programs, thereby allowing a very productive utilization of the batch operation mode.

From this development the diary to be studied is formed as the collection comprising the problem analysis report, test notes, programs, and computer output, together with a record of the time spent on the project day by day. The magnitude of the total task is summarized in Table 1.

For the purposes of the following discussion the nature of errors found during the testing is particularly pertinent. For this reason the outline of the testing history is given in Table 2, and an overview of the corrections made in Table 3.

3) PROGRAM CORRECTIONS

Table 3 gives an overview of all corrections to the simulator program and to the test programs made as a result of the program testing. In the following notes these corrections will be discussed, with special attention to the psychological issues that seem relevant to an understanding of them.

The most conspicuous overall feature of Table 3 is the wide difference in the number of corrections in the various groups. What will be argued here is that these differences

TABLE 1

Magnitude of Programming Task

Work phase	Time spent		Lines produced		
	Calendar days	Work hours	Free text	Comments in programs	Program
1. Design of program, writing of problem analysis and program text	24	38.5	666	154	679
2. Punching, proof reading	2	10.6	0	0	0
3. Writing of test notes and programs, doing test runs and corrections of errors	16	31.3	251	0	369
Total	42	80.6	917	154	1048

TABLE 2

Testing History

Run 1, 1980 June 4, 11.07. The Fortran compiler referred
to in the operating system was obsolete and produced large
numbers of spurious error messages.

Run 2, 1980 June 4, 16.50. Diagnostics: from Fortran
compiler: none; from loader: one undefined name (indfad, used
for infad).

Run 3, 1980 June 4, 17.02. No diagnostics. Execution of
one minimal test case, T20.

Run 4, 1980 June 4, 17.18. Execution of six minimal test
cases, T21 - T26. All fail because of the same error, viz.
destruction of argument in central input conversion function.

Run 5, 1980 June 9, 11.33. Execution of seven minimal and
two productive test cases, T1-T2. Essentially correct
execution. Errors in details of output format.

Run 6, 1980 June 9, 12.57. Execution of new test case, T3,
leads to infinite loop, because of error in test data.

Run 7, 1980 June 10, 14.12. Execution of seven minimal and
five productive test cases, T1 - T5. Everything worked
correctly.

Run 8, 1980 June 11, 13.57. Execution of six new test
cases, T6 - T11; no errors found.

Run 9, 1980 June 17, 15.36. Error in operating system
control instruction.

Run 10, 1980 June 17, 16.55. Execution of five new test
cases, T12 - T16. Four had trivial errors. No error in
simulator found.

Run 11. 1980 June 19, 13.57. Correct execution of four
corrected test cases, T12 - T15. No errors in simulator found.

TABLE 3

Corrections to Simulator Program and Test Programs

Test run in which error was noted	Number of corrections						
	2	5	6	9	10	11	Total
Group							
1 Error of simulator logic	3	1					4
2 Misspelt name	1						1
3 Error of program text format	14	1					15
4 Error of simulator output format	1	4					5
5 Error in test program		1	1	1	4	2	9

closely reflect the author's conscious judgement of the
importance of each group, in the sense that the larger
numbers of corrections are found in groups that the author
knows full well are less vitally dependent on correctness.
This rule is seen confirmed in several ways. First, the most
numerous group of corrections is 3, errors of program text
format, which is concerned purely with the appearance of the
printed program text, and which in no way influences the
operation or correctness of the program. Second, the second
group according to size is 5, error in test program, which
shows 9 corrections to the 369 lines of test program. This
may be compared with the total number of corrections to the
simulator program itself, groups 1, 2, and 4, with altogether
10 corrections to 679 program lines, of which the 5 corrections of group 4 are concerned only with the relatively
inconsequential matters of output format. It seems quite clear
that when working out the test programs the author's awareness
that errors entering at this stage would have only slight
consequences has led to a much increased error rate. Third,
as already noted, of the total number of corrections to the
logic of the simulator program, groups 1, 2, and 4, half come
from the relatively unimportant group 4.

Considering now the core errors of the simulator program,
corresponding to the 5 corrections of groups 1 and 2 of Table
3, it is remarkable that none of them has been found later
than test run 5. As seen from Table 2 this means that the
work on test programs T3 to T15 did not reveal any further
errors in the simulator. This observation becomes still more
remarkable by a closer inspection of the details of the
errors behind the five corrections. One was a spelling error,
detected by the loader as an undefined name. Three errors
were detected fortuitously by inspection of the simulator
program. Only one error was found by its influence on the
execution. Every one of these errors was a purely local slip
of the pen or mind. In other words, every part of the
simulator, from the overall plan, via the control table, to
every detail of the instruction word analysis, execution and
addressing, worked perfectly according to the design, without
any modification or correction whatsoever.

In view of the general interest in program correctness and
the attention given to it in works on programming methodology,
this positive result of the present program development will
be further looked into in the following section.

4) PROBLEM ANALYSIS WORK MODE

As background for the consideration of the problem analysis
that led to a flawless program design, some knowledge of the

underlying author attitude may be illuminating. This attitude
has, as one important component, the view that since programming must finally rest on the programmer's direct, intuitive
understanding, the criteria for the program produced being
"right" must be based, ultimately, on the programmer's
looking at what he or she has done and accepting it. From
this view it follows that for helping the programmer in his
or her task, what is important is anything that may make the
programmer retain his or her alertness in the face of the
mass of detail constituting the program, and that may make
every one of these details relevant to his or her direct
understanding. The ideal situation is one in which the
programmer may take any part of the program, look at it, and
decide that it is right or wrong. Where this ideal cannot be
realized because the algorithmic means available in the
programming language are too remote from the actions that the
programmer directly sees to be required for solving the
problem, the programmer will have to bridge the conceptual
distance by means of a suitable intermediate platform of
concepts. This, then, is the task to be done in the problem
analysis: the programmer must consider each aspect of the
problem in turn, and for each decide whether it can be
realized directly by programming or whether a conceptual
bridge is required, and in the latter case, he or she must
build the bridge.

As the work mode for accomplishing this task the present
program development has used a technique of problem analysis
according to which every part of the program is developed
through a conscious process, the steps of which are recorded,
as far as possible, as a fully articulated written argumentation. In this process the development of each part of the
solution is allowed to proceed along its own path, informal
or formal, restricted only by the one basic guiding principle,
that every part of the documentation must be made to appear
such that the validity of the underlying argumentation is
intuitively obvious. As shown in Table 1, in the present case
this manner of developing the program has led to the
formulation of 666 lines of problem analysis text, which is
roughly the same number of lines as in the program itself.
As a concrete illustration, Fig. 1 shows a sample of the
problem analysis text. As apparent from this figure
formalization is used quite freely in the problem analysis
text. The amount of formalization used in the complete
problem analysis is summarized in Table 4. What is most
noteworthy in this table is the fact that so many different
kinds of formalization have been found useful. Since clearly
each such kind can only be used as a result of a deliberate

2.6. Addressing of storage locations and registers.

In section 2.1. above it was assumed that the simulator treats the store and registers of the simulated machine in such a manner that to a large extent the operations themselves are executed in the same manner, irrespective of whether the operands are to be found in the store or in a register. This is achieved primarily by placing the registers side by side with the locations of the store, in such a manner that within the simulator the same kind of *place index* may refer to either kind of operand.

The details of the storage simulation for convenience as far as possible will be arranged so as to allow easy determination of the *place index* for the various forms of instruction words. In the first instance it is obvious that a location in the simulated store must correspond to an internal place having an index that can be directly derived from the storage address. Making the natural assumption that an integer Fortran variable is used for each 8-bit word, we get the correspondence:

INTEL 8080	Fortran simulator
Storage location, address Q	PLACE(PI), where the place index PI = -STRBAS + Q

where STRBAS is a suitable constant, the store base.

In allocating the registers of the simulated machine we have to consider the handling of both single registers and register pairs. It is further desirable that the registers be held in places whose indices can be derived from the fields of the instruction words in a simple manner. In particular it is desirable that the difference of the place indices for the two parts of a register pair be the same as the corresponding difference for the two parts of a pair of storage locations. In other words, what we wish to achieve is that the place index of the more significant part of a pair of registers or storage locations can be derived from the place index of the less significant part by addition of the same constant. In order to achieve this we note that for storage locations the place index of the more significant part of a pair is 1 greater than that of the less significant part. For the two parts of a register pair, on the other hand, the value of the DDD or SSS field of the instruction word of the more significant part is 1 less than that of the less significant part. Consequently the registers will most conveniently be held in places whose place indices are formed as a constant minus the corresponding DDD or SSS field value. Continuing from here we can derive how the place indices of each register pair can be derived from the corresponding RP field value. The desired connections can be derived from the following display, which is developed line by line, starting from the ordered series of the non-negative values of 7-(value of the DDD or SSS field of instruction word).

7-DDD = 7-SSS, decimal	0	1	2	3	4	5	6	7
DDD = SSS, binary	111	110	101	100	011	010	001	000
Single registers	A	none	L	H	E	D	C	B
Register pair	none		H-L		D-E		B-C	
RP, binary			10		01		00	
2 x (3-RP), decimal			2		4		6	

In this display, in each register pair the less significant part is the one to the left. A comparison of the first and last lines of the display shows that except for references to the special register pair SP all references can be derived from the corresponding instruction word field, DDD, SSS, or RP, in a simple manner.

The placement within the simulator of the storage locations, from address minadr to address maxadr, both included, and the registers shown above is now determined if we decide to place the storage locations in the simulator array PLACE starting at place index 1, followed immediately by the registers, ordered as shown above. In this manner we obtain the following mapping:

INTEL 8080	Fortran, place index
Store(minadr)	1
Store(q)	q-minadr+1 = q - STRBAS
Store(maxadr)	maxadr-minadr+1 = rbsind-8
Register A	aind = rbsind-7
(Not used)	rbsind-6
Register L	lind = rbsind-5
" H	hind = rbsind-4
" E	eind = rbsind-3
" D	dind = rbsind-2
" C	cind = rbsind-1
" B	bind = rbsind

where for the bracketed group: rbsind-DDD

In this picture the values of minadr and maxadr are supposed to be given. All remaining quantities are introduced and given values by the relations displayed in the mapping itself. Thus the constants of the mapping can be derived:

STRBAS = minadr -1
rbsind = maxadr - minadr + 9

The place index of the less significant part of a register pair whose RP value is given can be derived from the display above, which shows that

$$7-DDD = 2 \times (3-RP)$$

From the mapping we then get:

place index = rbsind - DDD = rbsind - 7 + 2 x (3-RP)
        = rbpind + 2 x (3-RP)

where we have introduced

rpbind - rpsind - 7.

Fig. 1 *Sample of problem analysis text for simulator program development.*

consideration of the manner in which a particular part of the
solution is most effectively described, the employment of
these several kinds indicates that in the manner in which the
problem analysis is carried out the choice of the most
suitable mode of expression appears prominently.

TABLE 4

Formalizations in problem analysis

Kind of formalization	Number of lines
Simple list of target machine instructions	30
Structured list of target machine instructions	60
Target machine store map	13
Arithmetic formula (address calculation, etc.)	8
Target machine word position display	3
Algorithm fragment	4
Control word format description table	16
Case enumeration table	17
Any formalization, total	151

In the problem analysis no conscious effort has been made to
follow either a top-down or a bottom-up procedure. In the
subsequent analysis of the development process these terms
appear to be largely inapplicable in that it is unclear
whether each item of the discussion belongs near the top or
the bottom. For example, in Fig. 1 the question of addressing
influences the overall structure of the simulator and thus
would appear to belong near the top. On the other hand, any
approach to it requires analysis of the details of representations and bit patterns, and so would seem to belong near
the bottom. The early decision to use an internal place index
that makes storage locations and registers look alike in
certain sections of the simulator might be claimed to be a
top-level one. However, I would never have made such a
decision without previous experience relating to the manner
in which such a solution can be realized at the level of detail.
    A more fruitful manner of describing the design procedure
would be talk of what one might perhaps call issue approaches.
The total design problem would in this manner divide itself
into several issues, for example storage allocation,
addressing, instruction word analysis, input, and output.
Each issue in turn would give rise to several alternative
approaches. Each approach would generally imply decisions at
all levels of detail, from the overall structure of the
program to the smallest matters of bit patterns. The design

process would consist in analysing and comparing the approaches, and then adopting one for each issue. This implies that the decision to adopt an approach would at one and the same time entail decisions related to many levels of detail.

The insistence that the problem analysis provide an intuitively obvious justification of each part of the program implies that the problem analysis effectively includes a proof of the validity and correctness of the program. In the present problem no explicit proof of any part has been given in the problem analysis, the solution having been proven correct by construction. This fact is a reflection of the nature of the problem. In solving other problems the same general approach might very well lead to a need for demonstrations that depend on such intermediate steps that are characteristic of proofs. Such demonstrations can be accommodated within the present frame of work without any difficulty.

In addition to the arguments for the correctness of the solution, the problem analysis must include arguments that justify the choice of each part of the solution. These arguments may be expressed in any appropriate manner, and in particular may include discussions of effectiveness and of alternative solutions.

More generally, the mode of work employed in the present program development may be said to conform closely to that employed in normal technical activity concerned with systematic development and construction.

5) RESULTS OF THE DIARY ANALYSIS

The diary analysis given as illustration above suggests, as one result, that when the programmer is fully aware of the implications of errors in various parts of a project, his or her error rate will be influenced strongly by the severity of the consequences of errors in each part, in the sense that more errors will be made where they matter less. This result accords well with common sense and with experience reported earlier (Smith, 1967).

As another result, a problem analysis aiming at a full justification of every program part in the most effective manner has resulted in an analysis report written mostly in prose, but making use of eight different kinds of formalization. This result may be viewed as a sceptical comment on some recent work aiming at establishing a single formalized notation for program specification (see, e.g., Liskov and Zilles, 1977).

The most striking result of the present study is the

indication of a high level of program design correctness
obtained by a problem analysis requiring a written,
articulated justification of every part of the program. This
result, if generally valid, would be highly important to
practical development. It therefore suggests further studies
aiming at clarifying whether a problem analysis of the kind
considered is a feasible approach to solving at least some of
the problems of error-free program construction. Such studies
should aim at finding out to what extent errors in programming
are related to the argumentation used when writing the program.
As another aspect, the further studies might attempt to yield
observations related to other persons and problems. In either
case the studies might very well make use of the diary
approach, and indeed, it might be difficult to pursue them
in any other way.

In conclusion it appears that several important aspects of
programming can be conveniently and effectively studied by
means of diaries, in the sense described above.

REFERENCES

Brooks, R.E. (1980). Studying programmer behaviour
    experimentally: the problems of proper methodology. *Comm.*
    ACM 23 (4), 207-213.
Liskov, B. and Zilles, S. (1977). An introduction to formal
    specifications of data abstractions. *In* "Current Trends in
    Programming Methodoloy". (Ed. R.T. Yeh), Vol. 1, pp. 1-32.
    Englewood Cliffs, New Jersey, Prentice-Hall.
Naur, P. (1972). An experiment on program construction. *BIT*
    12 (3), 347-365.
Naur, P. (1975). What happens during program development - an
    experiment. *In* "Systemeering 75". (Eds M. Lundeberg and
    J. Bubenko), pp. 269-289. Lund, Sweden, Studentlitteratur.
Smith, W.A. (1967). Nature and detection of errors in
    production data collection. Proc. AFIPS 1967 Spring Joint
    Computer Conf., 425-428.

MULTI-STYLE DIALOGUES AND CONTROL INDEPENDENCE IN INTERACTIVE SOFTWARE

STURE HÄGGLUND AND ROLAND TIBELL

*Software Systems Research Centre
Linköping University and Institute of Technology
Linköping, Sweden*

1) INTRODUCTION

Computing devices were originally thought of as *data processing* machines, where input is fed into the system and computed output delivered as a result. Characteristic of this view is that the computer system implements a mechanism for transforming input to output according to some algorithm. Parameters for the processing are elements of data, the management of which is considered secondary to the computations.

However, as data processing applications matured, the focus of interest was gradually shifted in favour of the *data management* aspects. Computers became more and more thought of as instrumental for handling repositories of data. Under this view, processing of the data is but one function available when storing, organizing and retrieving information. Database systems are becoming essential as parts of the software environments provided for implementation of various computerized services. The same evolution is reflected in the development of higher-level programming languages with the introduction of support for data abstractions, object-oriented computations and data-driven programs (Liskow *et al.*, 1977, Ingalls, 1978).

The current development seems to emphasize more and more the central role of *communication* in computer utilization. This fact is manifested by the increasing importance attributed to internal cooperation between different software systems or physical communication in distributed computer networks, as well as the need to understand and implement efficient human-machine communication using the computer as a responsive tool for human problem solving.

PSYCHOLOGY OF COMPUTER USE
ISBN 0-12-297420-4

This discussion brings us to the central topic of this paper. It appears that there are many cases, when a software system should be viewed as a realization of a communication system for an information repository where different kinds of data processing tasks can be initiated. Then conventional programming languages are inappropriate as tools for thought, since they are primarily suited for expressing algorithmic processing of data. Instead we need support for expressing models of human-computer communication (and other forms of process communication) and information management in a more declarative way than the procedural paradigm of typical programming languages, i.e. descriptions oriented more towards *properties* of a system rather than explicit specifications of *how* these properties are realized.

In the area of information management this goal is pursued along several lines within different areas of research. For instance, *data abstractions* are studied in connection with programming languages, *conceptual modelling* is a vital issue within the database community and *knowledge engineering* has emerged as a subject of great practical applicability from artificial intelligence research.

The rest of this paper will be concerned with models of human-computer communication and software architecture supporting such models. The need for adequate techniques for implementation of user interfaces should be apparent from the fact that typically something like two thirds of the program text in interacive application programs is concerned with some aspect of dialogue management. Guidelines for designing dialogues and tools for their implementation have been presented in numerous papers and some books, e.g. Martin (1973); Fitter (1979) and Shneiderman (1980). We will add to that tradition, but also supply some observations with general implications for the organization of interactive software, which we feel are of some importance.

The following list summarizes some properties, which we feel are important for a software system implementing a human-computer interface:

1) The internal structure of the software system should correspond as far as possible to the user's model of the system. Then requests for changes in the system's external behaviour are easily mapped to modifications of its internal definition.
2) The description of computations and internal data management should be separated as far as possible from the definition of the end-user dialogue, for reasons that will be detailed below.
3) Supply of ample help information, explanation facilities

and possibilities for rapid browsing of available
information and operations are important. The dialogue
designer should be encouraged to provide such user
assistance.
4) Different user categories should be accommodated and
systematic support for user growth included, in the sense
that more advanced techniques for utilizing the system are
naturally acquired over time.
5) Undoing of unintended actions due to misconceptions,
erroneous input or premature decisions is an important
option, both for the purpose of providing safety measures
and as a possibility for the end user to explore the
behaviour of a system.

In the following sections we will discuss the consequences
of such a view on the structure of software systems and on
the methodology and techniques needed to develop such
software. The two main issues to be treated are:

1) The utility of *control independence* as a principle for
implementation of human-computer interfaces. Under this
principle we can decide on the particulars of the dialogue
independently of the data processing aspects of our
application. In particular, *multi-style dialogues* can be
supported with dynamic adaption of the dialogue to the
preferences of the end user.
2) The utility of *state transition networks* for modelling the
dialogue behaviour of interactive software, in the
tradition reflected by the work of several others e.g.
Parnas (1969); Woods (1970); Wasserman (1979); Lucas (1980)
and Dehning *et al.* (1981).

The rest of this paper is organized as follows: in section 2
we discuss support for abstractions in the design of software
and the notion of control independence. Our approach to
modelling of dialogues is explained in section 3 and
experiences from developing and using some tools and systems
supporting the proposed approach are presented in section 4.

2) ABSTRACTIONS AND DIALOGUE CONTROL

One main trend during the history of programming languages
and systems has been a striving towards higher levels of
conceptual abstractions in order to promote more reliable and
maintainable software systems. Another way of expressing this
endeavour is as a search for an increased problem orientation
in the design of applications programs, leaving details of
implementation to lower levels of systems software.
Programming in one sense means transforming an abstract
requirements specification into a concrete executable
implementation. This process is simplified, if the number of

details that have to be added during the programming is
confined to a minimum, i.e. if *abstractions* are supported in
our programming environment.

Writing a program presumes the ability to describe a)
states (or *objects*) b) *operations* upon states (objects) and
c) *control* for sequencing operations. Traditional programming
languages have a certain degree of built-in support for using
abstractions when dealing with these three aspects of a program.
However there is also a need for programmer defined abstractions
as a means to improve software quality and productivity.
Conventionally the concept of a *procedure*, performing
parameterized processing of data, is the main abstraction
facility. Thus by writing a procedure and specifying its
input/output data relationships, a module is created which
can (hopefully) be used within different environments without
knowledge of its internal realization. A later generation of
emerging languages, e.g. CLU (Liskow, 1977) and Alphard
(Shaw, 1977), pioneered by Simula (Dahl, 1968), in addition
supports the concept of user-defined *data abstractions* for
the purpose of encapsulation of all information about the
abstraction and thus achieving representational independence.

Data abstractions, as well as the idea of schema-driven
interpretation of stored representations of data in database
systems, illuminate a very important concept, namely the
pursuit of *data independence* in software. This is to be understood as the encapsulation of the concrete representation of
data in such a way that it can be changed independently of
the programs which use the data. We feel that a similar
abstraction facility for the external interface for a human-
computer system is very useful. The idea is to separate the
description of the *contents* of a dialogue from the decision
on how the actual dialogue is to be performed. Then, for
instance, we can support multi-style dialogues based on either
VDU forms, menu-selection, command language, etc., using the
same underlying definitions of objects and operations. We will
use the term *control independence* to denote such an organization
of software.

A variation of the same principle is when we develop a data
processing application by building a *knowledge database* in the
tradition of artificial intelligence research, and then
implement the software as various interpreters for the same
knowledge base. Then each interpreter is imposing different
control and we have a realization of control independence in
the sense that the knowledge base and the set of interpreters
can evolve comparatively independently.

The principle of control independence is of course implicit
in much of the current work on human-computer interfaces,
since techniques for table-driven screen from dialogues,

command language parser generators, etc. are in wide-spread
use. However it seems to us that few systematic attempts have
been made to use a common internal description as a basis for
dialogues in different styles, as chosen dynamically by the
end user. This matter will be further discussed in the
following sections.

There are some significant short-comings associated with
most existing program packages which support implementation
of interactive software:

1) There is often a lack of hardware independence in an
   implemented dialogue system. Not only may a system restrict
   the dialogue to a certain type of terminal (e.g. with a
   particular local "intelligence"), but it may also be
   difficult to adapt the dialogue design to new generations
   of terminals, changing response times or transmission
   speeds etc.
2) Possibilities to adapt the dialogue style to the current
   background, knowledge and experience of the end user are
   seldom available.
3) Many tools are restricted in the sense that they support
   some specific kinds of dialogue types and exclude
   (definitely or almost) other dialogue organizations.
4) When dialogue management is supported by adding a set of
   specialized macros or a library of procedures to a general
   purpose language, there is no guarantee that dialogue
   management is uniform throughout an application system.

This discussion is intended to elucidate the fact that
there seems to be a shortage of dialogue design and
implementation tools in the intermediate area between general-
purpose programming languages extended with macro or program
libraries on the one hand and special-purpose systems
supporting the development of dialogue programs on the other.
The approach to dialogue development presented in the next
section represents an attempt to provide a comprehensive and
generally useful model for the task of dialogue design and
implementation. The model should be general enough to include
most of the customary techniques for man-machine dialogues.

3) MODELLING OF DIALOGUES

For the purpose of understanding how to design a human-
computer dialogue we may assume that it is performed according
to an explicit predefined *script*. The script defines which
input *messages* can be understood and processed by the system.
The interpretation of a message is made within a *message
context*, or a *mode* as it is often called. A dialogue script
contains a distinct number of such contexts and the inter-

pretation of identical messages may differ depending on
context. In addition the *response* following a given input
message also depends on the current *state* of the computation,
i.e. the history of the previous interactions.

Messages accepted by the system are either *simple*, i.e.
atomic tokens, or *compound*. In the latter case, we will
occasionally refer to the components as *message elements*.
Interactions may take place while the message is formulated.
Typical examples of compound messages are screen forms or
parameterized commands, while prompted responses or single
command parameters may be viewed as simple messages. It is a
matter of convenience, at which level we prefer to identify
the simple messages. For instance, it may be appropriate to
view single characters as message elements. A dialogue script
further defines the possible sequencing of messages, in
particular the *transitions* between message contexts.

The concepts of message, message context and context
transitions are extremely useful as a common basis for an
understanding of dialogue models used in current applications
software. Thus we may analyse a dialogue program from the
following aspects:

1) the number of message contexts implemented.
2) the pattern of possible transitions between contexts.
3) the support for compound messages.
4) the size of the set of messages valid in a given context.
5) the interplay between system prompts and message
   formulation.

Creating a description of the messages, contexts and
transition patterns can be understood as defining a grammar
for the dialogue. Since we have not yet discussed the *style*
of the dialogue (the dialogue technique in the sense of
Martin (1973)) we may view the description as the *deep
structure*. Various *surface structure* realizations of the
dialogue are then possible and can be selected depending on
the characteristics of the application or the preferences of
the end user.

For the purpose of this paper, we consider the following
dialogue styles, which are commonly used in interactive
applications software (for examples, see section 4):

1) *prompted input and menu selection*. The system guides the
   user through a series of questions. Menus can be used when
   the number of valid responses is reasonably restricted.
   This technique is often used in combination with some
   other, such as VDU forms or a command language.
2) *Command language*. The user controls the system by issuing
   commands. These commands are often parameterized, where

parameter values are either given in a predefined order or
else identified by preceding keywords. It is often useful
to distinguish between command language with *positional*
parameters and *keyword-identified* parameters respectively.
3) *VDU forms.* A form with empty fields is displayed on the
VDU screen and the user is expected to fill in values to
be entered. Often used for data entry and in combination
with menus for invoking the appropriate form.

We have not mentioned (restricted) *natural language,* which
may be used e.g. for database queries in some systems. Since
most practical implementations use a very restricted language,
we can for our purposes regard such a dialogue style as a
special case of a command language.
Let us now review the dialogue styles mentioned above in
the light of our previous discussion of messages and message
context. We will be interested in such things as whether
"user control", "ease of use", "user guidance", etc. have to
do with dialogue style or with context structure. The
following observations can be made:

1) *Prompted input and menu-selection.* In this case there is
usually a large number of contexts, one for each menu etc.,
and no specific notion of compound messages. Menus can be
used when there is a reasonably small set of valid
messages. Message formulation is then simplified since
numeric selection or pointing devices can be utilized. The
pattern of context transitions can be arbitrarily complex,
although auxiliary interactions (i.e. message contexts)
often have to be introduced if the sequencing of elementary
messages is to be conditional.
2) *Command language.* Commands are usually formulated as
compound messages, grouped together in a small number of
contexts often arranged in a hierarchy. Since there is a
finite set of commands valid within a given context, menus
may be requested for selection of the intended operation.
For each command with parameters, there is a substructure
of contexts corresponding to the set of parameters. The
transition between these contexts is sequential when
positional parameters are used. Otherwise there is an extra
context for the set of keywords for switching to the
appropriate keyword-identified parameter context.
3) *VDU forms.* This case resembles the previous one with respect
to the two-level structure of compound messages, although
the pattern of transitions between forms is usually more
varied. Often forms are arranged in hierarchical structures,
with menu selection in the internal nodes of the tree, and
forms in the leaves. Within a form, each field defines a
message context with transitions forced by positioning the

cursor on the screen. Notice, however, that some transitions may be prohibited, for instance when a display-only
field is not reachable with the cursor.

It should be clear from this exemplifying discussion, that
the degree of user unitiative in a human-computer dialogue is
related to the number of message contexts implemented and
especially the permitted transition patterns. If we assume a
certain *operational power* in an application system, i.e. a
given set of functions that can be invoked, then in general a
high degree of user initiative results from having few message
contexts and user-controlled transition patterns. On the other
hand more detailed messages have to be formulated in a large
context, which makes such a solution less attractive. In
practice, the important factor is of course how well the
structure of contexts and transitions corresponds to the
user's perception of the system and the way he wants to
perform his tasks.

It is often assumed that command languages give a high
degree of user initiative, while for example, prompted
response gives the user limited control over the dialogue. As
can be seen from the discussion above, such a statement is
misleading. The style of the dialogue can usually be changed
independently of the context structure.

The case where interactions between the user and the
system are allowed while a compound message is formulated
(for example correcting a validation error when entering a
value for a field in a form) may be viewed as an *embedded*
dialogue. Another instance of embedded dialogues may occur in
systems which recognize certain inputs as *exceptional,* for
example when interpreting a single question mark as a help
request instead of as a regular response. The handling of an
exceptional input message should usually not be defined
locally for a context, but globally for several contexts.

4) IMPLEMENTATION EXPERIENCES

We have performed several application-oriented projects based
on the approach to modelling of interactive software, which
were described in the previous sections. The general goal has
been to develop easy-to-use and flexible tools for construction
of interactive software, with a minimum of programming profi-
ciency required. Our experiences from organizing the software
according to the structure of the dialogue are definitely
encouraging.

In this section we will try to substantiate the previous
presentations, by giving brief descriptions of the IDECS
system for dialogue modelling and the MEDICS system for

educational simulations. The purpose of the discussion below
is primarily to communicate the basic architectural principles
underlying these systems, rather than to explain details of
their implementation.

4.1) *The IDECS System for Dialogue Prototyping*

The original IDECS system was developed around 1975 as a tool
for experimenting on the human-computer interface, before
implementing a full-scale on-line demographic database. Very
little was known about the potential end users of the database
system. Many could be characterized as casual users and they
could not be expected to receive very much training beforehand.
The IDECS system was designed to provide the possibility of
making rapid prototypes of the human-computer dialogue before
the final requirement specifications were to be settled. The
tool should support multi-style dialogues, be easy to use and
allow dynamic changes of the dialogue behaviour during
execution of the prototype system.

We based our work on the concept of a *conversation graph,*
i.e. a directed network where nodes represent message contexts
and the arcs correspond to valid transitions between contexts.
The graph structure acts as a grammar for the message
sequences, which may be accepted during a dialogue. The IDECS
system provides an interactive environment for creation and
interpretation of such descriptions (Hägglund, 1980). It is
implemented in Lisp (Sandewall, 1978).

The conversation graph resembles very much the idea of
augmented transition networks (ATN) in the sense of Woods
(1970), although tokens to be parsed are messages (simple or
compound) rather than single symbols. Another difference is
that the conditions for accepting a message are associated
with nodes and not with arcs, i.e. arc descriptions are
condensed into the predecessor node. The reason for this is
that interacting with a program is preferably viewed by end
users as an action performed *within* a certain state, rather
than as a *transition* between states. This is important for
the purpose of explaining the programmed dialogue model to
users and for the simplicity of the interactive tools used
for dialogue description and maintenance.

Different variations of state transition diagrams have
been used for the purpose of describing human-computer
interfaces, for example Parnas (1969); Wasserman (1979);
Lucas (1980) and Dehning (1981), or for syntax diagrams used
for specification of valid language constructs in for example
Pascal. It should be possible to support most of these
approaches with the tools provided by the IDECS system. The
basic idea in the IDECS system is that an application program

is organized according to the structure of the end user
dialogue. Thus each message context defines a module in the
system, a *node* in the conversation graph. All information
which has to do with end user interactions is represented as
named *attributes* of the nodes. These attributes are interpreted by a special program, which acts as a *driver* or a
monitor for the dialogue. Attributes can have the character
of parameters (such as a text to be printed or coordinates
for positioning the cursor on the VDU screen) or else be
procedural code, which is evaluated by the dialogue monitor.
Additional programs, which should not be allowed to interact
directly with the end user, can be called when attributes are
evaluated.

Examples of attributes associated with nodes in the
conversation graph are:

1) *Prompts and guiding texts,* which may be dynamically
   selected for presentation depending on the current style
   of the dialogue or the preferences of the end user.
2) *Positioning information* for VDU interactions, to be used
   when a screen-oriented dialogue style is used.
3) *Type information* for the anticipated input from the end
   user. This information is used to direct parsing and may
   also be given in the form of an invocation of a lower level
   conversation graph, for example when a compound message is
   to be read from the terminal.
4) *Help information*, which can be requested as an aid for the
   user before the input message is formulated.
5) *Constraints and defaults,* which should apply to entered
   messages.
6) *Actions and responses,* which will be initiated when the
   message is processed.
7) *Transition instructions,* which direct the transfer to
   another or the same node in the graph. To be strict, this
   information is not part of the node definition, but rather
   the arc part of the conversation graph. However it is
   often convenient to handle information associated with
   outgoing arcs as an integral part of the predecessor node.

The set of attributes defined for nodes in the conversation
graph can be viewed as modular descriptions of various aspects
of a human-computer interaction. If we compare the node with
a traditional program, with attributes corresponding to fragments of the program text, we notice that there is no control
defined within the node. In a program, statements are executed
according to explicit control structures or else in sequential
order. When a node in a conversation graph is executed, the
dialogue monitor imposes control, i.e. decides which attributes
should be evaluated and in which order. Thus control is

abstracted into the dialogue monitor, and control independence
is realized in the sense that we can change the rules and
style of the dialogue independently (to a certain extent) of
the declarative descriptions in the conversation graph. The
example in the next subsection is intendend to give a more
concrete illustration of our approach.

In order to write an interactive program in IDECS, we thus
have to create a set of interaction nodes and assign
attributes to these nodes. For actual execution of the program
a node interpreter is used. We have also experimented with
automated translations of a conversation graph to a procedural
program. The correspondence between the users model of the
system as a set of message contexts and the structure of the
implemented program has proven very useful as an aid when the
dialogue script has to be changed. Surprisingly enough
experiences with IDECS show that when such a tool is used,
conventional programming is almost completely eliminated for
a non-trivial range of applications (Hägglund, 1980).

An example of multi-style dialogues. The following simplified
example is intended to elucidate the previous discussion on
messages and message contexts, by showing how different
dialogue styles can be supported in a system based on the
IDECS approach.

Let us assume that we have to construct a human-computer
interface in a system for administration of a small scientific
library. The library contains books and technical reports and
we have to support for example registration, search, and
lending of books and reports. Typical approaches would be:

1) to construct a command language containing these operations,
   possibly combined with a prompted input of title, author
   etc.,
2) to design screen forms for each type of service, using a
   menu to select the appropriate form.

Following our approach, we may instead start with an analysis of the messages, which are to be accepted by the system.
For instance, we may define a book registration as a compound
message:

REG :: = ISBN CATEGORY AUTHOR TITLE YEAR PUBLISHER

with the obvious interpretation as a tuple of elementary
messages, where ISBN is a unique identification of the book
and CATEGORY is a local classification, etc. Before we make
any decision on how to interact with the system, we can start
defining a conversation graph with a node for each elementary
message. Then, for instance, we may decide that CATEGORY is
an *enumeration type,* i.e. there is a predefined set of values

acceptable as instances of such a message. The following
attributes may be associated with the CATEGORY elementary
message:

> *verbose prompt:*
>   "Enter local category classification for this book:"
> *short prompt:* "Category:"
> *identifying keyword:* "category"
> *prompt position:* 16,12
> *input type:* member of defined_categories
> *default:* "Not classified"
> *help:*
>   "Select at most one category among the legal
>   alternatives."
> *action:* save category
> *response:* acknowledge category
> *successors:* set of nodes

Example of node attributes

The informal description above should give an indication
of what kind of information can be used to characterize a
single interaction point in a human-computer dialogue. The
following discussion concerning different dialogue styles will
hopefully explain further how the information is used.

The other components of the book registration message, as
well as the other message types supported in our example
system, can be described in the same way. When we have defined
all elementary message contexts, it is time to introduce some
structure into the set of contexts. Structure is defined by
transition arcs and the notion of compound messages, which are
defined by connected subgraphs.

The previously discussed dialogue styles can be employed in
our example environment.

Prompted input (with menu-selection)

Let us assume that dialogue nodes have been defined for
each component of the book registration message, and that an
extra node is defined for selection of operation. Then we may
perform the following dialogue (user input in *italics*):

        ...

Select operation: *REG*

What is the ISBN number (blank if unknown): *91-7372-404-1*

Enter local category classification for this book

Select from the following list of alternatives:

1 General topics   5 Math. of computation
2 Computing milieu   6 Hardware

```
3 Applications        7 Analogue computers
4 Software            8 Functions

Enter alternative: 4

Author's last name:....

   ...
```

Incidentally, the same dialogue can be executed in a variation of the prompted input style, using a brief prompts option with a suppression of menus unless explicitly called for (by a help request):

```
* REG
ISBN: 91-7273-404-1
Category: Soft ( ==> SOFTWARE )
Author:
   ...
```

Comment: To execute the dialogue in this fashion, we have to define message context transitions in such a way that the dialogue monitor traverses the nodes in the appropriate order. In the IDECS system this information is represented as an extra attribute in the predecessor node. The evaluation of this attribute yields the name of the successor node to be selected next. For the attributes defined in the example in the beginning of this section, we may notice that the *prompt position* attribute is ignored and that the selection of *verbose prompt* or *short prompt* depends on the optional variation of the prompted input dialogue style.

Command language with positional parameters

In this case the selection of the intended operation is immediately followed by values for its parameters, i.e. the constituent elements of the compound message:

```
   ...
* REG 91-7372-404-1, SOFTWARE,...
   ...
```

Comment: Here the transition pattern should be sequential, i.e. we usually want to know in advance in which order to traverse the nodes and thus parse the message. There is no use of the *prompt* attributes, but menus or help information may be requested for each parameter as defined in the corresponding node.

Command language with keyword-identified parameters

The difference between this style and the preceding one is that the parameters of the operation may appear in an arbitrary order, i.e. we have to identify each elementary constituent in the compound message.

```
...
* REG ISBN=91-7372-404-1, CATEGORY=SOFTWARE, AUTHOR=...
...
```

Comment: This is where we use the *identifying keyword*
attribute, which is used to select next node from a set of
possible successors of the current one.

VDU screen forms

This dialogue style is the one which utilizes most of the
attributes in a dialogue node definition. A form corresponding
to a compound message is invoked after the intended operation
is selected.

```
ISBN:     91-7372-404-1 __

Author: _____

Title:  _____

        _____

Category: SOFTWARE        Year:____

Publisher:_____
```

Comment: Here we have to extend the notion of compound
message in the sense that we must know in advance which nodes
are part of the message corresponding to a screen form. This
information is used to traverse the nodes when *short prompts*
(guiding text) are written on the screen as a blank form
before values are filled in. Apart from that, this dialogue
style does not differ very much from prompted input.
(Although in practice, we would define some exceptional input
commands for tabulation between input fields.)

Summary of multi-style dialogue monitoring

The discussion above was intended to convince the reader that
it is reasonably useful to employ a view, where most aspects
of the individual interactions within a human-computer dialogue are recorded as a set of attributes for each interaction.
This set is a union of the slightly differing attribute sets
needed to support particular dialogue styles. In addition,
the structure of possible sequencing of interactions differs
depending on the dialogue style, but it is usually not
difficult to declare the transition pattern in such a way

that it can be interpreted appropriately for each dialogue
style. The main benefits of this view are that hybrid
dialogues can be implemented in a uniform way, and also that
end users can dynamically select the most efficient way to
interact with the system.

4.2) *Concluding Remarks on the IDECS Experience*

We have deliberately been quite vague in our description of
the IDECS system, which implements the approach to design of
human-computer dialogues advocated in this paper. That is
because there is not one specific system, which we would
propose as a universal tool for this purpose. We think that
it is more useful to think of the approach as a way to
structure dialogue-oriented software, where the tools needed
can be easily customized and adapted to the current class of
applications. In fact, our IDECS system is rather a family of
at least four different implementations, where the trade-offs
between simplicity, flexibility and expressional power are
tuned differently.

Several objections can be raised against our approach as
explained above. For instance, any realistic application will
result in a very large number of nodes in the conversation
graph, with an even larger number of attributes to be defined.
However, natural extensions in the direction of automating the
generation of nodes from a more compact description of the
grammar for the dialogue or using generic specialization
hierarchies for similar interactions (Sandewall, 1982) can be
used to remedy this situation. We may even prefer to use the
conversation graph only as a conceptual tool, with some
condensed notation for the dialogue definition and then compile
this notation to some efficient internal representation.

Another objection may be that although it is possible to
use a common dialogue description for several dialogue styles,
we have not demonstrated that the resulting human-computer
interface will be of high quality. This seems to be an open
question, but since so little is known about what is needed
to make a dialogue interface successful, we think that the
advantages of support for multi-style dialogues compensate
for some design compromises which may result.

Still our approach demonstrates the usefulness of a
specialized tool for construction of human-computer dialogues.
To conclude this discussion we will show an example of a node
definition, as it is seen by a programmer in one of our
implementations (master's thesis work by Tibell). This version
demonstrated the practical feasibility of multi-style dialogues, using a common conversation graph representation. The
system is intended to be used by a programmer (other versions

exist for non-expert users), and the attributes of a node are arranged in a hierarchy where the leaves contain expressions in a pseudo-Lisp notation.

CATEGORY

```
├─INITIALIZE : cat := retrieve (library, categories);
├─PROMPT ─┬─ POSITION : setpos (16, 2);
│         └─ MESSAGE ─┬─VERBOSE : print ("Enter local category
│                     │                   classification for this book:");
│                     │          menuprint (cat);
│                     └─BRIEF : print ("Category:");
├─INPUT ─┬─POSITION : setpos (16, 12);
│        └─ MESSAGE ─┬─TYPE : menuread (answer);
│                    ├─DEFAULT : answer := "Not classified";
│                    └─VALIDATION : member (answer,
│                                          union (cat, "Not classified"));
├─HELP ─┬─POSITION : setpos (18, 4);
│       └─TEXT : print ("Select at most one category
│                        among the legal alternatives.");
├─ACTION : current-book.category := answer;
└─TRANSITION ─┬─DEFAULT : next-node (author);
              └─SUCCESSORS : next-nodes (isbn, category, author,
                                         title, year, publisher);
```

Definition of the node CATEGORY

The *initialize* attribute is evaluated when the node is entered, but not when the node is re-interpreted after for example a help request, a validation error, or after some other exceptional input, which results in an embedded dialogue. In the example we assume that the names of valid category classifications are fetched from a database, to be used in a menu display and for validation of selections. The *input* and *help* attributes are used by the dialogue monitor in connection with processing and responding to the end user's input. In the *action* attribute arbitrary processing can be specified and the *transition* attribute is essentially a specification of out- going arcs from the node.

A table-driven interpreter is used for execution of the human-computer dialogue. The tables define which attributes are relevant under the current dialogue style and the order of their evaluation. The interpreter further defines how to handle exceptional inputs, such as help request, dialogue control commands etc. An extensive set of facilities for dialogue definition, modification, documentation and maintenance is part of the system.

4.3) *The MEDICS System for Educational Simulations*

As another example we will briefly mention the MEDICS system
(Elfström *et al.*, 1980). MEDICS supports interactive development, maintenance and executions of patient management
problems (PMPs), to be used for training medical students in
clinical decision making. Such simulations allow the student
to gather information about the patient and act in order to
provide the proper management of the case. The system is of
some interest for the topic of this paper, since it demonstrates how different types of control are applied to one
common description of a specific PMP. These matters are
further explained in Hägglund (1982).

MEDICS is implemented with the help of a slightly modified
version of the IDECS system described above. It uses the same
model of the software as organized around a transition network,
which defines the human-computer dialogue. However the contexts
appearing as nodes in the network are more complex than in the
IDECS case. Within each context the student can gather information and perform certain actions. Some actions explicitly
call for transitions to a new context. Such transitions can
also be forced by the current state of the simulation, rather
than actively selected by the user.

The experiences form the IDECS system regarding program
structure are definitely confirmed by the MEDICS project.
Programs for patient management simulation are realized as
structured contexts with different attributes acting as
parameters for the dialogue with the student and for the
simulation process. As in IDECS, the ability to change the
style of the human-computer dialogue, due to the control
independence resulting from this software architecture, has
proven very valuable. The programs which implement the control
processes, the simulation and dialogue monitors, are very
small and easy to change. At present medical students use a
version of MEDICS where the simulation monitor is rewritten
in Basic for a desk top computer, with simulation cases down
loaded from the Lisp development environment.

5) CONCLUSIONS

In this paper we have advanced the principle of *control
independence* as an important tool for realizing flexible
interactive software and multi-style human-computer dialogues.
In particular we have shown how a common style-independent
description of dialogue interactions can be handled as a
directed graph, where the nodes define contexts for inter-

pretation of input messages. The cardinality of the graph and
the pattern of possible transitions between message contexts
influence such qualities as the degree of user initiative and
ease of use. Our experiences from implementing tool systems
supporting this view indicate that the need for procedural
programming in application development is essentially
eliminated, while much of the flexibility is retained. The
usefulness of transition networks as a basis for dialogue
software is confirmed by our experiences.

ACKNOWLEDGEMENTS

Major contributions to the ideas and systems described in this
paper have been made by Östen Oskarsson, Hans Holmgren, and
Olle Rosin.

REFERENCES

Dahl, O.J., Myhrhaug, B. and Nygard, K. (1968). The SIMULA
    67 common base language. *Publ. No.* S-2, Norwegian Computing
    Center, Oslo.
Dehning, W., Essig, H. and Maas, S. (1981). "The Adaption of
    Virtual Man-Computer Interfaces to User Requirements in
    Dialogs". Springer-Verlag.
Elfström, J., Gillquist, J., Holmgren, H., Hägglund, S.,
    Rosin, O. and Wigertz, O. (1980). A customized programming
    environment for patient management simulations. *Proc. of
    the 3rd World Conf. on Medical Informatics,* pp. 328-332,
    North Holland Publ. Co.
Fitter, M. (1979). Towards more "natural" interactive Systems.,
    Int. J. of Man-Machine Studies 11, 339-350.
Hägglund, S. (1980). Contributions to the Development of
    Methods and Tools for Interactive Design of Applications
    Software. PhD dissertation, Linköping University.
Hägglund, S., *et al.* (1982). Specifying Control and Data in
    the Design of Educational Software. *Computers and Education,*
    6, no 1, Pergamon Press.
Ingalls, D.H.H. (1978). The Smalltalk-76 programming system
    design and implementation. *Proc 5th ACM Symp. on Principles
    of Programming Languages,* pp. 9-16.
Liskow, B., Snyder, A., Atkinson, R. and Scaffert, C. (1977).
    Abstraction mechanisms in CLU, *Comm. ACM 20,* 8, 564-576.
Lucas, P. (1980). On the structure of application programs.
    In "Abstract Software Specification," (Bjorner Ed.)
    Springer-Verlag.
Martin, J. (1973). Design of Man-Computer Dialogues,
    Prentice-Hall, Englewood Cliffs, New Jersey.
Parnas, D.L. (1969). On the use of transition diagrams in the

design of a user interface for an interactive computer system. *In "Proc. of the 24th ACM National Conference"*, pp. 379-385.

Sandewall, E. (1978). Programming in an interactive environment: the Lisp experience. *ACM Comp. Surveys,* 10, no. 1, 35-71.

Sandewall, E. (1982). Unified dialogue management in the Carousel system. *In "Office Information Systems"*, North Holland, (Ed. N. Naffah).

Shaw, M. and Wulf, W.A. (1977). Abstraction and verification in Alphard: defining and specifying iteration and Generators. *Comm. ACM 20,* 8, (Aug. 1977), 553-564.

Shneiderman, B. (1980). "Software Psychology", Whintrop Publishers, Cambridge, Mass.

Wasserman, A.I. (1979). USE: a methodology for the design and development of interactive information systems. *In "Formal Models and Practical Tools for Informations Systems Design"*, (Ed. H.J. Schneider) North Holland, pp. 31-50.

Woods, W.A. (1970). Transition network grammars for natural language analysis. *Comm. ACM,* 13, no. 10, 591-606.

THE EVALUATION OF A PROGRAMMING SUPPORT ENVIRONMENT

A.T. ARBLASTER

Queen Mary College,
*London, England**

* Now of: Bell Telephone Mfg Co, Antwerpen, Belgium

1) INTRODUCTION

The purpose of the project reported here was to evaluate the
design of one particular Ada Programming Support Environment
(Apse), which had been produced by a consortium of software
houses for the United Kingdom Department of Industry and the
UK Ministry of Defence. The design is therefore known as the
"UK Apse" (DOI 1981). We concentrate here on the methods used
to evaluate the design, and on the relative effectiveness of
these methods, rather than on the details of the design itself
or the recommendations made as a result of the study. The
study was required to aid government agencies in procuring
Apse software, and to examine all those aspects of the Apse
most strongly dependent on human factors.

The factors examined during the evaluation were (a) the
external, user interfaces, such as the design of the system
command language; (b) structural features of the Apse such as
the functions of components and the interactions between them;
and (c) the Apse as an organizational component in software
project management. When we consider all of these factors we
can see that the term "programming support environment" is
not entirely apt. "Programming", unless we radically widen
the definition of the word, is very far from the whole story
where software development is concerned. Consideration of
software tools presently implemented and of the structural
requirements of other existing environments demonstrates that
support is needed, and is often offered, for a much wider
range of activities than "programming". A support environment
intended to allow development of large scale computer systems
must provide support for activities throughout the software

PSYCHOLOGY OF COMPUTER USE
ISBN 0-12-297420-4

lifecycle. Most of these activities are influenced greatly by
human factors. In order to provide the context of the Apse
design evaluation, current ideas about the process of software
development will be summarized in the next section.

The study was conducted in three phases. First there was a
survey of the current state of knowledge of human factors as
applicable to programming support environments (PSEs),
together with a review of some existing PSEs such as Unix and
Interlisp. This survey led to the development of checklists
of human factors design criteria which were to be used in the
later phases of the project. In the second phase the original
basic requirements for Apses, embodied in a document called
STONEMAN (DOD 1980) were studied with the aim of determining
the human factors implications of these requirements. The
third phase of the study was the detailed evaluation proper
of the UK Apse design. It is not the intention here to touch
on all aspects of the project, but to give enough background
from the first phase for the reader to be able to appreciate
the context of the project, and enough information about the
evaluation methods employed to indicate their feasibility and
and usefulness. We will not touch on the second phase of the
project at all, and will neither give a detailed description
of the Apse design nor detailed recommendations, since in any
case the design was modified in the light of various reviews,
including this study.

The last phase included two "rapid prototyping" exercises;
one studied the implementation and use of the command language
interpreter, and the other a particular application of the
Apse Database. The study was therefore a survey of "applicable"
knowledge and an application of that knowledge to evaluation
of a very substantial software system at the design stage.

This form of "applied" project in the human factors field
is very much the exception rather than the rule: in this field
the aim of most empirical studies is to develop "applicable"
design principles, rather than to apply those principles to a
particular design. Of course, much anecdotal "work" also
exists - armchair musings which may have some value but which
can provide only the most fragile underpinnings for evaluation
of a software system design.

2) THE SURVEY

The survey phase of the study outlined the factors to be
considered from the point of view of the comparatively new
field of software engineering, then from the point of view of
human factors work, after which a synthesis was attempted.
The design of programming environments was then considered
within the framework which had been built up. Finally, critical

elements of the framework were incorporated in two checklists,
the first relating a software engineering taxonomy of software
quality to human factors issues and the second a consolidation
and abstraction of different checklists which have been
proposed for interactive systems design criteria. These checklists were developed for use in later phases of the study as
evaluation guidelines.

Outline of Software Engineering

We will provisionally define software engineering as the
application of scientific knowledge to the specification,
design, implementation, testing and operation of computer
programs. This definition already embodies one of the unifying
and central concepts of software engineering: that of the
software development lifecycle. Influenced by systems theoretic
ideas such as the concepts of feedback, subsystem decomposition, and control, modern software development practices and
standards emphasize a decomposition of the development process
into identifiable stages, each stage having its own characteristic identifiable inputs and outputs. Technical reviews
during and after each stage are used to control changes and to
impose formal configuration on code and documentation. The
lifecycle is defined slightly differently according to the
needs of the organization using such a view. An archetypal
view in shown in Figs 1 and 2.

The software tools and their support environment together
make up a "programming support environment". One of the basic
requirements of an Apse is that it should be open-ended - that
is, that it must be possible to add new tools easily, so that
one may begin with a Minimal Apse (Mapse) and let it grow in
an evolutionary fashion. To do this, the basic facilities
provided must be capable of supporting a wide variety of
different sorts of tools, since different tools will be
appropriate during different stages of software development.

It is also very important that the Mapse should allow tools
to be "composed"; that is, that the output of one tool should
be the input to another. (The term comes from mathematics,
where the expression $\underline{f}(\underline{g}(x))$ is described as the *composition*
of the functions $\underline{f}$ and $\underline{g}$.)

This rather obvious point has been overlooked in some
systems in the past. Composition is, however, central to
system usability and will often be referred to in this study.
For these sorts of tools we can achieve the necessary flexibility in two ways. The first is to use a very simple format
for the exchange of information between tools, such as a byte
stream. The disadvantage of this is that information about
the structure of the data has then to be communicated by some

PHASE	INPUT	OUTPUT
INITIATION	NO FORMAL DOCUMENT	INITIAL SOLUTION REPORT
REQUIREMENT	INITIAL SOLUTION	SOFTWARE REQUIREMENT DOCUMENT
HIGH LEVEL	SOFTWARE REQUIREMENT DEFINITION	SOFTWARE DESIGN DOCUMENTS
LOW LEVEL DESIGN	SOFTWARE DEFINITION DOCUMENT	DETAILED DEFINITION DOCUMENTS
IMPLEMENTATION	DETAILED DESIGN DOCUMENTS	APPLICATIONS CODE; SOFTWARE SPECIFICATION DOCUMENT; SOFTWARE OPERATION MANUAL

TESTING – AN INTEGRAL PART OF SOFTWARE PRODUCTION BUT ALSO PART OF THE CONTROL PROCESS OF QA.

PHASE	INPUT	OUTPUT
MAINTENANCE	APPLICATIONS CODE, SPECIFICATIONS; OPERATIONS MANUALS, SOFTWARE TEST AND TRANSFER DOCUMENT	CODE AND DOCUMENT MODIFICATIONS

FIG. 1 *A view of the Software Lifecycle*

PHASE	*DOCUMENT*
INITIATION	OUTLINE PROJECT PLAN
	OUTLINE QUALITY PLAN
REQUIREMENT PLANNING	DETAILED LIFECYCLE PLAN (including detailed work breakdown, timetable and resources plan)
	QUALITY PLAN (including deliverable items, methodology for remaining work, documentation plan, definition of standards, definition of quality assurance organisation and procedures).
	OUTLINE TEST PLAN (related to requirement).
HIGH LEVEL DESIGN	ACCEPTANCE TEST SPECIFICATION (related to high level design)
	DESIGN REVIEW REPORTS
LOW LEVEL DESIGN	DETAILED ACCEPTANCE TEST
	DESCRIPTION
	DESIGN REVIEW REPORTS
	MODULE TEST DESCRIPTION
IMPLEMENTATION	REVIEW REPORTS
TESTING	MODULE TEST REPORTS
	ACCEPTANCE TEST REPORTS
	CONFORMANCE CERTIFICATE
MAINTENANCE	MAINTENANCE PLAN

FIG. 2 *Documents needed for Software Management*

form of *ad hoc* encoding within the byte stream. This form of
communicating then means that each tool (or its implementor)
has to know the encoding methods of other tools. There seems
to be no satisfactory stage between allowing data to be passed
only as a byte stream (with internal encoding to give the
information structure) and using some form of Database
Management (DBM) system, where structure information can be
kept in the form of a schema and accessed by each tool through
its own subschema. If the structure of the Database Management
system is well designed, then programs can have their own
independent view of the data, with detailed access being
mediated by the DBM system.

The UK Apse

Having looked at the wider context we are now in a position to
appreciate some of the reasons for the design concepts of
Apses, and some of the intentions behind some of the STONEMAN
ideas. The idea is that an Apse is structured in the form of
a Kernel Apse (Kapse), the basic toolbench, which itself is
intended to be portable to a variety of host systems. Some of
the host systems may be bare machines and others may be
machines with sophisticated operating systems. A conceptual
view of Apse organization is shown in Fig.3.

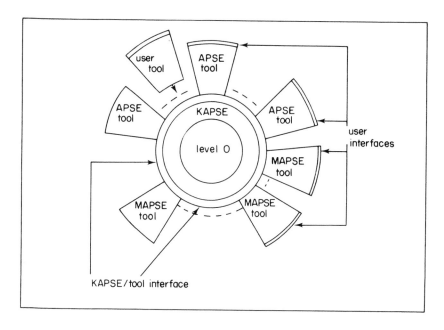

FIG. 3 *APSE Structure*

The Kapse (any Kapse) has facilities built into it for
retaining information in a database system. It also has
facilities for program initiation and intertool communication.
In the distributed Apse a basic "minimal" set of tools is
implemented. Such a system is called a "minimal Apse" (Mapse).
These tools are intended to enable basic use of the Apse for
editing, compilation, linking and debugging of programs,
including other, new tools which may be implemented. The Apse
should then grow by evolution into a "Mature Apse" (There
isn't any acronym for that!). For the UK Apse the decision
was taken to provide rather more than a minimum set of basic
tools, so that the Mapse would begin life as an attractive
and congenial system for users, even before its evolutionary
process had begun. All of the tools in a Mapse are guaranteed
to be available at all sites running an Apse derived from the
same root design.

The Kapse is the tool portability level. To move a Kapse
from one host to another may entail much work, but once that
is done an Apse should be portable without any reprogramming
of those tools which work to the Kapse interface. In the UK
Apse it was recognized that many of the tools would need a
man/machine interface, so an attempt was made to define a
common language interface for Apse tools, together with a
library preamble to provide the interface between the user
and any tool which is to use the common interface. It was also
recognized that more than a simple filing system would be
needed, so the Kapse has an inbuilt database management system.
The major Mapse tools considered in the design were:

1) The Command Language Interpreter (CLI)
2) The Compiler and Domain Manager
3) The Linker
4) The Database Utility
5) Test and Debug Utility
6) Editor

An Outline of Human Factors Considerations

Most of the human factors involved in computing are psychological in nature. There is some involvement of physiological
and anatomical factors in such things as keyboard design or
finding an appropriate temperature for computer rooms so that
operators are comfortable, or in finding the correct
luminescence for VDU screens; but these are really concerned
with matters peripheral to the essential nature of computing.
This essential nature is concerned with the use of the
software tools discussed in the previous section in order to
solve real-world problems, an example of the deployment of

higher cognitive skills.

Some understanding of the nature of skill comes from analysis of perceptual-motor skills (skills of the type needed in operating physical machinery - a car, say or a milling machine) and the information obtained is useful in understanding some of the characteristics of higher level processes involved in thought and language. Perceptual-motor skills are also important because some of the experimental methods and orientation used in their study have been carried over to studies of human-computer interaction, and because there are still a good many perceptual motor skills involved in computer use.

In perceptual-motor activities there are four basic components:

1) receptor processes involving perceptual organisation of information from the senses;
2) effector processes, structures which translate from intentions to physical action;
3) decision making, the higher level formation of plans to deal with the current environmental situation;
4) feedback processes, where information from motor activity is fed back to control that activity.

In human-machine systems the receptor processes are normally presented with some pre-synthesized information via a *display* (the instrument panel of an aircraft, for example); the design of such displays is an important element in the study of skilled performance. Again, effector processes normally operate in man-machine systems on some control transducer which then effects the desired action. For normal skilled performance there are *internal* and *external* feedback loops. The internal loop controls the effector process and ensures that each activity is correctly executed. The external loop assesses the effect on the person's action and provokes further action as it is called for either in response to error or to environmental changes. The skilled operator does not just react to each item of information as it is presented. He develops an internal model of the process he is controlling which helps him to concentrate on the important (often exceptional) facets of the input. This modelling also helps him to anticipate future control actions before they must be made. However, even for the skilled operator we may have information overloading - if information, that is each item of which requires a response, arrives too rapidly then at a certain rate the performance of the operator will degrade catastrophically.

In the higher cognitive tasks which are the norm in computing, the basic operations of perception - feedback (internal and external) - decision - response are similar.

For a higher-level cognitive skill, however, perception
may be less immediate than for perceptual-motor skills.
The ideal is still that the person can perceive the
organization of his sensory input immediately, but in fact,
depending on circumstances, the organisation may need
considerable "working out". The concept of information
overload also applies here, not so much in the sense of rapid
serial input of information to the person as in the sense of
information being structured or displayed in such a way that
too much working out is needed.

With cognitive processes we again have a need for feedback,
both internal and external. In this case the internal feedback
is provided by a process of continually reviewing the intended
activity - understanding the code as it is produced, perhaps,
at the implementation stage - and correcting problems as they
arise.

For many computing activities there is a perceptual-motor
component. An example is the use of on-line editing devices.
Here the arrangement of the perceptual-motor task must be
such as to allow requisite feedback at the basic level, while
avoiding interference with the higher-level processes which
are also involved in the task. External feedback for higher-
level tasks is also necessary, and should be such as to allow
errors to be detected as rapidly as can be accomplished.

The need for feedback is of great importance. Many psychological studies of a variety of tasks have shown that people
can be greatly helped by appropriate, prompt knowledge of the
results of their actions, or conversely that they will be
heavily handicapped by lack of such knowledge. This is true
even when there is no "logical" need for it.

Relationship Between Human Factors and Software Development

In this section we will examine the human factors in the
tasks which have to be accomplished in software development
and their implications for the tools which must be used.
The shortcomings of previous systems helped to indicate the
sort of problems in basic programming support environment
structure that should be looked for and eliminated.

Considering tools in the order in which they are used
throughout the software lifecycle, the first phase uses
requirements analysis and design tools such as PSL/PSA, SREM
or SDS (Teichreow and Hershey, 1977; Alford, 1977). These have
been successful to some extent, but must be regarded as first
generation tools. Their drawbacks from a human factors point
of view are threefold. *Firstly* the information display
facilities are not flexible enough to present just what

information is needed in any particular case without
information overload on the user. The second human factors
deficiency is that the database structure is fixed, thus not
allowing different views of the structure of the system under
development, and therefore constraining the development
methodologies which may be used. This third major problem
experienced with the "first generation" requirements analysis
tools has been the problem of relating the constructs built
up and the information provided to the information used in
the next phases of the lifecycle itself, on the one hand, and
relating the information to the project management information
needed, on the other. This problem is related to the, as yet
not completely solved, problem of finding satisfactory ways
of composing high level software tools, discussed above.

In the design phase of the lifecycle we have tools for high
level and for low level design. The drawbacks of these tools
as they exist now are related to those discussed with
reference to requirements analysis. Some effort has been made
with the development of design discipline to provide extrinsic
support, by imposing methods of working not implicit in the
task itself in order to constrain the task manageably.

The next phase, the implementation phase of the lifecycle,
uses as one main tool the programming language. Other tools
are editors, and debugging tools such as trace packages and
program dump analysers. Partly because of the similarity in
use between word processing products and program editors
there has been a great deal of work on the human factors
aspects of both, dealing with such things as the desirable
speed of feedback, the structure of command languages and the
number of distinct modes that should be used. This research is
ably surveyed by Embley and Nagy (1981). Main results are:
that on-line editors are preferable, because of the rapid
feedback; that reasonably prompt system response is needed;
that the display should reflect faithfully the internal state
of the manuscript; that the system organization should be
such that the user can develop a model of that system which
is close to the reality; that a system description should aid
to develop such a psychological model; and that "screen
editing", such as word processors achieve, is preferable to
the use of a command language for simple word replacement and
character changing, but that a command language is acceptable
for higher-level operations such as string searching. In
addition it is claimed that there are advantages in being able
to change from the editor to other operations, such as
compilation or program analysis, so long as a return to the
editor level is easy after notification of error, say of
syntax errors. Little empirical evidence exists in support of
this assertion as such, but in the light of the need for a

consistent whole system, a good user's model and rapid
feedback and correction of program errors, it is a plausible
claim. Given the pervasiveness of editing operations in all
of the lifecycle phases, and in such tasks as production of
configuration management information and management operations,
the use of an editor which can be used as a general component
of these other tools would certainly seem to be sensible.

For the testing phase of the lifecycle we need to be able
to relate the final form of the program to all of the earlier
forms. The tools discussed earlier, test coverage monitors,
static analysers and so forth, are again in a relatively
early stage of development. Drawbacks reported for such tools
as DAVE (Osterweil and Fosdick, 1976), the most widespread
static analyser, and for other systems, are that, though the
analysis phase is accomplished adequately, the design of the
information display facilities is rudimentary. Such tools
deluge the user with information, some of which is useful but
most of which is not. Therefore the extrinsic aids for easy
perception and organization of information are lacking. This
might be rectified by arranging for the analyser to update a
program database, rather than printing all of the information
available. The database could be interrogated by a query
language. This is the approach used in one Fortran program
analyser (Logica, 1980a). Using this method also means that
it is easy to build and analyse the program in modules, since
the database continues to be available from run to run of the
analyser.

Dynamic analysers and test coverage monitors have proved
to be more acceptable to users than static analysers, perhaps
because the relevance of each item of information produced is
more manifest than for static analysers. However, here too an
approach based on the use of a test information database with
a query language has proved to be successful, as in the Logica
Fortran Test Coverage Monitor (Logica, 1980b). For more
conventional debugging programs we again have the problem that
the information produced can only be related to the source
program with difficulty. More sophisticated debugging devices
now exist, in the form of postmortem stack analysers and so
forth. These are part of the state of the art in compiler
writing, and depend on a variety of ways of keeping information
produced at compile time, such as symbol tables, in a form in
which they can be referred to at testing time by the postmortem
analysis programs.

For the last phase of the software lifecycle, operations
and maintenance, there are few software aids. The main problems
here are organizational. Above all this phase needs a carefully
designed configuration and maintenance system, where fault
reports are validated in a controlled way and disseminated to

the appropriate authority for rectification. The system must
then ensure that proposed changes, including enhancements,
are again disseminated and that the changes are reflected in
updated requirements, design and source documents. Appropriate
tools here are those which can aid and support such organization, such as some method of cross referencing all of the
affected parts of a system.

Summary of Evaluation Methods

In many previous programming support environments, users have
found it difficult to negotiate the plethora of different
input and output formats and to relate the information
produced from one tool to that needed by another. We have here
two problems - that of the external interface, the command,
input and output formats the user sees, and the internal
interfaces which allow composition of the software tools in
the system. The importance of human factors in the design of
the external interface is obvious, and is partly covered above
in the discussion of the external interfaces of the tools. The
main overall requirement, unrelated to requirements for the
interfaces of each separate tool, *is that there should be
enough design uniformity in the interfaces that the user can
capitalize on this knowledge of the use of one tool when
using another.*
    That part of the system interface we have not yet consid-
ered is the system command language. Some empirical research
has been done here, and several recommendations can be offered.
Command names should be congruent and hierarchical (Caroll,
1980); command languages should be organized according to
consistent principles (Payne and Green, 1983); where commands
take positional parameters, consistent ordering is preferred
(Barnard *et al.,* 1981); explicit markers to differentiate
between commands and literals may be of advantage (Thimbleby,
1982); and perceptual cues to the syntactic structure of a
command language will increase its usability (Sime *et al.,*
1982). In addition, command languages such as Unix's shell,
and that of our current concern, need some procedural
features to control tool composition.
    The internal interface for tool composition has two
interrelated aspects. The first is the facilities which the
system offers the software tools programmer for passing
information to other programs and for storing information.
The second is the external image, on the systems command
level, for casual tool composition. The first aspect can share
perceptual properties with procedures in the systems programming language to be used. The most important criterion for
this internal interface is that it should have a structure

which is as simple as possible consistent with the job the
system must do, and that it must support the necessary
consistent user's model. The second aspect must again provide
simple and consistent structure but must also, preferably,
provide a notation consistent with the command language for
the whole system.

The next feature of a desirable support system which really
must be mentioned is the filing system. Here again we have two
different and important main aspects, first the structure of
the filing system as reflected in the image presented to the
user, second the structure of the data which can be held in
those files.

From discussion of the known problems in existing systems,
together with known successes and the evidence from
experimental studies, a checklist was produced. This summarized
the human factors considerations which a good support environment should fulfil. The support environment must fulfil these
criteria from two points of view, as a software system in its
own right and as an aid in helping applications systems which
are developed with its help to fulfil these criteria.
Inevitably the taxonomy we use and the criteria related to it
are somewhat *ad hoc*; we hope that the preceding discussion
will have indicated the complexity of the Gordian knot which
we propose to dissect here.

As a framework for development of the checklist we used
the taxonomy of software quality developed by Boehm *et al*.
(1978). This taxonomy is reproduced in Fig. 4. Our purpose
was to develop a checklist of human factors contributions to
software quality, and for that purpose we examined the association between human factors and each of the primitive
constructs in turn. Note, that Boehm's taxonomy assigns
"Human Engineering" to the utility of software system "as it
is".

Broadly, a software development environment has needs which
can be classified into:

1) perceptual needs: that the user should easily be able to
   perceive the current state of the system
2) operational needs: that the user should be able to take
   the actions necessary to accomplish his task
3) feedback: that the user should be informed in a timely way
   about the results of his actions and the system's response
4) understanding: that the user should be able to develop and
   maintain a psychological model of the operation of the
   system.

We must differ from Boehm in making such a clear-cut
distinction between human engineering and understandability,
at least with regard to programming support environments.

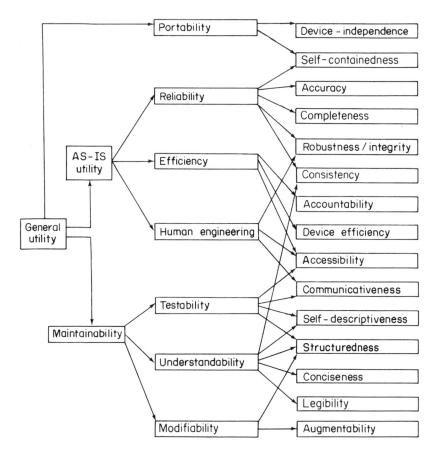

FIG. 4 *Software Quality Characteristics Tree*

Our checklist was organized by the primitive constructs of
Boehm's taxonomy, and within each construct we looked at the
contribution to be made by features aiding the user's
perception, feedback and understanding needs. Operational
needs are a matter of the technical design of the system,
except in so far as this design affects issues of understanding, perception and feedback.

3) THE EVALUATION

For the evaluation checklists (Appendix) each software
quality criterion was taken and the influence of human
factors related to *perception, feedback and understanding* was
considered. Then design features that, from our previous
discussion, were thought to be helpful in each case were
included in the checklist. A second checklist of detailed

recommendations for interactive systems design was formed by collating published lists of criteria, many of which exist, and adding to these. Naturally, some recommendations which were felt to be of no use in the present context were discarded.

From the results of the study phase some critical points for evaluation were determined:

1) the direct man-machine interface - in particular the general tool interface and the system command language interpreter.
2) the structure of the database system (really a database management system): how it could be understood by users.
3) The structure of the whole Mapse: how the user can compose subtasks to accomplish a task, for example how one would use a number of tools such as command language interpreter/ database utility/editor/compiler manager/linker/debugger. This influences the understandability of the system.

To evaluate the second area a rapid prototype of a database fragment was constructed. This is not described here. The first and third of these three critical areas are discussed in detail below. Their empirical evaluation hinges on two developments:

1) the building of a rapid prototype of a command language interpreter, in order to discover any problems in the command language definition, to check our intuition about the perceptual properties of the command language, and to provide a vehicle with which to try out the scripts described below.
2) the development of scripts for a scenario of use of the Apse. This scenario was based on a non-trivial test case project, the development of software engineering tools for program analysis. This project proceeded in parallel with the one described here and was done for a large aerospace organization. Activities of the project team developing software engineering tools were automatically logged, and the team was interviewed regularly. The Apse evaluation team then considered how these activities would be undertaken using the Apse. This method provided a focus for team discussion and consideration of likely patterns of use of the Apse. These activities also provided ideas of likely patterns of commands which be issued to the command language interpreter, and also the experimental scheme for the database prototype.

Three archetypal users were considered: a project manager concerned with requirements, management control and configuration management, an applications programmer, concerned with producing a system using Ada and the Apse as tools, but concerned in the main only with the use of the Apse rather than its structure; and a software toolsmith, concerned with

the development of new Apse tools and therefore needing a
good knowledge of the internal structure and of the internal
and external interfaces of the Apse.

*The General Tool Interface and the Command Language
Interpreter*

The command language in the UK Apse is a means of invoking
and controlling programs and Mapse/Apse tools. Our prototype
allowed most features of the command language to be tested.
    Invocation of programs in the UK Apse design is via a
system command. Programs can be invoked:

1) individually; the command language interpreter (CLI) waits
   for completion before prompting for a new command. This
   was fully implemented in the prototype.
2) several programs can be run concurrently, connected by
   "pipes" or by temporary files. These were not implemented
   in the prototype, though syntactic and semantic checking
   on such commands was performed fully, to establish their
   correctness and to indicate errors.

The UK Apse CLI also provides a number of "built-in"
commands that do not invoke programs but are obeyed directly.
These fall into five groups:

1) Program control
   These commands allow suspension and resumption of programs,
   abandonment, and so forth.
2) Variable and Status handling
   These allow the user to declare, set, display and extract
   the values of command language variables. All of these
   commands were fully implemented in the prototype.
3) Flow control commands
   These are available from within command files (not
   interactively) to implement conditional execution of
   commands and looping. Only the "return" command was
   implemented fully in the prototype.
4) Editing
   Command editing may be done using "recall" and editing
   commands. These allow the recall of previous commands,
   their modification and optional resubmission. These were
   fully implemented in the prototype.
5) Miscellaneous
   Other commands control current database mode settings. None
   of this was implemented fully, except for "logout".

All of the syntax for commands was parsed and most semantic
consistency was checked, even when the commands were not
implemented operationally.

The design and implementation of the CLI prototype was carried out iteratively, results from each stage being used as a basis for modification of the prototype. This allowed examination of alternative solutions to the problems posed, and in some cases showed up weaknesses in the design.

Much valuable information was gained both during the implementation and in the use of the prototype. Several more or less subtle problems were found in the syntax, and solutions were proposed. Some deeper problems were also discovered, particularly related to human factors, and solutions were proposed where possible. One problem that proved to be somewhat intractable is inherent in *any* system interfacing to Ada. An Ada program can accept a single string as a parameter on initiation, and, naturally, can interpret the string as integers or booleans or whatever it wants to. *But* the command language interpreter or whatever tool called the program may have had to decode its own parameters - evaluating variables, for example, concatenating strings, and so on. *Then* it must convert the whole lot back into a string to pass it on! The problem here is that the needs of the command language are reasonable - in fact other command languages such as Unix use a similar format - the specification for Ada is also reasonable - a language with strong types, very necessary for secure implementations - but at the interface we have an incompatibility.

In normal use the CLI proved to be a congenial tool, easy to understand and, generally, similar to the Unix shell in interactive use. However, some problems were observed; for example, the formal syntax gave rules for the writing of parameters to a command which made the use of quotes obligatory to delimit literals. A subsidiary rule made the omission of quotes possible. This was presumably an attempt to help the user, perhaps by avoiding problems of quote matching in a complicated command string. Unfortunately the rules for cases where quotes were obligatory were not easy to remember - in fact quotes could be omitted except in cases which caused problems of syntactic ambiguity. These cases were a set of exceptions, rather than subject to a consistent rule, and there was no assurance that all exceptions could be identified easily by the implementor of a CLI, let alone the user. In these circumstances the rule that quotes could be omitted was felt to be likely to lead to more problems for the user than it avoided. The language rules were modified in the light of this criterion.

The Structure of the Mapse

The Mapse structure was evaluated by considering separate
components in themselves and the composition of components to
accomplish whole software production tasks. To structure the
evaluation, the patterns of use of the support environment for
a parallel project were collected. This project was considered
to be particularly suitable, since it involved the production
of software of the sort that would be likely to take place
using Ada and the Apse when they become available. The
software was a set of software tools to aid the development
and technical evaluation of embedded systems. The tools were
intended to be portable to a set of operating systems and
machines, and hence problems of configuration and version
control were present in the development process. The development team were observed and their use of the development
system, comprising an operating system, database system,
editors, compilers and other utilities, and their use of a
text processing system for documentation, were noted. This
information, together with the checklist and some of the
experience gathered from development and use of the prototypes,
was used as the basis for group discussions of the use of the
Mapse tools to accomplish the same sort of tasks. This process
helped to focus on concrete issues concerned with the use of
the Mapse tools separately and together. The review team
members also had considerable experience of the production of
both applications and systems software. Attaining enough
familiarity with the details of the Apse to begin this phase
of the evaluation was in itself a not inconsiderable task.
The design was embodied in seven volumes, which, together with
review documents and appendixes, had to be assimilated. The
approach outlined above helped to structure the evaluation of
this mass of detail, lending concreteness to what otherwise
might have been an overly diffuse set of discussions.

Tool Commonality As the designers of the Mapse have perceived,
it is of the utmost importance to ensure that users see a
unified system, with a common command structure and a simple
conceptual model. In order to ensure this the designers have
provided recommendations and definitions for a generalized
tool interface. In effect a "command execution" machine is
being defined. As the final report (DOI, 1981) says, "there
are many occasions when a user of our Apse will *feel* he is
issuing a command" (our emphasis). The important point is
that the user *feels* that these occasions are similar in some
way, so a common conceptual framework must be provided which
does not clash with this intuition. The perceptual lexical and
syntactic properties of the interface must be used to support

this conceptual framework. The authors (of DOI, 1981) have
recognized this need.

First we deal with the lexical properties of the interface.
These are also related to the perceptual properties, in the
sense that the lexical definition defines the layout of
commands to some extent. The choice of separators, separator-1
being a space or tab and separator-2 a comma or one or more
spaces is time-honoured, and experience shows it to be
adequate. The lexical form defined for identifiers and
literals is more questionable. Identifiers are defined to take
normal Ada form. This is a valid choice, though it does clash
with the definition for the lexical form of CLI variables. A
few problems were identified and solutions recommended. A
good feature of the design is a set of guidelines for tool
implementors (who can be ordinary users, it will be remembered).
This covers choice of names, ordering of parameter types,
methods of prompting for further information, pattern of use
for tools which provide a new command environment and
discussion of the conditons under which tools should report
success or failure. Command prompting and help facilities are
also discussed.

Command Language Interpreter Most of the issues here have
been discussed earlier. The CLI is a good, if conservative
approach to the problem of defining a user interface.

Editor The editor design concentrates only on the problem
of maintaining derivation records. These are a set of files
which give the history of modification of a file. Each time
a file is edited the changes from its predecessor are recorded.
The idea was that the whole history of the file could be
reconstructed from these traces. The review team felt that
these derivations only recorded part of the information about
dependencies between database objects that would be needed for
configuration control purposes, a minor part. It was suggested
that the more important function of an editor is to
conveniently allow files to be created and modified, and some
human factors design recommendations were made.

Compiler Manager and Domain The design proposals for the
compiler manager (CM) and domain utility (DU) are excellent.
The separate compilation features specified in the Ada
language definition are intended to aid structured system
development, to save time and effort in creating and
maintaining large systems, and as a corollary to aid in
configuration control for large systems. This latter aim is
helped by the requirement that dependent compilation units
must be recompiled when the compilation unit on which they

are dependent is modified. The objective of separate
compilation with control of the unit dependencies has complex
ramifications and poses problems for the human factors design
of the system. The user must on the one hand have a simple,
consistent cognitive model of the system, helping him be aware
of the consequences of his actions in terms he understands and
on the other hand he must be protected from the tedious details
of domain management.

   This is a complex problem in human factors design. It
involves the design of a good user model, provision of
requisite feedback, and provision of a user interface which
at the same time protects the user from unnecessary detail but
gives him adequate information about what is happening. It
also involves ensuring that the user model is *progressively*
consistent: that as the user grows in experience of the system
and needs to know more about the details, he is not suddenly
faced with a quite different user model at some stage or a
need to acquire a very large amount of new knowledge about a
variety of aspects of the system all at once. This last need
is a common problem with systems which use many default
actions: the user has suddenly to know how to specify and
understand options for a large number of parts of the system
for which he could previously use defaults. The designers of
the compiler manager and domain succeeded in meeting these
human factors needs very well indeed. The design decisions
were well thought out and the explanations were clear and
well written, as were the more detailed and technical
discussions in the section dealing with the features of the
compiler itself (indeed the sections of the report dealing
with compilation are of such quality that they could almost
be used as the basis for a course on compiler writing).

The Linker   The requirements for the linker are predominantly
technical. The primary human factors need is that the
objective and functions of the linker are clear to the user.
In addition to this the linker provides information which the
user needs for other phases of program production. The linker
also has a role in the larger human factors considerations
related to software management and software engineering
methods, since it implements a major part of the mechanism
for controlling the complexity of the system under production
by allowing it to be split into manageable units.

Symbolic Test and Debug   Testing is a process which is met at
several different levels in software system development.
Recalling our discussion of the role of feedback in system
development, we note that testing provides an inner loop
relative to the implementation phase of the lifecycle itself.

In this phase testing is checking the correct implementation
of a design. Testing at the next level checks the design
itself to ensure that the software performs as it is intended
to. Finally testing relates back to the requirements specification phase of system development, to ensure that the
requirements for the system are met. Testing of this last sort
is very frequently done as one element in formal acceptance
tests in organizations (such as those where Ada may be expected
to find wide use) where software with critical reliability and
other quality requirements is developed.

The UK Apse report (DOI, 1981) concentrates on the inmost
loop of this testing process in the main, though the tools
specified may also be used to a large extent for testing the
design of software and to a lesser extent for checking against
requirements. This approach is entirely appropriate in the
context of the design of Mapse tools. As is noted in the report
a compromise is needed between the desire to include the widest
possible range of tools and the concept of the Mapse as a
minimum toolset. The decision was reached to provide as a Mapse
tool a single symbolic test and debug tool. This decision
cannot be faulted. The further decisions on the range of
facilities to be provided in the test and debug tool are again
good. The test and debug tool specified meets the need that
the users should have good facilities in order to be able to
do the basic operations of system development well, without
either compromising the quality of these tools in order to
allow the provision of more complex and sophisticated tools
or precluding the provision of these higher level tools at a
later stage.

4) CONCLUSION

The project was surprisingly successful, particularly in view
of the tight timescale and relatively limited resources with
which it was undertaken. A very large, ambitious and complex
software project was reviewed at the design stage, in order
to evaluate the human factors design of the product. It was
established that the design was generally of high quality. A
few problems were identified and solutions were proposed. The
worth of identifying and eliminating problems as early as
possible in the software lifecycle is well established, and
the evaluation project succeeded in this.

Turning to the evaluation methods used, these were on the
whole successful. The project was accomplished promptly and
with relatively limited resources. The checklist of quality
criteria for human factors proved to be useful as a method
for focussing attention on points of detail, which was
necessary given the huge amount of design information that

had to be absorbed and considered. The checklist of
interactive system design criteria was less useful in general,
since it dealt only with the simplest aspects of the user
view, not mainly with the structure of the system. This second
checklist also dealt with many aspects of the system which
would only be defined in the next, detailed, design stage,
following the review.

The prototyping exercises were remarkably successful,
particularly that of the CLI. In the field of human factors
work, no matter how excellent the design principles or the
theoretical predictions, the issues involved are so complex,
and the factors interact to such a great extent, that there
is no substitute for actual experimental evaluation. Another
interesting finding was that a great many of the problems were
identified during the implementation phase of the CLI prototype, even before experimental use of the system. The method
of implementation also proved to be so flexible that alternative solutions to problems could be easily explored. The
success of the prototyping exercises owed much to the software
tools available for the implementation of the prototypes.

The script discussions were helpful in guiding the project
team through a plethora of information about this major system.
It was found that the evaluation team needed considerable
expertise both in applications and software systems development to be able to discuss the system which was being evaluated.
Paradoxically it transpired that very high expertise in systems
software sometimes led to greater uncertainty about the meaning
of some section, or the structure of some utility: an
experienced systems designer could see ways of implementing
quite strange things to fit in with apparent interpretations
of the design specifications! The problem was that more than
one interpretation was sometimes reasonable. This effect can
never be eliminated until specifications are routinely
presented in a formal way - and not even then, probably.

To sum up, it was found that the evaluation methods used
were successful, particularly the use of prototyping, but the
software tools necessary should already be available on one
system and should be known to the implementation team. In our
case the team members were familiar with the tools used. If
they had not been, the project would have taken much longer.
Lastly, if the prototyping is being undertaken to assess human
factors design, a multi-disciplinary team might be necessary.

ACKNOWLEDGEMENTS

This project was helped by many people. I would like to thank
Ian Gooding and Alan Levy, for heroic feats of implementation;
Annette Hughes, Project Supervisor; David Brown, Project
Manager; Robert Worden, Divisional Manager, Program Products;

and Chris Dain, Divisional Manager, Technical Division, all of whom are Logica staff. Also Tim Lyons, from the DOI consortium, and Philip Weatherall, of the Royal Signals and Radar Establishment, and the editors of this book for their use of the thumbscrew. The project was supported by the UK Royal Signals and Radar Establishment, under contract A61B/3183. The contractor was Logica Limited.

REFERENCES

Alford, M.W. (1977). A requirements engineering methodology for real time processing requirements. *IEEE Trans. on Software Engineering SE-3*.

Barnard, P.J., Hammond N.V., Morton, J. and Long, J. (1981). Consistency and compatibility in command languages. *Int. J. Man-Machine Studies*, 15, 87-134.

Boehm, B.W., Brown, J.R., Kasper, H., Lipow, M., Macleod, G.J. and Merrit, M.J. (1978) *"Characteristics of Software Quality."* North-Holland, Amsterdam.

Carroll, J.M. (1980). Learning, using and designing command paradigms. IBM Watson Research Centre Report RC 8141.

DOI (1981). *UK Ada Study Final Report*. Department of Industry, London.

Embley, D.W. and Nagy, G. (1981). Behavioral aspects of text editors. *ACM Computing Surveys* 13, 33-70.

Logica (1980a). *The Fortran Program Analyser: User Manual*. Logica Ltd, London.

Logica (1980b). *The Fortran Test Coverage Monitor:User Manual*. Logica Ltd, London.

Osterweil, L.J. and Fosdick, L.D. (1976). Some experience with DAVE, a Fortran program analyser. *Proceedings of National Computer Conference*.

Payne, S.J. and Green, T.R.G. (1983). Organizing principles in command languages. MRC/SSRC Social and Applied Psychology Unit, University of Sheffield, Memo 555.

Sime, M.E. Payne, S.J. and Green, T.R.G. (1982). Perceptual structure-cueing in a simple command language. MRC/SSRC Social and Applied Psychology Unit, Memo 550.

STONEMAN (1980). Stoneman, Ada Programming Support Environment, (Ed. J. Buxton) ISIE, Arlington, Virginia.

Teichroew, D. and Hershey, E.A. (1977). PSL/PSA: a computer aided technique for structured documentation and analysis of information processing systems. *IEEE Transactions on Software Engineering, SE-3*.

Thimbleby, H. (1982). Character level ambiguity: consequences for user interface design. *Int. J. Man-Machine Studies*, 16, 211-225.

APPENDIX

HUMAN FACTORS OF SOFTWARE QUALITY CRITERIA

DEVICE INDEPENDENCE

Perception

1. Are devices to be used expressed as mnemonics? (So that the user can specify the type of a device, e.g. a line printer, rather than a system-dependent channel number.)

2. Are systems parameters easily accessed? (For example, number of I/O devices, linewidth of a display.)

3. Can the notation used for system interaction be used on any device? If not, are the different notations compatible?

Feedback

1. Are device interfaces automatically provided so that feedback on use of that device is available? (For example, if different VDU's are being used for editing, are responses acknowledged in terms which are compatible with that VDU?).

Understanding

1. Are the characteristics of various devices easily available to the user in terms which make it clear which tools may be used with which devices?

SELF-CONTAINEDNESS

Perception

1. Does the support environment provide interfaces which are independent of any characteristics of underlying software? (e.g. if the environment is built onto an existing operating system does it depend on the existing system's formatting conventions for messages?)

Feedback

1. Is feedback provided from the support environment itself? (If so, is there a conflict between the feedback provided by the environment and that of the underlying software?)

Understanding

1. Can the operation of the environment be understood without reference to the operation of external software?

ACCURACY

This construct does not really apply in this context, at least in the sense of numerical accuracy. The support tools should, of course, fulfil the claimed functions: for example a compiler should provide a reliable, semantically correct translation.

Non-numeric "accuracy" is perhaps better described as "consistency".

COMPLETENESS

Perception

1. Does the system provide an adequate notation for each of the operations it is supposed to support?

Feedback

1. Is adequate feedback provided so that the response of the system to each input is clear?

Understanding

1. Is the system integrated: can each subsystem communicate adequately with other subsystems?

2. Are facilities available for all of the operations which must be performed?

ROBUSTNESS

Perception

1. Are perceptual cues provided to help the user avoid errors?

2. Are command inputs designed to reduce memory load?   (e.g. by providing menu selection for system functions.)

Feedback

1. Are inputs fully screened for errors?

2. Are error diagnostics clear and informative?

3. Is the current state of the system made clear to the user?

4. Will the software handle unspecified inputs properly?

5. Are singularities handled correctly? (e.g. specification of empty sets in the database.)

6. In case of system failure are diagnostic aids provided?

7. Are database diagnostics provided for checking consistency and completeness of the database?

Understanding

1. Are safeguards provided against accidental specification of undesired actions?

2. Are 'help' options provided?

3. Are there adequate provisions for backup and recovery? (Both of the transaction the user is attempting and of the whole system.)

CONSISTENCY

Perception

1. Is the notation used for communication with the rest of the system consistent?

2. Are the interfaces for tool composition, provided internally to the tools and externally through the command language, consistent?

3. Are notations for communication with different tools consistent with each other?

Feedback

1. Do similar erors result in similar feedback and similar error action?

Understanding

1. Is the system structure such that a simple, consistent user model can be maintained?

2. Are apparently acausal system responses avoided?

3. Are the actions necessary to use various subsystems mutually compatible?

ACCOUNTABILITY

Not applicable, in the sense in which it is used by Boehm *et al.* (1976): their meaning is that the system should provide for the collection of performance information in order to assess efficiency. This has no direct effect on human factors, although the indirect effects of the system's efficiency may be considerable. We will assume that the system functions with 'reasonable' efficiency and that some way of monitoring this is needed. This is related to the next point also.

In the sense of being "accountable for its actions" or providing explanations for its behaviour, there are strong human factors requirements. These, however, may be classified within Self-Containedness and Self-Descriptiveness.

DEVICE EFFICIENCY

This does not relate directly to human factors needs, but perhaps indirectly in respect of ensuring timely response during interaction. This requirement is much more general, however, embracing the total system; as such it is included within Accessibilty.

ACCESSIBILITY

Perception

1. Does the notation used to invoke systems functions and tools make it clear what is being invoked?

2. Are default options clearly defined?

3. Is a labelled display of input options and defaults available?

Feedback

1. Does the system allow modification of erroneous commands, or must the user re-input?

Understanding

1. Are the system facilities clearly defined?

2. Do the formats used for tool invocation and composition make the operations to be accomplished clear?

3. Is adequate training available? (Maybe not <u>within</u> the system, but the system should be structured to aid training.)

4. Is the complexity of the system within the capability of the user?

5. Does system documentation (including user manuals and online 'help' facilities) have a high readability index?

COMMUNICATIVENESS

Perception

1. Are the inputs and outputs of the system sufficient to be able to distinguish different messages clearly?

2. Does the system take full advantage of modern peripherals? (e.g. colour graphics terminals.)

3. Are outputs formatted in such a way as to be easily understood? (For example it may be necessary to format output differently depending on whether interactive query or off line report is being prepared - this should be user-definable.)

4. Are perceptual cues used to help the user disambiguate input and output?

Feedback

1. Are error diagnostics clear, informative, and given in the user's terms?

2. Does error action leave the system in a clearly defined state?

3. Does the system provide clear cues about what state it is in?

SELF-DESCRIPTIVENESS

Perception

1. Does the appearance of system input and output make the system's structure and function clear?

Feedback

1. Is help available from the system for tool use and composition when requested?

2. Do error messages make the fault which has occurred easy to identify?

Understanding

1. Can the user determine the objectives, assumptions, inputs, outputs constraints and components of the system and of software tools from information that the system provides?

STRUCTUREDNESS

Perception

The structure of the system is not really subject to perceptual cues, except those which have been dealt with under the headings of Consistency and Self-Descriptiveness.

Feedback

Not applicable.

Understanding

1. Does the structure of the system lend itself to a simple user's model?

2. Is the structure of the system as simple as it may be, consistent with its purpose?

3. Is the structure consistent?

CONCISENESS

Perception

1. Does the command interface allow concise expression?

2. Is the conciseness or verbosity of the system under the user's control?

Feedback

1. Can the information available in error messages be expanded as desired?

2. Is simple, concise information available about the correct action of the system?

Understanding

Not Applicable.

LEGIBILITY

Legibility, or readability, derives from self descriptiveness, consistency and, to some extent, conciseness (although, especially with respect to command languages, the latter concern is more directly aimed at 'writeability').

AUGMENTABILITY

Perception

1. Is it possible to modify the notation used to communicate with the system?

Feedback

1. May the user add to the messages the system uses to provide feedback in such a way that feedback remains consistent?

Understanding

1. May the user add tool fragments or tools to the basic system library?

2. May the user easily compose tools or tool fragments?

SUBJECT INDEX